KRISTEN

The UnFinished Book

Some of the greater things in life are Unseen

RABBITRAIL PUBLISHING

The UnFinished Book
Copyright © 2018 by Kristen Wambach

This title is also available eBook. Visit https://www.kristenwambach.com/
Requests for information should be addressed to:
Rabbitrail Publishing 2365 NE Merloy Ave. Corvallis, Oregon 97330
https://www.kristenwambach.com/rabbitrailpublishing.html

Library of Congress Cataloging-in-Publication Data
Wambach, Kristen, 1959
The UnFinished Book
TXu 2-091-040 March 23, 2018

All Scripture quotations, unless otherwise indicated, NASB are taken from the Holy Bible, New American Standard Copyright (C) 1960, 1962, 1963, 1968, 1971, 1972, 1973, 1975, 1977,1995 by THE LOCKMAN FOUNDATION. Used by permission.
Other Bible translations quoted in this book are listed within Bible Translations page, which hereby becomes a part of the copyright page.

Any Internet addresses (websites, blogs, etc.) and telephone numbers in this book are offered as a resource. They are not intended in any way to be or imply an endorsement by Rabbitrail Publishing, nor does Rabbitrail Publishing vouch for the content of these sites and numbers for the life of this book.

ISBN-13: 978-0-692-14198-4
Cover Design: Kristen Wambach and Mona Alhamood
Editor Laure Fabre
Proofreading John Bugni
Visit https://www.kristenwambach.com/

First printing June 2018 / Printed in the United States of America

Endorsements

Many of us have had an opportunity to touch Revival in our lifetime; few encountered a Reformation. The UnFinished Book, in its earliest stage, crossed my path a little over ten years ago. Kristen wrote me a letter asking if I would read and consider endorsing her first "UnFinished book." I responded with a massive yes. Many intervening years passed but she hung onto that letter of hope. That same request copied and mailed to me, resurfaced as she crossed the finish line removing the "Un" to her Finished work. I'm inspired by her journey as if she had met Martin Luther himself somewhere in the pages penned. She has wrestled and nailed many thesis upon the door of what we call church. Her text will challenge the "established" boundary line of eternity with experiences that could only be authored by the Master. The race she has run is one that I am honored to be part of.

Tommy Barnett
Author; Co-Pastor Dream City Church Phoenix;
Founder and Co-Pastor Los Angeles Dream Center

"If you have traveled in the supernatural realm of the spirit and encountered God there, you will find in this book a kindred spirit in Kristen. If you have desired to embrace the realm of the spirit that you have read about in the scriptures and sensed it is real, but aren't sure how to pursue it, Kristen has given you a roadmap to follow. As Bill Johnson has said, "we live in parallel realities, the natural and the supernatural, and the supernatural is the superior reality." The UnFinished Book will lead you on a journey into that superior reality. If you are unaware of this superior reality, let this be your introduction. It will lead you to amazing and awe-inspiring encounters with the Lord. Kristen has paid the price of seeking God in His native realm at a time when few people were "taling" about it. Her journey took her deep into the heart of God, and she has done the hard work of putting her experiences into words with impressive persistence and a "lay it all down" attitude. Come journey with her in the experience of a lifetime, an eternal experience of an eternal lifetime."

John Bugni DMD
Governing Bench of Heart of the Valley
Community Church, Co-Editor

The Christian journey is a long and winding road, where you never know what will be around the next spiritual bend. Kristen has done a masterful job of helping us as she describes her unique journey of sold-out passion, while at times experiencing disillusionment and disappointment. Using humor and hope, Kristen has managed to challenge us to go beyond our own religious box of who God is and what He desires to do in our lives. Enjoy your journey through her 'UnFinished Book'!

Mike Lindell
Senior Pastor One Life Family
Fellowship Yakima, Washington

I have gotten to know Kristen over the past few years through our online conversations where we have shared our supernatural journeys towards deeper intimacy with our loving heavenly Father. I thoroughly recommend following her journey as shared so eloquently and passionately within "The UnFinished Book" so that you too can discover your place within the intimacy of our Father's heart. On this incredible adventure, God desires that we all discover our identity as a son or daughter of the King within a face to face relationship of restored innocence that you too would add another chapter to this amazing story of God's love. I would without hesitation recommend this book as an oasis in the wilderness to be inspired to continue your journey into the promise land of mystical secrets that God has hidden for us to discover.

Mike Parsons
Governing Bench Freedom Church, Freedom
Apostolic Resource Center, Barnstaple, England

It has been an honor and a pleasure to edit and proofread Kristen's book. Her testimony is such an inspiration and an encouragement for all of us who are hungry for more of God every day and not only for more of God but the truth about Him, about Heaven and us.

My walk with Kristen was ordered by God, I know it. French native, my heart goes to France and the Francophonie around the world - over 250 million people -who will have the opportunity to share these words as our next partnership project is to translate The UnFinished Book into French. Like myself, Kristen has a call for France, and we are walking it together. God wanted us to be in a relationship because He is relational. In God's kingdom, everything revolves around Love. So I love her, and it is effortless. We enjoy learning about heaven together and discover what Abba has for us.

We are children of God; we have untapped authority and power to partner with the angelic and the cloud of witnesses. They are there to teach us, encourage, build up and operate and play with us. We are learning to live in both realms - on earth and in Heaven - at the same time. Kristen's book is just what we need to go further and understand what God has prepared for us. There is no limit. Our maturity as sons of God, what we carry in our heart and our hunger for intimacy with Father is what opens doors. So let's play.

Laure Fabre
Editor & Proofreader, Bath, England

You don't simply read The UnFinished Book; you experience it. And reading this book is an invitation to join the author on her creatively chronicled journey--past, present, and future--of continuous discoveries of the realms of heaven, and her living, breathing relationship with Papa God, Jesus, and Holy Spirit. Enter into these pages, embark upon this journey, and you will be expanded. Kristen has been my Pastor and mentor for nearly four years; she is a "fleet-footed" forerunner, and this book is a breakthrough, a voice that needs to be heard, and a "crowning" achievement.

Yvonne Mutch
Heart of the Valley Community
Church, Corvallis, Oregon

Father blessed me in the spring of 2013 with one of the most influential & precious friendships I have ever known. Her name is Kristen Wambach. Knowing Kristen, watching her life, and in community with her teaching these past 5+ years has brought me (& continues to bring me) into an understanding of the spirit realm that Father wants His sons & daughters to experience daily & intimately as a lifestyle. Kristen is a dynamic forerunner of forerunners, teaching us "how to" consciously & consistently walk in, work in, & experience the heavenly realm. 'The UnFinished Book' provides delightful insight, in Kristen's transparently vulnerable style, as to what this lifestyle looks like. She shares her journey, her questions, her growth in understanding... or not! You'll laugh. You'll cry. You'll learn. You'll be set to think, encouraged to explore! Two quotes from this fascinating book provide an excellent summation as to what the reader can expect:

"No longer can we cast off the responsibility of our inheritance of seeing in the spirit."
"Your spiritual self has encounters far beyond what your understanding has yet grasped."
Let us pursue with diligence, our heavenly inheritance! Be blessed & enjoy!

Julie Lauchner
Heart of the Valley Community Church, Phoenix, Arizona

Kristen Wambach is one of the most real people that you will ever meet. A woman with both feet on the ground, a mother, and wife of a healthy active family, yet the Father has chosen her to open the gates of Heaven for so many of us. In her new book "The UnFinished Book," she has invited us along to experience the marvelous opportunity that we all have to step into the Heavenly realms and speak to the Father, face to face. Thank you, Kristen, for opening your heart and revealing so many simple keys that continue to unlock the mysteries of Heaven and the many realms of the Kingdom of God.

Dr. George Watkins
Faith Producers International Mt Vernon, Washington State

Psalms 139, Ephesians 2, & James 1:22,
Don't be just hearers of the word, but a doer!

Kristen Wambach author and longtime friend: Bible toting, to dreams, visions, encounters, and stepping out to fulfill the Book/Scroll written about her before the foundation of the world, bold and courageous, believing all things are possible for those who believe! Her passion for knowing God, linked with sincere desire that we each fulfill God's created destiny. Passionate, honorable, a forerunner, one who flies with the wind, to testify of our Father's involvement in our lives!

With great honor and love for this friend,
Sandy Jeffers
Fellow citizen of Heaven! Heart of the Valley Community Church, Corvallis, Oregon

The pen is a powerful stick to lay down realms on "flat" surfaces. Engage your spirit with the "strokes" of the pen in THE UNFINISHED BOOK, and the realms become vibrantly alive and multi-dimensional. Changing you! Kristen Wambach guides you on an adventure of life from here to beyond the veil. Read these compelling accounts with Holy Spirit and let the encounters heal and flow through you. Engage # 1!!! You are worth it!

Susan Schoonover
Governing Bench Heart of the Valley Community Church, Corvallis, Oregon

It has been my privilege to share in Kristen's continuing journey of transformation, to witness her navigating the realms of heaven and drawing on heaven's provision, always seeking to accomplish the destiny that God ordained for her: And now, through The UnFinished Book, you're invited to participate too: not only in her quest, but also in your own.

Jeremy Westcott
Freedom Apostolic Resources Center, Barnstaple UK

The UnFinished Book is a life-story of a profound spiritual awakening. It will open up your heart to new ways of intimacy with God. It will test your religious boundaries and challenge you into new divine arenas. You will love Kristen's great sense of humor and her creativity.

Kim Snell
Benjamin Testimony, Princeton, Texas

If someone told me I would be happily married for 33 years and have four amazing sons, I would not have believed it. Thanks to God He moved a beautiful young lady into the house in front of me. I have seen many unusual things but I will always thank God for my wife and life. Thank you Kristen for writing such a moving book for anyone who wants to be closer to God.

Donald J.
The pastor's wife, Corvallis, Oregon

For Don,

Who patiently believed I could write a book; until I did

Forethoughts

I sensed it was important to share a few forethoughts, to assist the reader finding the hands-on-place to my journal notations and testimonies found in this book.

1. https://www.kristenwambach.com/ The UnFinished Book Community: photos, sketches & live links, to help you navigate the text. Also, a place for you to share your testimony experiences while reading the book.
2. "Notes" page, found in the rear of the book with links more on a teaching "note".
3. RABBIT TRAIL, learning to "See" and "Hear" the Lord's path. It takes some experience and relationship time, to understand the intent He was trying to make all along. The journey is always worth it!

My invitation to the reader beforehand is set your agreement to encounter the hidden things of the spirit. You already hold a key; hunger drew you here, use that key to unlock the resources within.

Jesus many times gives this same open door, "The Kingdom of Heaven is like…"? Quiet your heart, read from a place of rest. Ask questions of Him after your spirit absorbs. Believe the Jesus in you.

In the spirit of writing out of an "experience," the unseen realm is pregnant with eternity, questions, answers and curiosities. I too ask many questions about how does this pertain to the purposes of my life and what just happened? Again, allow your spirit to drink in and your mind/understanding to wait.

Knowing is the relationship conversation He loves having with you.

I may touch on a matter that you are unfamiliar with, and it doesn't fall within the mandate of my book to teach principals at length. Experience is a testimony He desires all of us to make personal. You need no man or woman to teach you.

Rely on Holy Spirit and the anointing.

Read to experience Him saying; "The Kingdom of Heaven is like…"; gathering more than a day's manna or regurgitated information never fed life to the soul and spirit. Happy encountering Him!

Contents

CHAPTER 1

Introduction to Indulgences
"the window box"

If you want to change the world,
pick up your pen and write. "Martin Luther"

My hands hover over the keys while tears rise from my heart to my eyes. Typing is comfortable and one of few classes that I would share the grades on my report card. I could fly over the keys, typing at almost a hundred words a minute. But why is writing so difficult? I have written the beginning of several books, but never completed them or seen the end. Promises have been made to God, Don, and myself as regret rounds the corner each time I do not follow through. I'm struggling with balance, I have authored many excuses real-time, unseen blockages, or is it just me not hunkering down and paying the cost to walk in integrity. "Unfinished books," they gnaw at my heart. Is mercy still indeed extended to me by my faith-filled husband, Don, who still believes in me? He sees me wrestling with this elusive monster. A fight that steals my voice, dulls the imagination, and doubt that lunges its fists deep into my destiny. Hope and words cower and are whisked away into a corner emoji called the recycle bin. My un-written words fester as weapons against a wavering heart. Pages, chapters and sentence structure set traps in the battle of my mind. A blank page is a failure, a paragraph cut, sliced and misunderstood.

Words in my hearing have eyes. Audibly received, words paint scenes, like colors of the rainbow. Thoughts fathom a pot of gold, spilling its riches underneath an overgrown apple tree kissing the earth. I hear and see a picture sum is worth a thousand words. I struggle to get them contained in the frame: held inside the limitations of punctuation. My internal camera ponders the spring moss caressing a weathered 2x4, weakly framing the neighbor's gate. I either see beauty or necessity of needing a new fence. How do you explain that? I've smelled the roses and the fact that you have too gathers in my mind. I'm waging war; a voice wanting to be heard, understood, sharing, teaching, creative, agreement. I muse the outcome: Will I find a gift of honor in readers, in exchange rewarded with spiritual understanding? Or does a list of book reviews banish the eye before the shutter closes?

How audacious a pen must be; to write words that persuade any transformation with which I must bravely concur to have illumination! Do I have pride or proof? If I ask myself the question; why would I allow anyone to crawl into my head in an attempt to perceive my heart where misunderstandings are so ready to wrinkle red squiggle lines under my collection of thoughts. Countless times those squiggle lines have mattered: fear of man, fear of failure, fear of self.

Negative thoughts gather saying:
There's no music, and you're not graceful so why dance.
My spirit cheer-leads: "Take up ballet!"

Fear bellows in the wind: "Don't sing like that unless you have a bucket at your disposal."
A bold heart decrees: "Cut out the bottom of the bucket and make it a megaphone."

Thoughts wrangle in the everyday mundane of lies, like brushing one's teeth to ward off decay yet you still eat the sweet.

Hidden in a word is a secret under lock and key.
Pack a box of Kleenex if you want to read the heart, for its savory is in the salt that flavors each tear.

Otherwise, in the long and the short of it, I might misspell words and talk in parables because isn't it all Greek!

I rarely read a book for the sheer enjoyment of it. As an adult, Jane Austen or Charlotte Bronte would accompany me on those rare summer camping trips. Most books I choose to read are for self-improvement. I can remember difficulties during my grammar school years; letters were switching around in my head; numbers in twos would play like a game of tag, left me feeling like I was never ready or not, to be Olly Oxen free. This curious phrase is a corruption of the German "Alle, alle auch sind frei" which, when translated, means "Everyone, everyone also is free. "OH, how urban language slurs on the tongue. I'd cry in the silence of my heart, Can't I be free? Reading and writing never made me feel free. Elementary school was challenging because of a mild case of dyslexia: i's and e's still argued who comes after C, p's and b's dance the polka, t's reverse mirror around f's, j's turn somersault with y's. I can balance a checkbook but don't ask me to reconcile.

How do you begin to change the world if you struggle to talk to it? And write down those shape-shifting figures! Everyone is correcting your spelling, offering to say: "Oh she means this?" It's my world held in, desiring change. Eagerly looking to be unveiled. Loosed, "Alle, alle auch sind frei."

> *"If you want to change the world,*
> *Pick up your pen and write." Martin Luther's*

Compels me towards an act of courage that breaks my molds of the mundane. It stirs up the question: "How does one birth a reformation project inside of you, which has carousel'd round and round, failed repeatedly." You press in to reform your mind and understanding yet your fight comes up vain, measured, always a measured of self in time past, almost fifteen years.

I had heard about the infamous "95 theses" nailed to the door of the Castle Church on October 31, 1517, in which he denounced the sale of indulgences. It sparked my curiosity. So, I began to inquire. In my imagination I visualized Martin Luther breaking the rules by audaciously nailing papers that were blasphemous. In this day and age, the "Nailed post" or soon to be You Tube video caught on a bystanders phone would have gone viral on Facebook in less than twenty-four hours. Not so in those days. Nailing documents on the church door was very much like our social media, a public tradition of communication where they challenged each other's thoughts, opinions in this manner. Nailed to a community door for many to read. He, nailed his objection to the practice of selling indulgences?

What indulgences were they "selling," Have I sold out to similar procrastinations webbed over my life?

Roman Catholic definition; "Remission of part or all of the temporal and especially purgatorial punishment that is due for sins whose eternal punishment has been remitted (Christ) and whose guilt are pardoned" (as through the sacrament of reconciliation).

Kristen's definition: I didn't want to take responsibility for my communication with God or mistake/sin, so I paid or traded to procrastination, weakness valid of otherwise in hopes of reducing the "purgatorial" to lessen the punishment on another day. Destiny pushed further away.

The church during Martin Luther's day paid men dressed in a man appointed priest-covering, to absolve them and their responsibility. Indulgences.

God did not have any part. Authentic heaven appointed forgiver, imitates Christ in His ministry before the Father. Mercy triumphs over judgment because someone went to stand judged.

Martin Luther was challenging a local religious structure that was making money off people who believed the clergy had power with God to undo or lessen the outcome of sin. Have I a question for you? Can I ask for forgiveness on your behalf to God? Yes, from the position of a priest. We are all priests and Kings, right! I have another question for you. Does my repentance bring transformation to you? Who's indulging whom now? And how does that come about without the purgatorial system of my time spent? Time spent before the one who sacrificed. If I'm going to over think this, I'll share a short tale. Christmas Eve "Santa" had filled the stockings and set them on the floor in front of the fireplace, for they were too laden with treats to hang. Come Christmas a party arrived before the children did. Ants! Wrapped candy or not they were contending in the masses. The next day I picked up some ant bait and placed it on the trail of said army. The following day with disgust the traps were blackened with troops. I suffered the grossness for several days and imagined them carrying their poisoned bounty back to the evil queen. Success! However, relatives showed up in the bathroom. I picked up one of the ant baits and relocated it behind the toilet, still filled with the casualties of war. Same ant strategy abounds as they followed the repetitive path even with the evidence of death laid at their feet.

Martin Luther's infamy to sever and cut away the rubbish. A means that isn't changing the heart. I might think of it in this way. I'm writing on the door of myself; I want a reformation inside of me. I'm challenging that status quo, the innate repetition; I am guilty of focusing on the temporal to persuade the eternal. Indulgences that are being paid off when all the today's blend into tomorrow's and all I do is look at yesterday, without consequence that inanimate fear is controlling my destiny. Now, who's acting like an ant?

I am picking up my pen:
Tho' sharing may stir things in me I'm unfamiliar with,
Searching for truths,
Consider they may get misconstrued,
"Pen," you allow eyes to look at my weakness or strength of soul to find.
Pen let's change the world.

Change the world: first, change me.

My husband Don gave me a pound of superb chocolates for Valentine's Day; bought from our renowned local Chocolatier. One might say that a pound of chocolates is an indulgence. The day before Valentines I had a conversation with the Lord feeling that "flowers" would serve my "Getting fit" season better than the familiar "go to" favorite. Don has a well-worn path to the chocolatier. Good Chocolate! It was about ten minutes before the noon hour, I thought about texting him suggesting such, that candy was counterproductive to my efforts. An indulgence I didn't need. Remember: Kristen's definition: I didn't want to take responsibility for my communication with God or mistake/sin, so I paid or traded to procrastination, weakness valid of otherwise in hopes of reducing the "purgatorial" to lessen the punishment on another day. My destiny pushed further away.

I struggled and tossed the conversation with Don in my head. How would I approach grace towards a gift that I had not yet received? Happy I was "Getting Fit": Patting myself on the back for following through on a consistent routine of exercise; desiring a smaller more "in good condition" me for the coming summer months. More critical communication is to witness the giving than the receiving on this occasion, so I kept my texting-fingers off of my phone. You guessed it, he came home that evening with a pound of truffles, delighted with himself for conquering his quest before the Valentine masses.

Just a thought? Girls, we ought not to mess up the years of invested training, I should have been dropping hints way before the day arrived.

Odd thing, after Don had given me my "Be Mine" treat; he mentioned that maybe flowers would have been a more appropriate sign of affection. Oh well, aren't we ever learning about marital communication? The joys and trials of it all. Typically, a box of chocolate from a husband doesn't make front page news? Hidden are the thanksgiving kisses shared in secret. With God unwraps in it all, I've created a unique window box with the empty chocolate container. Yes empty! I shared! Sweet in many ways, heart-shaped, brown, with a border of red matting locking tight the cellophane, see-through lid to display the confections at hand. Today, it's posted before my desk and filled with a craft collection of cutouts, taped here and there, making a lovely spiritual reminder puzzle collage similar to Martin Luther's thesis nailed to the door of my heart: indulgences of a divine nature. We started with five, but the end of the book brought six. Cut out-collection, listed in order of appearance:

1. A scribbled note from Don jotted from my Paris notepad on my desk a Christmas gift received from my brother and sister- in-law.
2. A photo of a birds nest with three tiny light blue and brown speckled eggs.
3. A pristine photo of a slice of Champagne wedding cake, with two oranges in the background, looking just picked, leaves intact.
4. A photo of red converse shoes, All Star logo on the heel, low-top with soft-back.
5. New this morning, a small red envelope with a birthday card nestled inside addressed to me and a photo tucked inside of four $50 bills. Corners of the 50 spot, decorated with a single petite sea pearl.
6. Picture, cut out of a set of World War II pilots wings. Added during the manuscript proofreading.

This collection of "Prophetic cut-outs" displayed inside my "Valentine" window box, alongside a rough draft outline of my book cover original title, The Watchmaker. Add in a graphic picture of pink tulips, reminding me of His gift to me. What do they mean? They are living goal markers or change of heart markers that through our relationship God brings them to pass, as I write this book.

I am surrounding myself with the Lords words, how He has expressed His affection towards this "book" project. It helps me to focus. I have known for over 20 years that in me should be a kindred spirit for writing. Hmm, God's affection? Is it possible the Lord knows things about you that you haven't discovered yet in yourself? I say absolutely. Creativity or creating begins with a picture, a collage, a place: they are living letters that I hang on the wall of my heart. Our habits of life can act like a robot. We function with the same actions again and again and achieve the same product. My issue was getting these living markers to yell louder than the inadequacy I felt inside. As a living stone built and attached to Christ corner-ship, I desire to accomplish the destiny that God ordained for me. To fulfill one's future, I have learned to engage (experientially know) what I am destined to be. My conversations with God reveal the plans He has for me. They're not hidden to be a secret; they are un-lit needing lights beam to produce intimacy. Transformations journey involves growing and maturing through; relationships failed, loved, misunderstood at times, from laughter, through tears. When you love people, and people return that affection to you, staying the same is impossible. Because all life has seasons and cycles, seeds fall into the ground for sowing, which is the result of harvest gathering. I've indulged in Him to discover how He has "indulged" in me. I should ask myself where I have planted those seeds. That ought to change the world. If only in my neck of the woods.

How He activates me: I've changed a bit since I first shared the "feared" pages of "indulgences." I also have pinned my book "road-map" on the wall that I received from God. It tells me where the book is going, so the "pen" is working, positioned and pointed. I'll share later in the book how I received the map, and it mystically gets orchestrated in the chapter on Being Seeded or Seated, Prophetic words and Dreams.

I want to highlight number five in the window box Heart. The red birthday envelope picture with four fifty-dollar bills. I received the 200 dollars, yes physically, just a few days after God showed me in the spirit. Faith is active. His words are yes, yes and amen. But I couldn't figure out the Birthday card part! What was curious is that the card had an intuitive "feeling" of being sent from someone who knew me. I couldn't shake the notion.

I have a great relationship with my Mom. She is quite technically modern for her senior years. She is always sending me emails with articles on gardening, decorating, heartfelt and motivational finds. For over a week she had sent me reminders saying: "did you get the e-card?" I was busy and let it just slip by; she reminded me again. Did I get the "e-card" she had sent? No Mom I haven't seen it. Even looked in the junk mail folder to make sure it hadn't been blocked and deposited there. So I asked her to send it again. Well, it still didn't seem to make it through cyberspace and Mom was checking a couple of times daily "Did you get the cute card with the animated birds on it yet?" No, Mom! Well, I am not sure what held it in la la land, but it arrived in my email inbox. I opened a sweet animated card, with birds flying and singing. Guess what? The merry tune to this little e-card was Happy Birthday to you, Happy Birthday to you, da da da da da da da, Happy Birthday to you. I just smiled. Lord, I did get a birthday card from someone who knew me well, even months away from my Birthday. Mom sent it because the birds were adorable. There are other hidden treasures God has loaded into the little red card. I know that it is a window of four's, a window of Jubilee, multiplied fours of pearls of a high price.

Twenty-One thousand six hundred and fifty-five words since I confessed my problems with my pen. And if I think about it, it's somewhat mind-boggling someone/you are reading this journey with me. Thank you. Let's establish some "New friend" guidelines; and cut each other momentary "venting" rights which in this case have focused on me, me, me, myself and I's. Change is difficult. Writing challenging, but getting better.

Ok, can I tell you another heaven story pretty much off topic, from Introduction to Indulgences? It's just that I am reminded of it when I mention you being part of my pen.

During the New Year season, I set aside some quiet time to be with the Lord; hearing and procuring goals, promises, and provisions for the upcoming year as our focus. I had never stepped in ahead of time to heaven for divine resources to fill the year ahead. So, it's a kind of a rookie journey: supply and demand for this vision at heart. Odd how you spend years praying for things that you desired yesterday. What a different concept to apprehend them according to His plans for you before the need occurs. Yippee! Often, inside of me, when engaging new "heavenly" territory of heart, Old framework/mindsets arise and feel like somebody is going to "catch" me and say, what are you doing here? Like the proverbial iniquity of getting caught with your hand in the cookie jar.

To transform, I apply myself and do the work to change how I am responding. Protective habits of "feelings of hiding spiritual experiences" had to change. Time well spent in His presence has apprehended faith in my experiences in heaven, and their fruit was gaining significant ground.

For the upcoming year and project in writing, I met Jesus on the Sea of Glass. He has that look, with a shy smile on His face, of knowing your intent. Hidden conversations in my heart are saying; Yes, Sirree I'm not doing this year without asking, seeking, knocking and walking through the door. So off to the treasury room. We walk to meet up with Melchizedek, Chancellor of Gods Treasury Room. Chancellor= A priest in charge of public (heavenly) records. If you read in Genesis and meditate on the offering given to him from Abraham, you will begin to see his original origin. No, teaching here. Back to my encounter. I'll share an anchor from (my) perspective; the Treasury room door is much like I would walk into a cave opening at the base of a majestic mountain. I have always met Melchizedek at the entrance. He is regal, unpretentious, humorous, purposeful, ready to teach, patient for you to learn, and inquiring about your story. In my different encounters with Him, I have experienced both, a human looking man and also a brightly light-filled spirit. It's just a different lens that develops in your seeing. You'll get there. So, here I am at the door, we exchange our greetings, hugs and such, my purposeful self-shining bright with intent. I have my marching orders from God and need supplies. The cave lined in gold, I'm sure that it has many things to discover within it but currently, my experiences have been teaching me just to receive (without over thinking it) provision. Most items, scrolls, index cards, tools, resources... have been within the cave-like-room at hand. Getting to know Melchizedek in his foyer - so to speak - the relationship has been a focused key. There are manners and etiquettes in heaven: Being invited into "more" of someone's abode is offered through relationship. I have eternity to venture into discoveries. I pass the large index file cabinet on the left of the entry. There are what look like apple boxes sitting on the floor, filled with treasures lining the side of the room. Immediately I am given a treasure chest full of gold coins; my spirit pours the coins out on a portable table as we have for my church, said table has folding chairs around it. Heaven is a fascinating place, a place of generous permission. That is what my spirit perceives, permissions far beyond the imagination. My spirit-eyes seem to hone in on what I was meant to seek. I see a sword hanging on the wall. Heaven is alive, so your perception "feels" and communicates emotions via your spirit, bubbling over with real touch-impressions to your body. Secretly fixated on the sword, I can feel might, value and an extraordinary history I'd love to hear from its former handlers. It's an awe moment for sure. Easy to be overwhelmed in a good sense from this glorious place. Experience knees are wobbly, so I ask Melchizedek for his wisdom and help to guide me for what I am going to need. Changing your DNA from lack to abundance requires lots of capable tutors. Amen! He smiled at me, and both our eyes were drawn back like a magnet to the sword on the wall. Well forged steel, simple design, balanced handle with turned grips and a single narrow leather strip tied around its neck. Heaven is listening: conversations; my conversation is heard and spoken from the heart, through lips never moving as my spirit is moving toward the sword for a closer look. With my questions spoken in thought: "What's the significance of the leather straps?" I asked Melchizedek. My answer arrived in no time? "The strap is a portion of David's leather slingshot." Well that takes your breath away now doesn't it. My next question of its ownership arose with a surprising audaciousness, not that I needed the sword, but may I have it? His/Melchezidek's response was humbling: "Nobody else has come to get it..." Selah. My journal notes say: what an odd statement Sir King of Salem. When I said this to him, he held out his left hand to me and in it was a small round ancient pure gold snuff or pill box, the size of a fifty-cent-piece, fitting petite-lay in the palm of his hand. My first impressions feel like there is gold dust inside? He smiled at me as we exchanged gifts, I gestured forward and covered both our hands with my left hand to hug-hand-shake the exchange. Thank you. I put the mighty sword on my back and thanked him for the golden box. It feels like a personal gift. I must have been twenty inches taller than when I came in. A remnant of greatness (the sword) hung on my back, my clothes mysteriously transformed in the exchange as I walked out with a new suit of armor and a personal treasure in my hand. As I was going from there to here, or back to my humble prayer pillow, in the spirit, I examine his gift, a little gold snuffbox. Pondering if it could hear my thoughts: What do you do? And what do you hold, for what purpose will I learn to unleash your beauty? Question opened the answer as my eyes accessed it like a key. Unlocked my sight to view laying in-hand a lens. I saw a realm of rooms having tiled floors of mathematical patterns. While drowning in the glories laying in my hand, I heard laughing and conversation around me. "She got it!" From heavenly witnesses. I saw circles of seals of authority stacked one on top of the other like a tunnel of DNA. A tunnel, no a spiral staircase of transformation!

PROTOCOL ACTIVATION: Today, I've journaled the unexplainable and received my provision from heaven. All the mandates (scrolls, assignments) I've received need recording, so I stepped into the Record room to see Edward (Scribe) and then release what I experienced to my angels. Receive, agree, record, release. Write the declaration.

In moments not governed by time, I'm back sitting on my prayer pillow. Even re-writing the encounter rekindles the fantastic of spirit. Heaven is alive, today I can step back into the life that I lived when I was in its dimension of wonder. I'm basking in its surprises and mystery, with a few tears, bowing down to the greatness, the personalized details and the pleasure I feel; Father to daughter. God, maturing His child.
I'm so glad I asked.

So, why did I take a fantastic rabbit trail with you? Rabbit trails just lead to another opening in the "family" burrow. The little gold, which I call snuff box, I highly doubt they need snuff in heaven. Giggle giggle! Since that day I activated it by spiritually setting the paper cutout "snuff box" on my table/desk with me, surrounded and encouraged by my menagerie of heart-window-box of motivational promises. I've changed and found boldness from what I said before the adventure:

Twenty-One thousand six hundred and fifty-five words since I confessed the problems I felt with my pen with you. And if I think about it, it's pretty mind-boggling that you are sharing this journey with me. Thank you. Thus far it's been focused on me, myself and I's. Would I suggest many parts could be your story? I've read the end of the book, chuckle and together were in for a life-changing treat.

RABBIT TRAIL, YOU READY? OK, from the Introduction to Indulgences "the window box." I included you being part of my pen. A little over a week ago I was writing, struggling to write and I saw God's hand reached over my shoulder from behind. He opened the small gold "snuff" box, grabbed my pen in the spirit with my hand on it and with both our hands holding the pen, dipped into it like an inkwell: writers together to write, pen filled with heavenly ink.

You are now part of my pen. You are part of His pen.

Another goal accomplished: my first time setting a target of two thousand words per day. Day one. Two thousand one hundred and sixteen just today. One fifty-one in the morning. Current Project: twenty-three thousand and five. Only forty-seven thousand, seven hundred and forty-five left to pen. Blessings

CHAPTER 2

In the beginning, God

Suffix: "Something added to the end of something else."
ists, ism's and atics. Birthed and raised in a "suffix" realm.
Baptists, Fundamentalists, Charismatics, Pentecostalism...

When you're a child, you never question why we attend community buildings, week after week, year after year. It's what "Christians" do: Go to church. However, your neighbors just down the gravel road from you gather their children much the same every Sunday morning; They go to the building just around the corner from yours. Even Grandma and Grandpa's building has a similar sign post perched for view by local traffic. We go in and out and celebrate weddings, funerals, Sunday school in the basement, anniversaries, Mother-Daughter teas, choir practice, and baptisms. No questions, really: that's all I knew. Maybe that is what my parents knew? There is comfort in the structure of repetition and traditions. When I started having children, I jolted awake looking into the eyes of loin of my loin, flesh of my flesh; I began to question. My broken heart responding to a "cry" for wholeness, and I did the same thing, jumped back onto the train of "Church." For me, church in itself has mostly lovely memories: the gathering, and getting together with people who form a community around you. I love His presence with and within His kids. Making "Truth" my own, I found the "suffix" man added to the Gospel and differences started to show.

From the "ists" house, I felt Him most when Mom sang special music. Helen, Joyce, my Mom, if I remember the names right, were a familiar trio that stepped out from within the choir for special music. The familiar and melodic music would float into the comfort of my heart and say: "That's God and isn't my Mom pretty." Hymns would carve a chasm of "church" that today when I hear the music, memories wash like a river filled with spring rain. Rushing songs, married with the frequencies of my heart, like photos in the cyber clouds hidden in a touch of an application. Memories: The ultimate weather system with infinite storage.

Mom did all the driving, checking for dirt behind the ears, hurrying to be on time, and fear-of-God looks from the choir loft if my brothers and I were jostling outside of invisible chalk boundaries on the pew. I am the only girl, number three in the birth line up. As young-un's hands would fidget: elbows collided as premeditated irritation weapons, and we doodled with that tiny pencil conveniently placed on the back of the bench before you, drawing on resources provided on the front and back of little offering envelope. Oops! Clunk, as I dropped the hymnal and its balanced doodling content of small pouches, Sunday school papers sliding from my lap. Moving in slow motion, it allows me to use up two more minutes of monotonous time to retrieve it. I can feel Mom's Superman eyes peering from the choir loft while I casually, in my own "sweet time," return to view from my seat. Oh, the kid drama in the pew: makes me smile.

Don and I began looking, searching, or "shopping," for a "church." We didn't even have enough language to know what flavors were out there. We searched for a blend of the familiar patterns that bring us tradition and hope. What a shuddering image in the mindsets we steward, church shopping! That proverbial "seeking" Sunday morning torment, trying to manage time, stepping into a community aristocracy feeling like you're the court jester come to entertain the king: The new kid on the block of a relationship. Church-Relationship and God, there must be a better way! Our top trophy memory is awarded and held by our son Jacob. We were between the (ists) moving toward the (ism's) at this foursquare breakfast. Opening the sanctuary door: hurried, and late, we bumped into venerated generations of a lay person's backside position, of His Father, Father's Father "USHER," like Jimmy Stewart in the movie Shenandoah. Always in haste, juggling kids and ignoring husband's comments to get back into the car and drive home. We were always trying not to make a scene, sitting, in the second to the last back row pew. Many of us have been there. I'm holding baby boy number four in my arms, his two older brothers able to sit the saddle and two-ish Jacob is on his knees, head on the bench, drifting in and out of sleep from the drone of the monotone message. Don and I are pretending not to "feel" curious eyes on the back of heads all around us. Breathe, Kristen. This family drama is trying to put a good face on for the Joneses and Smiths. Let's liven the story a bit, draw more unwanted attention. Well, you certainly know what boys do, in that lucid-sleep place of la la land. Yes, our sweet little one ripped a stinker that vibrated the sacred row. The silent reverence broke without an invitation; muzzled shoulder laughs, domino effect waved through, boys, humiliated parents and the row of our maybe "new best friends." With lost dignity and lack of control, you held your breath, in and out to control its urge.

The smell awakens those sleeping with their eyes open in front of you and their "sweet little" ones turn around to begin searching for the guilty party. Silence, judgment, and shame are ousted every time a shoulder shakes, and the "wave" starts all over again. We didn't wait to shake the Pastor's hand and couldn't get to the safety of our car fast enough.

I'm sure somebody needs a-little inner healing from all that! In the scheme of "church shopping," Don pleaded with me and "I," the "obedient one" (smirk), compromised to his request, and agreed to his same old same old building, attending the historic local Lutheran church. Who would have guessed its serving pastorate were a "Closet," Holy Ghost, tongue talkin' Reverend and his lovely wife? But don't tell anybody I told you! (Sad to say we keep those pure Holy Ghost manifestations secret.) His hand even in the "same ole." God's, perfect match: I could stretch my wings and visit the "atics" on less than sacred days and practice the new-found gifts on unsuspecting Lutheran "ism". What a gas!

I hear you. I can laugh now and appreciate learning from my strange seeking journey: I suppose a host of you may shudder. Others of you never returned to the faith of your fathers, never making Him personal, your own. Many have no history or family story. My kids have often said: "Mom you forced us to go to church." Oh, the trauma that has unfolded surrounding buildings as we repetitively heeded the magnetic call. Many sides of a story, what does the heart say?

In the beginning, God, it was good, very good. Did we focus and build doctrines that enforced consequences from a garden we didn't understand? Wasn't the garden of Eden a window between here and there where Adam walked with God? I'm guilty of not personally having asked, Him the questions, and took doctrines, generationally handed down, as truth. Is it all good? Depends on whose blood it's washed in?

I had fun along the pathway. My, "In the beginning, God." I managed to find healing for my broken heart, wings broken a time or two in the politics of it all. I messed up my kids I'm sure, and I purchased every spiritual book I thought would "enlighten" my husband.

Have I just continued the legacy of adding a suffix on the name post of the building in which I gathered? No! Let me share with you another life story that has me suggesting that maybe we started at the wrong "starting line."

It takes place in the same pew where I giggled, fidgeted, and was visually threatened by my Mom from the choir loft to sit still: North West corner of Main and Monmouth Avenue. The sign said it was first in all the "ist's." There was a cement ramp off to the side leading from the sidewalk to double doors. A darkly suited usher and his wife with outstretched hands, greeting. Pastor Whiting, from my grammar school memory, was tall, lean, always-in-a-dark-suit, Abe Lincoln looking man. His spirit was gentle, a passion descended into the pages of his bible and ascended with a voice of grace. I heard it! His wife smelled like violets, barely seen behind the keys of the church organ, eyes twinkling under a small pastel bonnet with a swish of veil brooched up to the left. I think my great-grandma Coffman had at least ten of them in her closet. I'm the daughter of a grocery man, growing up on an Oregon farm, seated with my family seven rows back, left-hand side. We are taking up most of the pew except for a brave "in love" college couple who would fill the end by the stain-glass windows. In my memory, nothing was amiss, from foyer to silver communion set, prominently placed on the "In Remembrance of Me" table. Same old, same old followed generationally, all the way from Keota Iowa, visiting the California shores, down Boone's Ferry road to Independence Oregon; church.

Let's get to the end of the story. A percentage of you will read the end of the book first anyway, so I might as well put the ending up front so we can begin, at "Christ's victorious manifestation" on earth, the wilderness experience didn't benefit those who traveled its path.

After months of struggle, God coordinated my overly mystical self and gave me a map to follow, for writing this book. In the spirit, I encountered a vehicle with the "Book" map; a train numbered 161. That's what "Papa," Father God, called it. The locomotive is running on a single set of railroad tracks stretching across a rain forsaken land. It wasn't modern and if I visualize the word "Locomotive" it presents the picture of a vintage, powerful engine, with a bit of nostalgic smoking character. The numbers were stenciled and painted in gold "161" on the side of a regal, black, coal powered workhorse with a collection of cars linked and trailing behind. It seemed more like a freight train than a passenger train as most of the cars were shallow and open. I did a bit of Google searching for different kind of railway cars to see if I could find what I pictured in my spirit? Hmm, I'm not finding it, the name of the type of cars I perceive. Thinking back, I remember; my brothers and husband Don all still having their original Lionel train sets. There it is, I found it. Identified as? "Barrel and Gondola cars". They were short sided paneled cars for carrying and loading supplies, open-air to allow entry for cumbersome crane and forklift access. That is what Father, showed me. I don't know if it has any "Prophetic" hoopla at all. I didn't add the numbers up to see if they meant this or that. Mostly I just listened and didn't second-guess what He was saying, just train 161.

Here's some clarity and understanding; that's His part of the story. You see, well maybe you haven't "seen" yet? Ask Nicodemus and Jesus about the importance of seeing in the spirit? Do-the-dance and wrestle with the "doctrine," recover your "visual" seeing-in-the-spirit inheritance and you'll be "seeing" before this story ends. OK!

The day before yesterday I was given this map, a spiritual plan to navigate this book project. Which is very helpful, because I have been wrestling mindsets and mud for a few months trying with all my strength to put this book together. God was pleased with my progress. However, my measuring stick was on a different scale than His. I have been pressing in on this project for almost eight months. From my perspective, it should have been virtually finished "yesterday." Oh, the plumblines we drop on ourselves!

I've already shared with you where the "train" 161 picked me up. Corner church anywhere, USA, right! The map showed a pathway crossing a wilderness. No surprise, eh? Wilderness mindsets or man-made additions of ists, ism's and atics, all those suffixes neatly attached to my thinking, added to titles, for building, movements, revivals. Remember what's added to the "END." In many of the chapters of this book, you'll read the different circumstances I walked through. We have similar experiences I have no doubt. Changing the title from The Watchmaker to The Unfinished Book seems fitting. Even if I did write two different beginnings. Crossing the wilderness is not a new concept. It didn't benefit the Israelites too much, did it? Let's go over the river and get to the mountain.

A couple of years back I asked the Lord about my "conversion" experience. Yes, when I got saved! I invited Jesus into my heart and said the sinner's prayer. I shared with you the bits and pieces of those memories or as much as my sanctified imagination has provided. I was eight years old: couldn't tell you what Pastor Whiting was preaching about but I heard and answered His call. The pastor invited me to come forward and meet Jesus. So, I did. I raised my hand from the seventh row, left-hand side, began to move out of my seat. Most of us are familiar with this step of faith and probably prayed with a Pastor/leader. That part I don't remember, the upfront praying stuff. That is why I asked the Lord, what "actually" (from the perspective of the realm of the Kingdom) happened on that day? My day? In the spirit of it all? We've heard about angels having a party in heaven. I have never heard testimony from the spirit realm on this transition. So, He showed me.

Stepping into the picture/encounter with Him: He whisked me away (in the spirit) back into First Baptist Church, Monmouth, Oregon, through an invisible door. The divine meeting altered me, my eyes spiritually opened, measured time surrendered, and I found myself once again standing in front of my seat: Row seven, left side pew. Kristy Richards-Wambach, 55 years old, looking from my heart-eyes inside myself, seeing myself age 8. I could still see my family sitting in the pew; I was standing. The sanctuary was filled, well attended with all familiar folks. They were in time: I was "outside" of time. It appears as if the molecules of my body and the people around me were moving at different speeds. The invitation-sound of the call to Him has transformed me, changed my hearing and sight. Coming down the aisle, moving around Pastor Whiting, was Jesus. He was dressed in a beautiful white robe, with a simple gold woven thread belt, wavy darker brown hair about shoulder length. Yes, that was Jesus, and He was walking towards me, Blue eyes with transforming fire: they didn't appear like I'm-going-to-burn-up fire or flames: they were pools of love, on fire love cisterns, overflowing into the room, into my inner being. Jesus's right hand stretched forward to meet mine. My thoughts seemed spoken out loud. "Did Pastor Whiting have any idea that He was "really" there?" Jesus' smile was filled with outstretched mystical hands as if touching people as He passed them sitting in their row. I took hold of His extended hand, the room filled with the flame of ten thousand candles, (Angels & Glory). I was unaware. All irrelevant to seeing Him, looking at me. Jesus just smiled at me as I took in the atmosphere, seeing, feeling, sensing heaven opening on earth. My curious nature squeezed tight to His hand. I was safe. It felt like His arms were hugging and holding me with more than just His hand. Curiosity in me surveyed everywhere to capture the room in my spirit. I caught the directional shift of His eyes: I turned my head left. The colors of the stained glass window panes moved and changed into a bright living liquid. I have never seen them that way on a Sunday morning. Then "they" stepped through: larger than life! As windows became doors giving access. At 8, I didn't recognize the two of them, my understanding at age fifty-five did. Both of them were dressed as Jesus was, white linen robes tied at the waist, their tan leather belts not gold like His. The one standing next to Jesus and on my left was tall, six-foot-something, strong, sturdy, muscular. His robe just gracing his knees: hair a wash of ash blonde with streaks of brown loosely trimmed up over his neck. Regal in demeanor. He looked at Jesus, his eyes honored and bowed. When Jesus looked at him, they appeared to be old friends, trusted, faithful. (My eyes, at this moment, seemed to have many lenses or visions which viewed "extra sightedness.") In one lens, I could look at this larger than life man wearing armor and sword. In another lens-instance, he was prostrated on his face receiving instruction, notable in council. There was an awe about him as we met, eye to eye: not a man to trifle with, a man of excellent standing.

In awe, my spiritual-eyes moved on, to meet with my next heavenly introduction. His spirit-man felt familiar. I liked him right away. Many things about him were similar to me, and I wasn't sure how I knew this. 5'9 or 5'10 wiry, more unkempt but very keenly aware. His hair color was like Jesus, messy, just below chin length. A grin from ear to ear, with a mischievous persona, like he's the guy from your youth that you hung out with if you wanted to jump the fence to avoid paying for tickets to get into an outdoor concert: No boundaries, break rules that need breaking, great faith. His, and Jesus's eyes met, and they exchanged thoughts simultaneously. Jesus nudged me over toward my new friend, and he put his arm around my shoulders. I found myself standing between them, watching a conversation shared without a word spoken. Did I keep eye contact with Jesus; in a good-nervously way, saying in my spirit you are staying close right? Absolutely. *Moses looked at me, mentor to student, Elijah grinned and chuckled as a friend with water under the bridge, foreseeing my destiny and what I would forerun. Selah.*

As swiftly as I had been taken through to another realm, I was once again back through the mystical doorway, sitting in my living room on my prayer pillow. By this time, I was weeping. Jesus had shown me what happened on that day of salvation. Now that's a conversion experience! Amen. It took me fifty-five years to encounter it. My head is whirling with questions, but the emotion of the encounter is fresh, bubbling up. I know where I was and the type and shadow it created.

Tomorrow's another day.

I figured out my spiritual eyes years ago and took off the training wheels with a bit of confidence. Encounters have become a familiar everyday language in my relationship with the Godhead. Visions/sight/seeing whether a picture, video or translation. To this day, I can move in and out of the experience because it remains alive. Heaven is alive. Through divine mentoring, much practice and learning the arm's reach of time. The Kingdom of Heaven is at hand: how to step in, around, out and in.

Ian Clayton, a great forerunner, gives wise counsel: "up and down first" into the realms of heaven, in and through relationship, then "to and fro," on the timeline of history, life, and ages."

All movement is part of the length, breadth, width, height, depth of His love. Up and down is through the veil into the Kingdom of Heaven, back and forth, practice, practice, practice. Relationship births responsibility. To and Fro is on the timeline, going with Jesus is always a safe, win-win situation, never out of His perfect "timing." He will introduce tutors into your life.

When I penned this day, I hadn't re-engaged with Moses. Of course, that statement has changed while walking out this book-project. Elijah: yes, I have met up with him again in the Discovery Chancellor House. I hear your questions. Please ask Him. More information/teaching does not benefit us. We do not want to create another "map" of knowledge without experience. Isn't that what initially got us off the relationship path?

What has challenged me, and Jesus knew I would chew on it and eat it, was that my new-birth, salvation beginning, was His earthly end. Or shall we say, His heavenly re-start. So how much of His Kingdom-in-eternity am I opened too? He was crucified before the foundation of the world, before the Mount of Transfiguration. He revealed it through a relationship in our understanding. To this day I feel very privileged to experience encounters like the ones that Jesus drew close to Himself: Peter, James, and John. That mountaintop remains open and alive in my spirit, treasured as a very personal encouragement: Who needs a prophetic word after that? I am firmly suggesting that it's not a "select" experience, or that He is a respecter of persons. No longer can we cast off the responsibility of our inheritance of seeing in the spirit. Our ignorance attached in our perception of the kingdom "realms," has cast aspersion toward a host of people we have labeled:

1. Nuts, fruits, and flakes
2. Mystics
3. Super spiritual ones
4. Operating within a Prophetic Office
5. From an orphan mentality saying: it's because of favor or calling.

How far did He rent the veil? And for whom? The answer is "All" to both questions. Spiritual sight is your inheritance. I suggest we are stretching our perceptions of what evangelism is meant to be? I hope so.

Not quite thirty years after I jumped on board His train, 161, I frequently stop at a lot of suffix like "encampments" along the way, like so many people do: getting on and off. I wasn't out of the wilderness till I crossed the bridge of His torn flesh. That is where we should all have our beginnings: Through the veil, not the wilderness. Start on the mountain of transfiguration.

ANOTHER TESTIMONY: I changed her name to Bonnie. I'm still in a relationship with her, and she knows that I am sharing part of her story.

Bonnie, is rough around the edges, tough as nails unless she lets you into her heart. She's a diamond in the making, tender, kind, encouraging, beautiful, creative and I love her. I met her over ten years ago while hiring staff members to work for me at the local youth summer camp. Her Mom came to the interview looking a little disheveled by her strong-willed daughter. I loved her immediately and hired Bonnie.

"Believing in someone is a transformational exchange. Bonnie had no references until I gave her one. Metamorphosis occurs when they see you sign your name on their reference papers."

Summer camp is a great experience but dealing with negative parenting style issues (the lack of discipline or controlling spirit) is immense. Bus driving and Camp Director are both ministries that receive a host of colorful and graphic words. I thought, maybe I am warming up to try umpiring baseball! Appreciate your bus driver today, please.

After "pre-camp" training, it was time to run the race. Parents happily dropped off a new set of campers every week. Bonnie was an ace, though not as a model employee. You could sense that her thoughts were always somewhere else. But she continued to come back to camp after breaks. I was amazed. I'd assign her the trying, terrible campers, the ornery cases, the chip on the shoulder ones, the bullies and brilliant children who manipulated and controlled any possible authority. Bonnie had a nack: brilliantly dealing with special needs children who knew they were special and could work the system, broken children that could vomit on cue to get their point across, parents label of (she's allergic) to everything children. I worked Bonnie hard, and she was marvelous. Her fellow camp counselors and the campers loved her because she was tough and knew the drill by personal experience (been there, done that, burned the T-shirt). Sadly, she only worked for me for one season: Memories forever embedded in my heart. I lost track of Bonnie through her final high school years. Then she started popping up erratically now and again, which turned into divine coincidences as we kept running into each other, even outside of our local coming and going's. I Love it: Holy Spirit's moments. What clinched the relationship to mentorship was my church leased offices and worship place which were in the same building as her Mom's office. Bonnie worked for her on and off. The mentorship birthed. After denying and wrestling with the pull, Bonnie began to find herself seated in my office, tears running down her face and amazed that somebody would listen. It was usually on a whim of desperation, but my door was open. Over the course of a few months, we started walking through some inner healing. I asked her when she said a derogatory statement about herself, "Are you OK with that?" She'd respond with "Why; what do you think?" I threw the ball (negative confession) right back, time to listen to your own heart and deal with what it's saying. From what I know about her, the only "ism" or church structure she got exposed to was a generational one. Weddings and funerals, you went to church. It was more her nationality than a conviction from her parents, less "religious" structural damage. The pattern of her popping into my office on a whim was transparent. She was missing the ownership and responsibility, I needed to show her how she could meet with Jesus without me being in the room. The next time a situation pushed her into my office, she said: "Do that thing that you do and make it go away," meaning the torment, distraction, shame. The enemy always has an auto start setting filled with YouTube's of our lives. I got up from my desk and motioned, let's go hang out in the prayer room for a bit. We settled ourselves comfortably on the floor pillows, leaning against the wall and she began to "dump." Up went my hand, nope, before you share we need to step into heaven so you can share with Him. She said OK. How do you do that? In brief, I shared with her that when Jesus died on the cross, she was familiar with that, His death ripped through and removed what had separated us from Father God. Because of Jesus, we have complete access to Father God. It's called the veil. We can step through by faith in Jesus. She didn't need a middleman, or me: Only Him. I asked her if she believed that Jesus wanted to talk to her. She said yes. We bowed our heads and closed our eyes for honor and focus purposes. I mentioned to her that Jesus was going to show her a particular thought, feeling or a picture! Just believe what He shows you. We waited for just a moment, and she was spiritually inside, crossed over (The gospel is simple, easy to recognize His love.) I asked her what she was perceiving. She began to share a particular room and Jesus was there with her. She went on to describe in part as emotion began to consume her. Bonnie sharing out loud, grew less a part of her experience as I watched her like she was viewing a 3D movie: Tears, recognition, emotions. She only asked me a few times "What should I do?" I just directed her back to the Author and Finisher of her faith. She heard, saw in the spirit and responded like a champ. Jesus spoke, answered, and guided her brilliantly. The best inner healing meeting to date, I have had the privilege to observe. She had clarity of all that went on. I think we were in the prayer room for maybe forty minutes. When Jesus ended that particular conversation, she sat wiping her wet cheeks, free, loved, a little stunned, and emotionally spent. Bonnie looked at me and said: "I was in heaven, wasn't I?" I smiled, knowing the gentle hand of Savior and friend. Yes!

Life and Bonnie still wrestle with each other. She is holding down a good job, rents an apartment and is making a home for her and her son. I don't see her as often because our paths have changed. She texts me now and again, and we get together when she is in town. Yes, I still listen to her struggles. The listening reminds her that I love her, so she quiets, and we always meander back to that moment when Jesus sat with her in a secret place. She talks about Him, how He made her feel, how gentle and real that encounter was and is. He remains alive, practical and accessible to her today. She still is discovering that relationships walk together over a period of time/life. I am so proud of her and thankful to have introduced her to Jesus on the mountain. He - already transfigured in her heart, the only cross she will ever know - is the One who through experiential relationship, brings victory, love, destiny, resolve, unity, and why He chose to carry it. The Jesus she knows is alive, ruling and reigning and willing to remove any brokenness. There is no "Suffix: Something added to the end of something else," No Jesus-ists, Jesus-isms or Jesus-atics, just Jesus and all of heaven to begin to live from, in, and to.

He is a great friend,
Holy Spirit an excellent teacher and
Father God, loving, long-suffering until we are ready to be fathered.
They thought of everything! And then created:
In the Beginning God!

Three thousand nine hundred and forty-four words in this chapter, Twenty-four thousand two hundred and ninety words entirely.

SIMPLE ACTIVATIONS: "BARREL AND GONDOLA CARS."

Step in by faith: I wait for Him to prepare the communion "elements." In the spirit!

My perceptions: You are welcome to join us. I'll share an anchor for you to grab if that'll help. Then He will paint a personal place for you. It's entirely OK if the scene takes on changes and looks different from mine. Trust Jesus in you.

I'm sitting with Jesus, high on a mountain. You can see mountains cascading behind mountains as the range goes forth. The lush hillside is rolling and green, making me feel like I imagine Ireland is which I have yet to discover outside of the Dublin airport. He, Jesus, hands me/you a Twinkie, representing His body (I smirk bending my cheek and only one dimple. He's so not-super-spiritual).

Back to the Twinkie: when He passes it to me, Jesus hangs on to His portion, and the Twinkie rips between our grasp. The filling is exposed and I hear Him saying:

"Brokenness was always supposed to reveal the cream center." My confession: Jesus, I hand you debris that I have loaded onto my life, like the barrel and gondola cars across the wilderness. I was never supposed to carry it. Forgive me for choosing to ride the rails across a desert of disobedience. I exchange it for the true riches and divine resources that I receive by faith in the mystery of this communion. I receive everything You, and Father have already "thought" of and placed into this divine manna for my journey.

Well, you know what you do with a Twinkie? You suck out the cream. I know; super spiritual.

The cup: Jesus hands me one of those new-fangled Hydro Flask water bottles, smiles, and says:

"I prepared this a long time ago: it's still cold and refreshing."

I thank Him for His body and blood... in me, changing and transforming me into His likeness.

CHAPTER 3

A Lady in Waiting

"You have my undivided attention, again."

My first attempt to write a book came much like the season of transition I am walking during the writing of this book. Familiar doors I have traveled through for over seven years have closed so I must learn/believe and seek to reroute in alignment with my destiny path. At times hard transitions in the moment make me feel like Father has sat me down to have a good talk, yet I'm the only one in the room. My thoughts in this season tend to lean to what did I do wrong instead of what did I do write - right. We are notorious for evaluating ourselves harshly saying: "I must have missed God, I heard Him wrong. You are out of God's timing." Sounds like a Lady in waiting.

For those of you with whom I am on email terms with, you know this Chapter title as a portion of my private email address. That said, my email address dates me, on the email and technological calendar. How long have you had your original email addresses? In today's busy technical language, we usually have more than one Cyber-address: Home, business, ministry. Life certainly has sped up since Tom Hanks and Meg Ryan starred in the movie "You've Got Mail". Easy to remember the sound of that old "Dial-up noise." Now we get impatient if a website doesn't load in nanoseconds. Ladies in Waiting have been around much longer than emails.

On my journey with inward acknowledgment, I was broken; I did experience His hand of mercy. Two ways for me to unpack the broken milestone.

1. I'm not being "led" at all, but walking a route determined by making or following a trail of debris. Brokenness resulting in remains of rubble is woundedness without a relationship with the healer. Or:

2. Brokenness in the hands of the Master framed in the life of a vintage flower vase which has been sitting on a shelf, specially chosen to hold a bouquet that He planted a long time ago. If you have a sincere desire for wholeness, pursuit sets you on a course of seeking. I never agreed with "praying" for "brokenness." Life offers enough without beating my chest for it. Yes, He is close to those with a broken and contrite heart.

His near presence I found through intimacy without pain. Authentic brokenness is a conversation with Jesus standing in the room; love reveals sight of the glories He planned for you. Love manifest brings confession, and I fess up to having made my own choices and go for it alone.

How far can any of us outrun a trail of debris run from the Lover of our souls; refuse love, dissuade our hearts, reject His love? In our past, we've all run, what might be to the ends of the world, maybe in the severest opposite direction from God. We kid ourselves to think that He, Father God, hasn't prepared well in advance to be a better parent in the grand scheme of things. In no course of our running, could we ever muster up enough deceit, rebellion, ignorance, or hate towards Him that can outmaneuver His love.

We have not accurately perceived His loving kindness or the places that death's gate appears to usher us too. That is if death in your doctrinal understanding is His chosen means to cross over from this age into the age of eternity. I died with Him on the cross didn't I? If Jesus led captivity captive, did we ask "for whom"? And if He led out captivity why would He leave some behind? And what about the promise of "Greater Works"?

I'll share a story that I have penned several times. Her story marks my attempts at writing a book. Originally a book now singled out in this chapter, "Lady in Waiting," has jumped off, again and again into the recycle bin. My alpha undertaking probably still sitting on the hard drive of my old pink Dell computer. Where to look to find the notes? I mull over my thoughts on her story: daydreaming again, trying to rekindle where I recorded her, when did I share about (her) recently, took a moment to find my notations. Hmm? What words would I use to search for the story? Ah ha! I found the notes in my journals. Searching my journal under Portland Art scene.

INFOMERCIAL HERE! Being a journaler is imagining that you are on a date with Jesus, and He escorts you to "Your" heavenly library of books. If you could pick out one book today, which would you choose to read first? Mystically, your experiences have been written by the hand of God, outside of time, in the beginning, and the end of the "Was was"; in "I Am." Your/His written words about you were spoken/written before you poured your morning coffee and sat leaning on your prayer pillow. Journaling: writing it down, making a note; It's a divinely invaluable lifestyle. Press in, honor hearing God and what He has written about you. Join Him in Journaling. Pick up your pen or iPad today. Ok, roll your eyes at me, throw an excuse my way; I have numerous testimonies from friends and people I mentor about how much their encounters skyrocketed when they began to journal. I challenge you!

Back to the story I was searching for.

Here she is, in my journal. What would we do without "Search bars"? I had recently shared her story with a new friend in an introductory type email. It turns out that this friend is one of the editors of this manuscript. Thank you, Laure. When I was introduced to her; re-phrase that thought? Divine happenstance had already stepped in. I met my European friend during a season when I felt the least capable of stewarding a new relationship. Those emotional times when everything on the inside of you has taken up residency on your shoulders. We all stare at them from time to time. A coat of paint or more makeup won't even make you look shinier to start. I guess I was emitting a heart sound that only Gods selected few could hear. Grace was divinely calling forth what I had sown faithfully in prior seasons. Truth can discern even through brokenness.

I cut and paste bits of that email to my new friend: "I'm sitting with the Lord this morning outside under our freshly completed pergola. The temperature is probably a bit more like your cool English weather; I've dug out of the storage cabinet and plugged in my electric blanket; tuck it around me, cozied in on my rattan settee, to sit with Him." I'm drawing on the atmosphere in my garden which fills me with a sensation of comfort more than the coolness of the morning might detour partaking-sitting within her back-yard beauty. My husband is out the door to work with lunch in hand. Our church, my church belongings just having been packed up in 10x20 storage place; which represents almost ten years of my life. That is my musings and conversations with the Lord this morning. Leaving me saying to Him: "You have my undivided attention "again.""

It has taken me a couple of days to collect myself to share on the pages of this manuscript, contemplating the question; do I want to bridge the sensitive issues rising to the surface in the next paragraphs? In rereading what I have already penned, it's uncanny that I just wrapped myself in that electric blanket again. The house seems cool. Writing is a sedentary action.

I quote again: changing the word brokenness to woundedness. What I perceive in the hands of the Master is I'm a vintage flower vase which has been sitting on a shelf, chosen to hold a bouquet that He planted a long time ago. At times, brokenness & woundedness may squeeze next to each other in the same "VINTAGE VASE." Through years of relationship I rise and say: Search my heart oh Lord, if there be any vexing pathway, lead me into all right standing. My resounding spirit-heart responds with a picture, even my tampered-with insides pick up this rare vase, holding it like a megaphone to my mouth. I release the wail of my heart beat which resounds as an ocean, a seashell echoing. No tear uncaught in His Kingdom.

I was a school bus driver for eight years when my boys were going to grammar school. Convenient, seasonal schedule so I could still be a shadow of a stay at home Mom. Don and I had agreed we wanted this lifestyle for the growing up years of our boys. Bus driving has few perks. It's early, thankless, subject to weather conditions, parent influenced, an excellent job to thicken your skin. Seriously! I'm purposefully sarcastic. To help your pocketbook with a little extra income, you're able to sign up to drive for field trips, athletic events, and extracurricular excursions. During a season of an intense study of the Bible, one of the perks was when I drove students to location, dropped them off, only returning for the designated pick up time, I was free to enjoy my surroundings and getting paid for it. If we get a chance to have coffee together, I have bus story after bus story to share. Miraculous stories, good, bad, and the ugliest of stories. The touching ones have made it into blog posts. You can go and have a look. If I haven't already asked you, and you or your kids ride a bus, thank your bus driver. I'll just ignore for the sake of this simple story the problematic parts of that profession.

I was next up on the "field trip" list and was scheduled to take a noisy bus of 5th graders to downtown Portland for a walking excursion through the local art scene. *Can't help sharing a perspective: you are traveling at 55 miles an hour down the highway with hundreds of hurried drivers wanting to get around your forty-foot yellowness and the only sight of control you have over your noisy "seat changing passengers" is from behind; looking up at your mirror cocked over your head. AAAAh....* Back to the story: I dropped off students and parked the forty foot bus in a little tiny downtown parking space. Bus drivers in the days I drove, were always welcomed to participate in the activities, including any entry fee required. I loved driving for field trips to the Portland Zoo, Rose Garden at Washington Park, OMSI, and my favorite was Oaks Park Amusement where I could sit along the river bank. This particular "Art-scene" trip had my attention, so I traded my alone time with "Him," and offered some "chaperoning" skills to see what creative canvas rested in the Portland Art community. This country girl dropped a curious question and made it a Father-daughter quest. Lord, is there a "Masterpiece" available that I would "shell" out a large amount of hard earned money? Will I find anything that moves my soul? Will I discover an artistic expression that I would give prized wall space or shelf space too, creative "Work," a note of spontaneity that I wanted to be part of my life? Can I imagine a piece hanging in my home that I could meditate on, get lost pondering and share time and time again with friends, its connection to my heart? High expectations, mine are ground level, "I am doubting any possibility of coming upon such a treasure." So, we began our pilgrimage.

Fast forward. Travel to Portland an hour and a half, park bus, kids and teacher on the move, now walking through different art galleries. It didn't take very long for me to be offended and questioned what was called "art". I saw a heavy hand of demonically influenced, pornographic and seriously confused pallets of people who needed some hours of inner healing. I do not consider myself a prude even though feeling a bit art sheltered, as a country mom of four busy boys. I guess you could say: Yes, this art moved me, right to a box of matches outside in the dumpster. That is just the "offense" wanting to talk, of course. I discovered many attractive modes & mediums, original watercolor collections, mother nature's depictions of God's glory; seascapes, majestic mountains, weathered barns, pueblos and flowers in vases. Obviously one of the more memorable field trips that I can recall almost twenty some odd years later. Despite looking at a loud voice of the deterioration of moral society, I was intrigued by my quest and felt sure that my "money" with a smile, was safely hidden in my pocketbook. Today, "art" or artist couldn't pry it loose. Though in the back of my thoughts, I hoped: God's creative painting-portrait-psalmist inevitably must rise! Let's still believe and hope that "He" has a willing vessel with a brush in hand, to speak to me through, by His heavenly handed gift of creativity. By this time, we must have walked through at least five galleries, kids in tow, lunch over, isn't it nap time? Down another alley, following directions scribbled on a small sticky note, carried by a weary teacher. Turn the corner to yet another alley, old pavement path, the smell of urban perfume, rich with history, as we discover a hung staircase, iron bracketed on the side of a city sooted brick building. "This is it," the teacher snapped, up and inside we ventured. I'm trailing behind the group, corralling the lolly-gaggers of spring twitter-pated girls and boys to keep pace. Inside the entry it was vast and airy, industrial beams showing, open studio with natural light, high ceiling, windows set in and around exposed pipes and plumbing. This room led to that room in a maze of false walls, each proudly displaying the fluid of heart to hand. I would suggest, "starving artist." Redundantly and carrying a bit of attitude by now, I ventured around the corner. The day is waning, kids are ready for a snooze trip home, floating atop the vibrating drone of "the wheels on the bus go round and round." Selah! And there "She" was: Suspended breathlessly reaching what seemed floor to ceiling. Divine interruption, I'm frozen! This "Lady in Waiting," the wait was no more. Halted! Noise evaporated within divine hush, kids melted, the room became singular. Selah! Pause and think about that! She was coalesced on a canvas of moist ocean blue-green, layered with ticking smudges and specks of brown/neutral hues, with matter like oatmeal and slivers of shredded cardboard clinging to its stretched cloth. Color, new at birth, like a robin's eggs, nested. Smooth brush strokes, brilliantly painted in springtime, held, caressed and camouflage protected in the precise weave of its parent's design. The canvas cradled "her" in secret attention. Distraction was the softness of her face; smudge circled frame. Long lovely hands are embracing surf interlude. Her body is hidden, silent, no outline except a wisp of suggested fabric masked, and hue between sea-light foam over stirred sand. Pulled in hands cupped around her breast, inches above a delicate oval face with eyes glancing down. I was speechless; even without an audience to speak. Moved, "re-" moved into a noise canceling realm, far from my pubescent passengers sound. "She" made me feel things that I would just as soon keep buried from manifesting in public places: even withhold from His secret places. I starred, pushed back swelling tears that dug up deep emotions. I was mesmerized, my quest conceded to all of "heaven," saying intimately, "Lord, You win, I would love to have her." I stole every moment to stand in her presence while the immature tour loitered round, till teachers looked for my assistance. With a price tag of

$5000, well worth it, I claimed her in my heart for free. I secretly owned her, displaying her in a tall-ceilinged room, hung over a mantle for all to meet.

You're invited into that room today. Sadly, after so many years gone by, I have misplaced a scrap of paper on which I evidently must have written down the artist particulars. Notations I remember: The model's name, "Jane," sister to the Artist, a portrait of a relationship full of color, heart spoken mysteries released in the build-up layers of paint, texture, and simple "face" of a heart. The title of the painting is something like "Blue of sky green of Ocean." My memory recalls the artist, a guest from the Chicago area. Bus trip complete and arriving home that evening I google searched this Artist Portland showing, advertised on the website of the gallery. She - "Jane" - stole my heart and in trade, I copied and pasted to print a 5x7 size, to mere and unworthy office paper, framed in a free cardboard frame that has sat on my "Church" cubicle shelf for 7 1/2 years. I have muddled back over it through the years and haven't been able to relocate painter or painted.

At the time of the email sent to my friend, I continued to say that the inexpensive faux "Jane" I just described to you is also packed and moved into a storage unit as of yesterday. If I had a subtitle for the painting, I would name her "Vulnerable," a picture of beauty trying to veil what the heart is susceptible too. That is what this sister "artist" voice pulled from me that day, 20 years later, now unearthed in the pages of my book. Vulnerable, that is how I feel and have felt in my walk of life, and currently with Him. That is how I "feel" today. Journal post 8/8/16.

Eight thousand two hundred and forty words till I reach halfway. I believe the expression of Jane, can hear!

I'm Vulnerable.

Chapter title, my first (recycle-bin) book title, A "Lady in Waiting," reflects my affection for British aristocracy. I've read horrid historical reports that many "Ladies in waiting" had a reputation within the monarchy. King Henry the VIII is the most notorious backdrop to the hierarchy of "Ladies in

Waiting" that I know. They waited with the threat of being beheaded. My endearment towards this title is more romantic than British bureaucracy.

I'd discovered the promises of a savior: rescuer from myself, my bad choices and now felt like the doctrines I sat hearing, alluded that, I was "waiting." Hope rekindled a journey towards wholeness for which I was willing to pay the price, seek more, know more, undo the trauma triggers and negative DNA that resonated a sound, a generational typeset over my life. I still experience vulnerability with Him, knowing I can't hide my thoughts, but neither can He. I now am exposed to a revelation through communion with Him, that changes that encoding. My image didn't look very much like the original design He knitted in my mother's womb, an opus with thousands of lyrics about my future. I'd been the one making "Him" wait. One can never understand long-suffering until one has "waited" for their child. I was beginning to understand the pain I had caused a blameless parent. As mentioned earlier I ran back to "church," embracing all that I had known before. It seemed to help; finding a bit of comfort in the familiar traditions reminded me of those implanted memories. The Gospel sounded different listening as an adult. I began to visit and briefly attend different houses of worship. I tried to conform to all the doctrinal "Buzz" words reinforcing that a lady, must "wait."

She waits for God because it's always about God's timing.
She waits for her husband because he is head of the wife,
She wants to express the Gospel to others,
but her place is in the home, and not behind the pulpit.
She waits in faith, patiently for her husband to desire
the things she has already discovered,
She waits in quiet spirit for her words are not welcome in God's house.
She waits for God to "save" him. So, she can be correctly aligned.
She waits because her husband is to teach her
and wash her with the water of the word.
She waits for him to discover his destiny.
She waits in support, submission, and service because her desire
is for her husband.
She waits...

Do you know how hopeless & angry that "doctrine" can make a "lady" feel? How ridiculous it is to have a relationship with God, the Spirit transforming you in intimate areas of your life, His Kingdom beginning to manifest around you, yet your experiences must be silenced and on wait mode. Do you know how that leads "ladies" into a place trading onto a platform of manipulation and control? No wonder so many women become "Missionaries;" they are not welcomed in their "own" hometown. Been there, done that; purchased the T-shirt and read the books written by men about "Women in the church." Again and again, I tried to fit the "Cinderella shoe" in obedient submission. How faithful, how many prayers I could pray for my husband. I set my life on hold because, without the "unity" of my husband, I was out of order. Sin was crouching at the door because we were unequally yoked. We were both unequally yoked when we met. I convinced myself that, Faith, great faith, fasting, and prayer would dump the prayer bowls in my favor. I sacrificed, wee hours of the morning, food, read the word, read the word, read the word, confessed the word, declared the word, memorized the word, learned how to bite my tongue because Jesus would respond to my great faith. Even in giving (confession to be noticed by the King) I have made every mistake under the sun, I was trying to get somebody's attention. Without marital unity, I was cursed, and my giving was cursed until my husband got a revelation of giving. I spent so much time trying to be the quiet, gentle unspoken expression of the Gospel that my husband would recognize, I honestly think I got louder and more displeased with the marriage God had ordained, blessed between us. I set myself on a course of repentance for things I couldn't change, couldn't control and a deceived doctrine making God, a respecter of person; that always left me in second place no matter how hard I ran and trained. An orphan spirit: "Looking for permission to be me." I'm supposed to be happy in this subservient world. I was following a written doctrine still cursed from the fall. You know how much grace that takes? But mercy never seems to rain/reign from this throne of grace. I'm so good at "waiting" at this point in my walk that women are seeking me out to help them pray for their homes, families and their husbands. Crazy! His reassuring voice would say, Kristen, you are the one who is listening. Come, follow Me. Not man's structure. It was like the Lady in Waiting of ole', they have a position in court with no voice unless they are seduced or do the seducing of the King. Wait on the Lord, and He will give you the desires of your heart and my desires were for my husband and church to get a clue. Seriously, can we say get a clue! A heart that was supposed to be set free found more bondage in doctrines that didn't know the freedom Jesus lived, died and lives to ever impart. I needed to be healthy, whole and loving Jesus and internally knew Jesus needed to be allowed to love me in truth. You can see why I only made it halfway through the writing of that book. I didn't want to write less than, or who would read about stifled complaining and unmet expectation. A voice of truth shined in me. I carried a revelation of Jesus, who I met, morning after morning, that is different than the Bible interpreted in the particular denominations (ist & ism's) I was attending. I would sit at my piano for hours letting His presence wash over me. We would write songs together, and I sang them over and over again till the walls dripped with the dew of heaven. Hurt was hidden deep in my heart. Jesus and I sang together in the safety of "Truth" the darkness revealed. He illuminated love and lifted burdens. I wrote over a hundred healing hymn or human type songs during those birthing years, waiting years. Hymns: human songs, focused on the personal suffering, aspect or sin. Lyrics, sharing the humanity of life. We sang about hurt, misunderstanding, hopelessness, and neglect. I wrote songs about the shortcomings and mistakes I made in my life. I focused on the problems in my life. Still, the grace of God healed, touched and instructed me. Jesus didn't seem to concentrate on the junk, He just loved my voice and that we were doing something new: A song to the One who saves. Amen.

During this "Lady in waiting" season, I purchased every "save my husband books" and brought them home for him to read; how to love your wife, communication skills, love languages, how to walk in honor. Don't all "Ladies in Waiting"go through that? Oh, Honey, this is an excellent book. They were all written by a man's man about being a godly husband, a godly father, a man of character and integrity. Bah, how much money did I spend? That was back when we use to stand in line after church service to get copies of tapes. I'd bring them home with high hopes that a nugget of truth and light of hunger would flicker. How does one spouse heart get "bitten" so to speak and the other is oblivious to the need for personal relationship? I asked Don years later: "Honey if you would have known when we met and before we got married I would turn into a Jesus freak would you still have married me?" What do you think he said? Dangerous question yeh! He stated that he loved the Jesus in me. He said I was a bit (Jesus) obnoxious at times. He admired my conviction and follow-through.

(Side note: Developing my spirit and healing my soul taught me how God communicates, I learned God's voice and also how God was talking to my husband. Each individual ear has differences compared to than my personal language or communion, and I needed to trust Him with Don. Not hearing God is a different issue.)

In this "Lady in Waiting" season, everything I read/heard and perceived in my mindset in scripture was bent toward a tomorrow, promises were for tomorrow. God is faithful, but it was always tomorrow. God always hears our prayers, but any delay was "God's will" or "God's timing." Again, I was a Lady in Waiting. Everything that seemed promised was in the spirit, for another day, in heaven. I was laying up treasure in heaven, right? Even marriage vows polluted a given life-promise "until death do you part." Take a very emotionally needy mom of 4 young children, feeling bound by man's doctrine of the Gospel that is supposed to set her free and put death in front of her as an escape? If we are transparently honest here, it knocked on my door more than once. The enemy pulls no punches. He knows what kind of sword will be carried into battle one day; he spared no expense to try any hindrance to take me out. Or destroy my testimony of family which would leave me on clean up, brokenness and survival mode for years. Grace indeed stewarded my heart and mercy was tremendously assisting my immaturity.

I'm painting myself as an emotional basket case. Interesting to read over your words that you wrote several days before. How you interpret the condition of your own heart.

I left all the romance and glory out of My Lady in Waiting season.
Hunger drives you, and nothing can dampen promises in the thought of living for Him in an arena of "less than."

His Glories Stories:

"Healing and seeing in the Spirit."

"Gretchen" was the first person in which I witnessed physical healing. I was attending an "ism" church. I met her over a sink of dishes "In the Spirit." Couldn't even begin to tell you what "In the Spirit," "Trans-relocation" meant in those days. Choir practice was on the proverbial Thursday night. Humble in numbers, I overheard members mentioning that they missed

Gretchen's singing voice. New to the congregation, I was quickly caught up with the local news. Her alto voice was laid aside when an injury to her back left her bedridden. For weeks Holy Spirit would bring up a Gretchen conversation during church activities with me standing near enough to hear. So, I began to pray. One evening, our little ones upstairs, Don outside and me having dominion over a counter full of dinner dishes, Holy Spirit "fell" on me. Strange the word fell. Anyhow, I think you understand, a "spirit of intercession" we called it in those days. I began to weep uncontrollably. Ask Don. He remembers walking by the kitchen window and seeing me in tears. In the atmosphere of intercession, I could "see" Gretchen in her home, lying on her bed suffering great pain. I noticed the clock on the kitchen wall said 8:00 pm. I could sense the Lord touching her and Holy Spirit moving up and down her body. She sat up. Intercession realm closed. My tears dried up leaving me with many questions and intimate knowledge of a future dear friend I had not met yet. (Sadly, I had already wised up and buttoned up my mouth when it came to sharing my experiences elsewhere, having discovered unbecoming resistance). Well, Thursday night choir practice rolled around, and the small chorale group convened, standing before the altar in a U-shape, men in the back, women up front to prepare for Sunday's worship. A hesitated push to the heavy double doors in the back of the sanctuary caught all our attention as a young Scandinavian woman with a cane in hand made her way down the aisle. I knew that I knew, while excitedly slapping my friend Steve's arm, "Its Gretchen, it's Gretchen," as her friends gathered around. I was beside myself. Before she joined us, she inquired if anyone could give her a ride home. My hand shot up, and my voice spoke with no regards for social etiquette and said I would. I was bursting with a secret and helping the divine get it shared. My friend Steve smoothed over my anxious faux pas, introduced me and put Gretchen at ease from my zealous outburst. She agreed to let me drive her home. I was elated to have a captive audience, in high hopes that the Lord was orchestrating our rendezvous. A couple of hours later we pulled in front of her little riverfront farm home, and I shut off the car. It was hardly silent because my heart was beating so loud. My emotions rose with a fearful effort to find the right words; tears opened hearts. I shared my "dishwashing experience." and to my surprise, she'd already encountered the same experience from the hand of the Master. We both confirmed looking at our clocks same time; same Spirit, a glorious miracle. Weeks later after another "prayer" meeting, the cane was no longer needed.

"And it Came to Pass."

Holy Spirit and I were enjoying discovering each other. "Renewal Days," though I was outside of the hub. Full-time Mom with one boy in diapers, another in pull-ups and the two oldest running full steam ahead on our small farm. Don wasn't an expert in this Holy Spirit stuff either, and I made him roll his eyes more than a time or two. The story begins with me getting dinner on the table for the Wambach clan. Don had just arrived home from a tiring day at the shop. I've had another "off the charts encounter" and was bursting to share about the crazy "like I was there" dream. A good friend of ours from "church" bravely joined us at our active and boisterous meal. You know how quiet the room gets when their mouths are full? It's perfect time to burst open the daily secrets revealed from Jesus' heart. I shared last night happenings to the life-like vision. It was so real. The Lord showed me a little girl crossing the street after school. She stepped out onto a busy afternoon street not using the crosswalk and a white car collided with her leaving her unconscious under its bumper. I saw myself witnessing the accident, jumping out of my car and running over and laying hands on her praying for her recovery. She lived. The dream hit deaf ears and rolling eyes when I shared it. And like so many other happenings I began to bottle up the experiences I so desperately wanted to share. Three months to the date after the vision, I had just picked up my two big boys from school. We were rounding the block heading to visit Dad at the shop, and it happened. The girl was hit just like in the dream. I instructed my boys to stay in the car. I leaped out, heart pounding and laid hands on her unconscious body. People were yelling, calling for help. I didn't leave, praying loudly without fear or thought of my surroundings. It began to pour, what you might say "Raining cats and dogs." I remained constant until she regained consciousness, the paramedics arrived and took her to the hospital. I'm left drenched, my body quivering from His power. I began to notice a few glaring eyes through my tears mixed with rain. And it came to pass!

"Because I offered Him my feet."

I was serving as the worship leader at Don's/our, comfortable "same old same ole" church, with the closet Holy-Ghost-filled Reverend and his wife. We, a dear friend who could play every key on the piano and myself, were invited to attend a worship conference in Irvine Texas. It was my joy to fly to attend a conference with some 3000 worship leaders and musicians in one large room. "My cup of tea; worship, discovering new places and more of Him." Funny I was thinking about this particular event.

May I take a rabbit trail for the sake of "Bow and Poof" humor? It got coined in Texas, and many of you are familiar with my "coined term." Bow and Poof? What I refer to as the ministry of making nothing (like tulle/ wedding netting and ribbon) into a lovely table and room decorations, into something. Bow and Poof! Many a Pastor's wives have coveted this gift. We arrived in Irvine an afternoon early to the conference and peeked into the large hotel gathering room. It was still a bustle of preparation, setting up chairs, staging the sound on the platform and some hotel "construction" type guys on a 20ft ladder attempting to "Bow and Poof" some fabric to frame the platform. Purely cosmetic and they didn't have a clue what they were doing! Well, my "Bow and Poof" gift was screaming pretty loud these days. The notion of looking at a stage that was off center and ugly for three days was enough to drive me mad. Well, so I'm a little decor obsessive! Where was that hospitality management anyway? So, leaving the doorway, my friend confused as to what I was doing, I marched up to the ladder crew and shouted assertively: "Excuse me, Excuse me? Sir would you please come down here?" I don't remember any resistance. They responded by climbing down the ladder like a well-trained husband. Without a blink, I proceed up the ladder, take the fabric in hand, scrunched it, adhered it to frame and balanced the room with the platform before they figured out I wasn't a hotel employee. I can still hear my friend saying: "Kristen I can't believe you did that." I was satisfied to look at it, pleased with myself for three days! Remember, I'm growing in the Lord!

Back to the conference at hand. From "ists to atics" it was a big deal to raise your hands in church. You felt like you were standing in your underwear. I was breaking into more freedom to love Him the way I loved the rhythm and anointing of the music. It must have been the second night of the conference. I was intimidated, and sure everybody was more qualified and gifted than I when it came to leading worship. We sat towards the back of the center, and I let the music lead me into His arms. My arms held heaven high and heart wrestling to give more. I'd never danced in worship publicly before. Can't say that I had ever noticed someone else dancing publicly before, conservative reverence racing through my blood. Love: it's an amazing thing. The alabaster box of my heart is brimming with an anointing, reminded of all He has forgiven and cast as far as the east is from the west. I must pour it over Him with my entire self. After moments of wrestling to step out from my seat, feeling a familiar heaviness and restraint; I boldly excuse myself in the midst of a song. With every step, tender freedom covered my eyes until all I saw was Him. My younger years of ballet gurgled free into gestures of fluid intimacy, rhythm released. I was confident too, affectionate communion, holding my breath for all eternity to see. I was His ballerina. Every move felt as grace-filled as my heart desired it to be. I remained out of my seat, for the rest of the worship, dancing on OUR back-of-the-room dance floor. Undone and sweaty, when the music stilled I made my way, keeping my eyes to myself, back to my seat, while preachers/teachers made their move towards the pulpit. But the rhythm in me didn't cease. I sat down from my dance offering and "He" stood up. His presence gushed like a pitcher pouring water on me, and my body began to quiver. I tried to contain and cover having no idea what was taking place. My friend and new acquaintances gently put their hands on my thighs to calm my vigorous spirit. To no avail! He dumped more. From quiver to violent shake I found myself on the floor as my friends were embarrassed by now, trying to set me back up in my chair. Immersed in His power, my body had no control over its response. It was like putting your finger into a light socket! His power felt all consuming to me, and I lived. I found it divinely encouraging that the following year I received another invitation brochure to this Worship Conference and when I open the three-fold, my picture, "filled with joy in His presence," was smack dab in the center-fold. The fear of man lost its battle that day, and a healthy fear of God opened a floodgate towards my destiny.

"Never argue with the Lord!"

My husband Don had a small auto repair shop nestled amongst other light industrial businesses in Newberg. During the evening hours, my honey would catch me up on the day, customers, broken cars and the lives of his different lunch companions. Through Don's stories, they, the lunch bunch, became a familiar community. During one evening report, concerned, Don mentioned Dave's pregnant wife, Pat. Her pregnancy had become fragile, confining her to hospitalization at Portland's OHSU, Oregon Health Science University. What pricked our hearts from Dave's conversation is that Pat was disappointed she hadn't had any friends visiting her during her month-long confinement. I think this is why Don told me; he knew I would volunteer to go. So, Don communicated our hearts to Dave, and he happily arranged a day. I love meeting new people and being God's "On Call" Samaritan. Arriving, this particular "Baby" hospital was floor after floor, room after room of fragile and bored mom's to be. Meeting Pat, she was easy to talk to, glad for some company and, much like Don's lunch community, happy to share about the different mothers she had met during her stay. A curious fact is every time she mentioned this one friend I would get a witness in my spirit. The afternoon sleep-zzz seemed to slow our visit, Pat was encouraged, prayed for and hope returned. I graciously inquired about this particular friend and boldly asked if she would introduce me. Gladly, knowing that all the mothers were hungry for any distraction, Pat laid hold of her wheelchair and we were off down the hallway. Beautifully, Pat maneuvered the introduction, and my new acquaintance set me at ease, happy for the company. Pat excused herself heeding the call to take an afternoon nap. Do you ever get so excited to meet someone that you miss hearing their name during introductions? Guilty. I have never remembered her name. For the sake of the story, I'll call her Jackie. Attractive young mom, dark long hair, she looked like she had been through the "ringer" with this pregnancy. Jackie told me that they were unable to stop her hemorrhaging which put the baby at risk for loss in the next 24 hours. I asked her if I could pray and lay hands on her and she agreed. I said a nice easy-to-be-entreated prayer. Nothing too earth-shaking, said Amen, thanking the Lord for healing her and delivering a healthy baby. As we lifted our bowed heads I "distinctly" heard the Lord say: "Pray for her in your prayer language." I was shocked. He repeated Himself, yes, pray for her in your prayer language. For a moment I felt like all the world could see the wrestle inside of me, as I had an internal conversation with the Lord. I argued His "Own" text with Him about the legalities of speaking in tongues publicly. To no avail, He repeated, pray for in your prayer language. I, conceding to possible misunderstanding and embarrassment, shared with Jackie that the Lord had given me a special prayer language, a wee bit of teaching before I jump off the cliff, and that He was prompting me to pray for her "again" using this prayer conversation. She agreed without concern. A very trusting and easy going spirit was obviously in the room. So we closed our eyes, and I spoke in another tongue, casting mysterious words over her. Maybe 30 seconds before I peeked with one eye to the Lord's intent, Jackie's face was wet with tears. We both looked up, I asked her if she was alright. It took her a moment to regain composure to speak. She shared: "When I was a little girl my Dad used to tell me stories in his native

Cherokee tongue, and you sound just like him. More tears flowed at the dearness of her memory. I waited till she was comforted. We hugged, and she thanked me for coming and praying for her. Next day Pat called Dave, Dave told Don and last but not least, Don shared with me that Jackie's hemorrhage dried up immediately and after an adequate amount of days later she gave birth to a healthy baby boy.

The relationship with being a "lady" inside your heart, a contending "Lady in Waiting," and what was written on my destiny scroll was calling me. A voice of Truth from a realm that I thought you only entered into at the retreat of a tired and decaying body. You see why the painting of "Jane" transfixed me. Like the feelings she exposed from my hidden self, I was in this vulnerable season in every way you look at it. Running on empty and trying so hard to get it right: Get it right with Him, at home and the church I'd come to love. *Jesus had to pass through my "Samaria" because a generous Father was seeking me. "Seeking His impassioned-for-"Truth" daughter, with a broken heart."*
Inheritance calls from a well of betrothal.

This morning I had a thought-provoking dream, which was my waking note for writing? Up before the chickens. I love the quietness of early morning; I love the peacefulness of a sleeping house, not a creature was stirring. Well, maybe a mouse. As I journaled the dream, I wasn't sure of its intent. Pizza dream, Paparazzi dream or Papa dream? They all have a message if I listen to the One who knows and mutters thoughts over my heart.

Three brief snapshots on how dreams reveal:

A PIZZA DREAM: processing about life, and what I'm fussing and focusing on....meditating and chewing in our night season, how daily circumstance affects me, where my own-self and feeling hides, and if another's person is involved, how their actions reverberated response. (Growing up in a testosterone environment it's easy to see how I developed an attitude of "Suck it up", "Toughen up", "No crying in Baseball." So, I learned that "Pizza" dreams tend to process the leaven in and around my heart. Jesus had to break me of that habit. No longer do I stash or bury my feelings. Holy Spirit is not able to be a comforter if I'm not admitting to needing comfort. The root of unmet needs will grow into hopelessness.

A PAPARAZZI DREAM: What the enemy has taken pictures of and gets paid big bucks for selling to the tabloids, photo-chopping software included. Your worst self, situated on magazine rack displayed at the check-out line at the grocery store. Fear of man, fear of self.

A PAPA GOD DREAM: His love and purposes revealed, openly, secretly, up the River of Life to the Kingdom of Heaven, transrelocation practice.

These days I take before His throne a majority of my night encounters; dreams, encounters or night visions to understand, bring clarity and expose the enemy. Protocols at hand;
Before the council of His might (Courts of Heaven).
Anything that "feels" out of order, I deal with it.
My enemies get revealed; I command them to tell me what right they have to bother me and remain; lies I have believed get talked about, uncovered, removed, and truth explained.

I love the courts of heaven. You want to know God and the power of His might, watch Him judge your (spiritual) enemies.

Yesterday I purchased a three-pair pack of garden gloves, pink gloves from a company promising to donate to Breast Cancer Awareness. The package also included a rubber wristband. On the band, it stated: "Work for Hope." Today I sit here writing to you about a season of my life much like this declaration. I was, "Working for Hope." Instead today, I work "From Hope."

Now that we have laid a bit of groundwork for dream language, I'll share and unpack what seems relevant to our journey.

My dream: I found myself living in an apartment with roommates. My roommates were out, returning later with plans to throw a party. I was home cleaning and preparing for the party. My first love, (represented as my high-school sweetheart) was Randy. He kept popping in and out of the dream. I desired to start dating again, and that we would get back together. It seemed like he was uninterested. With responsibilities I had taken on for the upcoming party, I was unable to spend time with "Randy," who I wanted to get re-acquainted. In the dream, I finally figured out that I didn't need to prepare for the party which my roommates were giving. They could arrange for preparation of the food, but I still went on cleaning.

I'm sure your interpretation is picking up certain things that I missed. My "Lady in Waiting" journey was so similar to the dream. I was always "working" for hope, for acceptance, in the hope that my first love, which represented my mindset towards Jesus, would give me the attention that I so hungered to receive. The orphan spirit lies I believed, that if I were responsible and cleaned up the mess, it would position me to change His mind.

I am very thankful for the path that I have walked. It is challenging while writing to be reminded of the mindset and wrong perceptions working through me at that time or the limits I put on my relationship with "knowing Him." God always seemed an arm's length away, because He was God. I was a "Lady in Waiting," still taking on responsibilities that weren't mine. My boundaries were all out of whack.

Remember, I had no understanding of a prophetic window yet. Awareness of the Baptism of Holy Spirit and His ministry were new to me and new to my generational line. I was pretty immature, hungry for God, loved how He "feels." Hunger is the key to growth. With disappointment, I sadly recall that in this season of atics-church-camp, "feeling" God was considered unstable and not based on the facts of the Word.

The romantic part of the dream is the endearment of your "first love," who in the dream is Jesus. Together we discovered an affection in youthful moments that forever is etched in the halls of "Firsts." You know those high school days where you would linger longer in hopes of catching a glimpse of each other. You premeditated to place yourself near a hallway or gym door where he might wander past. Kissing was an innocent discovery you took hours to perfect, at the expense of your parents flipping the porch lights on and off, time to come in. Nobody had ever told me that God could make you "feel" this way. He would look at you through your imperfections with such compassion and say: "Kristen, you do not need to carry that. Give it to me." The "four walls" had rules of governance leaving me feeling like the woman caught in adultery, forever in blame. Inside my spirit, I perceived truth and intimacy. I am as the woman with the "alabaster box," forever forgiven, pouring costly anointing oil over Him "forgiving." Over the course of years, we talked about the depth in which He continued to wash me free from mindsets. Sin is a manifestation of seeds that have spent years growing a negative tune. It takes a long time to kill the melody within and all the places you hummed it.

I finally did some growing up and set my husband free, years ago, from my expectations and wrong doctrine, forever discovering that being "One Flesh" is a mystery of unity. A secret not birthed on earth. Our spirits are ever entwined, learning to communicate, sharing without even opening our lips. One flesh, two spirits. Don survived those days of me learning to hear God's voice; being my greatest cheerleader. God's grace chose him for me during a season when I was unable to make a wise choice. God knew that Don had the faithfulness and strength to withstand my transformation.

Such a loving husband who has never expected me to wait for anything that Jesus wanted me to experience.

CHAPTER 4

Getting Permission

*"It is often easier to ask for forgiveness than
to ask for permission" Grace Hopper*

The thought crosses my mind, when did I first see? When did I begin to perceive the realms of mystery visually?

Your spiritual-self has encounters far beyond what your understanding has yet grasped. Thankfully, understanding does a bit of catching up. You begin to remember and recall places, and heavenly lessons take hold. The people (cloud of witnesses), heavenly places, and "light beings" start to come alive. Your spirit opens to His, flowing through into the gateways of your soul, flooding your physical senses. Heaven's tutors, the cloud of witnesses and their personalities, smiles, humor, and encouragement, become familiar just like a friendship does. The unique clothing they wear! It's a picture/sense/ remembrance to help you understand what they are conveying, what they are purposing with you, their assignment. Many tutors come to teach you. They have probably been standing in the wings for generations as your destiny scroll is lived out.

Finding a place to start; Hmm. Journaling.

I have begun my 14th year of journaling, which tells bits, pieces, stories, feelings: Invaluable opportunities for revisiting and referring to my journal notes time and time again. Your mind is similar to an index card cabinet in a library (pre-google). I can recall posts, tags and journal notes both by memory and "through my app search." A very high percentage have remained useful, His Kingdom lessons ingrained in the faith you remember through writing.

I'll re-read a tender story of a beginning, of an end, how a testimony came into being, how God asked me to participate, and how I saw His active faithfulness. I look back now and relish the first mentions and enjoy them as "first fruits," a treasure to tell, a lesson of love encounters in Heaven

47

remaining alive. Prophetically journaling shows a clear path over your walk with Him and how He shapes you, molds you, in trials of the heart. Hebrew thought is circular. The Alpha and Omega of our lives begins from an end. An eternal figure of eight of Jesus sacrifice is the crossing over a place of eternity. The Israelites went "around" a mountain choosing not to go up a mountain.

It's been roughly 11 years since my eldest brother, wife, and children were stationed in Seoul Korea during his 2nd tour of duty. Mike invited me and graciously paid for my plane tickets: My first time over an ocean. I enjoyed three weeks in a nation and amongst people where I had not imagined I could find a kindred spirit. A sea of dark hair, while my blonde locks stood out, standing several inches above most. To Koreans, I am the epitome of an "American;" blond, not blue-eyed, sunglass-wearing American. I was whispered about and treated like a movie star from their perspective, because of light hair, light eyes, and the self-assured gestures, raised-head of a strong woman. This chapter, Getting Permission, began there on the streets of Namdaemun open market, an ocean of black-haired heads, literally an ocean.

So many people lined the streets, filled the crevasses, and walked the alleys. I was a tourist, yet escorted by a prominent military presence, my career army brother. Watching people is a joy and lends a key to developing your senses in any cultural change of atmosphere. So much to see and perceive in learning about people, their traditions, culture, food culture, shopping culture. Korea is an entrepreneurial nation, family-focused, industrious, laborious, working in their market territory. Militant businessmen and women for which I also represented a U.S. dollar in their pocket, and you sensed their clever salesmanship. The Namdaemun market is filled with clothing, hats, bobbles, foods, baskets, belts, trousers, purses that looked almost like a designer but not quite, a knock-off of a knock-off. Each proprietor offered zealous bidding, creating "your" best deal. My favorite shop discovered, uniquely showcased in an upward staircase. Yes, a staircase! Koreans take an innovative idea or a learned family trade, add instinctual flair, thinking around corners to sell their merchandise. With fewer rules and more industry, you find their wares displayed within an arm-stretch of the competitor's booth. My favorite shop, an original, rising store, about twenty steps, only five feet wide, with gift-wrap/wrapping papers, hung, folded, draped, stacked everywhere, exquisitely organized. I wandered carefully up the staircase with only room for a single foot on each riser. A fantastic, delightful paper shop. Beautiful papers, gold embossed papers, florals, pastel polka dots, blues with the sun and green after green after green. Printed papers-saying: "Happy Birthday," Logo wrappings about Disneyland, papers written with words and poems and beautiful native writings. Korean symbols, Annamae, Hello Kitty, all in this 20 x 5ft staircase. I was enchanted. The proprietor's keen eyes never left me, following my ooh's and aah's, quickly reaching to show me just one more. Every shopkeeper was this way, "let me show you one more." Their wares were the best, least expensive, promising you couldn't find it anywhere else for this price. That was true in this case of a tiny paper store. Wrapping papers are found in other shops, but this creative-space obviously remained, treasured in my thoughts. I purchased several sheets of white linen paper printed with Hangul writings and enjoyed them for many years after. If I have portrayed a busy, industrious and spirited people in your minds, then I have written it well. I remember witnessing a very senior woman sitting cross-legged on the pavement, smack center of a "blocked off" street. She was selling vegetables from her basket. Her round face weathered, her eyes bright and body nimble from years of farming in the fields, she was selling her harvest. I can't even sit cross-legged like that, and she must have been in her 80s. I must confess my shopping eye was bouncing everywhere, as my brother commented I was in a "visual dither" of commerce, not currently drooling unless you smelled those vendors selling bean paste pancakes. As we visited street after street; I began to notice a bit of repetition from one stall to the next. My "shopping" head was moving like an owl; my peripheral view caught the releasing of a blue tarp like a sheet snapped in the summer wind. My head turned in full focus as the 12x12 piece of plastic was laid to the blacktop face of the street. Fabrics rolled loose as if Santa had dropped his sack: purses, blouses, and jeans in a heap. The drama unleashed ants to a picnic, as the free will shoppers digging commenced. I squeezed in for a position as my brother Mike just watched the "good deal" shopping "frenzy" exploding. My hands were tossing, lifting and looking for a bargain to unfold. Then out of the corner of my eye, a poof of fur, a flash of smooth leather stole my attention. I broke stride and pulled back from my station in the throng and kept my eyes attached to this mysterious pelt. Pushing my way, I saw other hands lift it and release back into the pile atop the blue tarp. I reached with determination down on one knee to catch my prize, while others watched to see my intent. Grabbed it, just as other hands lunge out waiting to see my decision. Triumph, my reward was a leather coat. Patch-worked together, reversed seams showing soft-tan hides, with an elegant fox collar and cuff. The waistline A-line tapered closure with wood toggle buttons, beautiful trouser length jacket, now cascading over and around my shoulders, a perfect match. I was in delightful victory.

Looking over my "stole" shoulder at Mike, he just grinned and rolled his eyes. Come on "little sister." With this coat on, I felt like that movie star watched by giggling Korean school children. The match divine, sealed both inside and out. My memory is foggy on the dickering part, but surely there must have been some. I have horse trading in my blood. I walked away that day with a leather fur-trimmed coat for $30; American dollars. The find of the century! I came, I saw, I conquered, I got a good deal, it must be time for lunch! Well, as you can tell I loved my visit to Korea desiring one day to return to the noble country. Now that you understand the back story regarding the "Varmint" coat, this allows us to take an earnest turn. One I hold very dearly unto the Lord.

Trying to retrace the timing: I believe I was in Korea during October as one of our outings was climbing Mount Seoraksan to experience the turning of the leaves, sarcastically, with all the rest of Korea there also. After returning home and a few months past, it must have been early the next year

I was walking through a difficult season with "church"! You know that place you get challenged or I am the challenge, with people, leaders, and doctrines. You love them on Sunday but the rest of the week is when the rubber meets the road. You serve and serve and serve, pray, lead, believe God together. We have all been there. We have all loved, lost, been lost and also saved. I've asked Him many times: What were "You" thinking Father? Anyway, Prophet Kim Clement (with great respect & honor as he recently and tragically joined heaven) and his prophetic team were scheduled to speak in Albany, a short twenty-minute drive from me, just across the river from my house. I had been a part of Kim's meetings many times before and attended his online ministry course for the school of the prophets. Very helpful in my early years of developing "seeing'. I felt prompted by Holy Spirit to be a part of this particular meeting. Don and I were newer to the Corvallis area, so I was still getting my feet wet within the greater Christian community. You know how you see familiar faces at conferences and such? The conference was a two evening meeting, and Holy Spirit was busy preparing my heart. As bold as I am in many ways, during unfamiliar gatherings I sit in the back of the room so that I may slip out of my seat for worship to not draw attention, only His. Life was in such transition. I was experiencing a difficult season with the pastor of my church. Holy Spirit was bubbling the gifts up in and through me. I knew things about people, words of knowledge, people getting healed, the spirit realm was squeezing into view, the whole prophetic enchilada. Many of us have been there, and most leaders have loved us, had dealings with us or misunderstood the "super spiritual" ones. I was hungry for Him! It was the days when many of my former pastors would say to me: "Kristen we love you, but we just don't know what to do with you! Hindsight today: they were unequipped to teach or share on the realms of the spirit. Again, remarkable back story.

Just pressing in and seeking hard, a word from God through His prophet would help to "settle" the season a bit. Feeling very misunderstood. Nobody to talk to regarding the things I am now seeing.

Getting ready for the meeting and a bit "me" focused, I desire to receive a word from God. Well I may sit in the back row, but I'll put a little "attention" on the matter, and I decided to wear my beloved navy-blue New York Yankees baseball hat with over-the-top orange bling NY emblem. I thought maybe God needed a little help to find me! Well, He found my heart and my pocketbook as I emptied it. He always is working on the more & less. Amen.

Day two, up early to have my devotional time with Father and I heard Him say; "I want you to dress to the "Nines" this evening." Seriously! My flesh was struggling with the fear of "women/church" what-would-man-think thing, all those opinions I would prefer not to run across. I obeyed, and grace helped me to be oblivious to anything on the inside of or the "outside." For me, this meant, favorite pair of jeans, snake-skin boots (also purchased in Korea) and yes, my "Varmint" coat, as I had endearingly named it. Found my same seat in the back of the sanctuary, took off my coat, lay it over the chair and entered into worship. It was delightful. The lights had been turned down a wee bit so you could disappear with God and be carried away by the sound of Kim Clement and his team. Worship lingered, a 3-point message seemed to have moved a position down the schedule of events. If you have had the privilege of being part of Kim's meetings you could just see the Lord drop His thoughts on him and a prophetic burst would scale the keyboard. Most of the hungry crowd had moved out of their seats and bunched up around the platform. It was elbow to elbow with delicious Holy Spirit. By this time Kim was rhythmically rocking back and forth under the anointing. He had called a few people forward to minister to them. Suddenly it seemed everything stopped. Kim straightened up in manner and said without any "romancing" the crowd: "Get out your pocketbooks, pull out your wallets (With a most earnest tone in his voice) we are taking an offering." Music was hushed, people untangled from the mystical air to listen to instruction. Voice lifted, Kim began a decree: "this is a Cornelius offering, this is a Cornelius offering." Rocking once more, again and again, repeating, "this is a Cornelius offering." With great fervency, he asked the crowd to go to their seats and prepare before the Lord. I stood there, heart engaged with the spirit, as people moved around me following the promptings of the Lord. I turned my heart even further to the Lord's attention and said: "Lord, I gave it all last night!" His answer heard in an atmosphere stilled at His response. I heard his heart without Him saying a word and I burst into tears. My spirit seemed to move without me as the vision of my offering played out. I saw it, hanging on the back of my chair, my Varmint coat and knew the instructions as to whom and to how to give it. I'm still stationed by the platform where the crowd had once gathered, with tears falling hard down my cheeks. I couldn't seem to hush my tears or gain my composure. I knew instantly I would obey, I turned myself towards my chair to gather my offering. Tears were uncontrollably washing down my cheeks as I picked up my coat and walked around to the side of the room towards the platform. I arrived next to the stage, a servant of the ministry helping to control the thronging crowd looked questioningly at my bewildered self. I motioned to my coat and then to the beautiful blond musician on the stage. He never questioned me but just caught the lady's attention and pointed to me. Without a word, I handed her my precious Varmint coat, still weeping and as she said before I walked away, "Is this for me?" She smiled, I turned, heading back to my seat. Thankfully the benediction came within five minutes, and I was the first one out the doors. What a mess I was... Through my tears I kept asking the Lord what my problem was, I have given offerings worth more than a 30 dollar coat countless times. Why couldn't I shut off the waterworks of my heart? I cried the entire 20-minute drive home. The house was dark, my family in bed. I paced the living room for a moment knowing that I would be unable to go to sleep. I prostrated my sobbing self onto the floor of the living room. Not knowing how long I laid there, the anointing resting and easing up until I could inquire again what had just happened to me. Selah. The Lord reminded me of Kim's declarations: "This is a Cornelius offering." I crawled over to my prayer basket and grabbed my bible to see what the Lord was highlighting. As my fingers type this text, I open my bible in Acts 10 to again recall the scribble notation about that offering.

Highlighted: Verse 4. What is it, Lord? Your prayers and alms have ascended as a memorial before God.

Let's set the scene of the Lord: Cornelius' Vision
Now at Caesarea [Maritima], there was a man named Cornelius, a centurion of what was known as the Italian Regiment, a devout man and one who, along with all his household, feared God. He made many charitable donations to the Jewish people and prayed to God always. About the ninth hour (3:00 p.m.) of the day, he clearly saw in a vision an angel of God who had come to him and said, "Cornelius!" Cornelius was frightened and stared intently at him and said, "What is it, lord (sir)?" And the angel said to him, "Your prayers and gifts of charity have ascended as a memorial offering before God [an offering made in remembrance of His past blessings]. Now send men to Joppa and have them call for a man named Simon, who is also called Peter [and invite him here]; he is staying with Simon the tanner, whose house is by the sea." When the angel who was speaking to him had gone, Cornelius called two of his servants and a devout soldier from among his own personal attendants; and after explaining everything to them, he sent them to Joppa. The next day, as they were on their way and were approaching the city, Peter went up on the roof of the house about the sixth hour (noon)to pray, but he became hungry and wanted something to eat. While the meal was being prepared he fell into a trance, and he saw the sky opened up, and an object like a great sheet descending, lowered by its four corners to the earth, and it contained all kinds of four-footed animals and crawling creatures of the earth and birds of the air. A voice came to him, "Get up, Peter, kill and eat!" But Peter said, "Not at all, Lord, for I have never eaten anything that is common (unholy) and [ceremonially]

unclean." And the voice came to him a second time, "What God has cleansed and pronounced clean, no longer consider common (unholy)." This happened three times, and then immediately the object was taken up into heaven. Now Peter was still perplexed and completely at a loss as to what his vision could mean when the men who had been sent by Cornelius, having asked directions to Simon's house, arrived at the gate. And they called out to ask whether Simon, who was also called Peter, was staying there. While Peter was thoughtfully considering the vision, the Spirit said to him, "Now listen, three men are looking for you. Get up, go downstairs and go with them without hesitating or doubting, because I have sent them Myself." Peter went down to the men and said, "I am the one you are looking for. For what reason have you come?" They said, "Cornelius, a centurion, an upright and God-fearing man well-spoken of by all the Jewish people, was divinely instructed by a holy angel to send for you to come to his house and hear what you have to say." So Peter invited them in and gave them lodging [for the night].

Peter recaps the story: *Now the apostles and the brethren who were throughout Judea heard that the Gentiles also had received the word of God. And when Peter came up to Jerusalem, those who were circumcised took issue with him, saying, "You went to uncircumcised men and ate with them." But Peter began speaking and proceeded to explain to them in orderly sequence, saying, "I was in the city of Joppa praying; and in a trance I saw a vision, an object coming down like a great sheet lowered by four corners from the sky, and it came right down to me, and when I had fixed my gaze on it and was observing it I saw the four-footed animals of the earth and the wild beasts and the crawling creatures and the birds of the air. I also heard a voice saying to me, 'Get up, Peter; kill and eat.' But I said, 'By no means, Lord, for nothing unholy or unclean has ever entered my mouth.' But a voice from heaven answered a second time, 'What God has cleansed, no longer consider unholy.' This happened three times, and everything was drawn back up into the sky. And behold, at that moment three men appeared at the house in which we were staying, having been sent to me from Caesarea. The Spirit told me to go with them without misgivings. These six brethren also went with me, and we entered the man's house. And he reported to us how he had seen the angel standing in his house, and saying, 'Send to Joppa and have Simon, who is also called Peter, brought here; and he will speak words to you by which you will be saved, you and all your household.' And as I began to speak, the Holy Spirit fell upon them just as He did upon us at the beginning. And I remembered the word of the Lord, how He used to say, 'John baptized with water, but you will be baptized with the Holy Spirit.' Therefore, if God gave them the same gift as He gave to us also after believing in the Lord Jesus Christ, who was I that I could stand in God's way?" When they heard this, they quieted down and glorified God, saying, "Well then, God has granted to the Gentiles also the repentance that leads to life."*   *(Acts 10)*

I summed it up this way. That goofy Varmint coat made me feel picked out of the crowd, unique, extravagant, favored, woven in my "coat" offering, irreplaceable memories created with my oldest brother. That is what I gave to Him. It still pulls my heartstrings today. This Cornelius offering opened the heavens for me to release & receive a revelation leading me into heaven that forever altered my "church," Your "church," the "Church." Rules, traditions, and doctrines changed. Like Peter's mindset melted.

Was it an invitation to reformation?
Reform how I, we, do things.

"Reform: the improvement or amendment of what is wrong, corrupt, unsatisfactory."

We have highlighted the core of my book. For years I have been aware of Jesus earthly ministry. That is the Gospel I shared in the first chapters. The Gospel that for generations my family had gathered around. A rich lineage I have received. Not only was I taught that He died for my sins and rose on the 3rd day but I was living to learn more profound truths that His death and resurrection provided. When I met Holy Spirit, I experienced Pentecost, the promise of the Father, and at that moment my spirit began following a path leading me towards mystery: Towards Jesus on the other side of the veil who rules and reigns. My discipleship and imitation of Him are not limited to just His earthly ministry. Jesus in the flesh didn't set me free! Jesus, seated at the right hand of the Father is what sets me free.

The "TRUTH" you personally "know" sets you free.
Truth is Jesus, who I know in continuation and encounter.
I asked the questions;

How did He overcome and fulfill His ministry?
How did He see what the Father was doing?
Tell me about Your kingdom?
How does it work, what about angels and beings, miracles and the transformation of the heart?
I want to know about the dominion of "My Jesus."

My Varmint coat has many representations, types, and shadows of the flesh given away. It felt like it on that day. Our flesh, our mindsets, are very similar to Peter arguing the law, pleading with God.

What shall we eat, by rules or what shall we consume, by the Spirit.

That day a seed was sown in me, and through me, it married me to a path of mystery. I received an invitation, from an offering, of extreme transformation.

Like Cornelius, my family received in both heaven and earth.

Like Peter, the four corners of the earth dropped down to reveal a sheet full of revelation.

A window of sight, a covering of change, the limitation in spiritual minds and kingdom of heaven doctrines that I thought wasn't allowed, we're just not so. Truth isn't "true" unless there is a witness. Otherwise, they are words that I only know how to repeat. And repeat I did!

Many of us, are framed in a bible of parrots and mockingbirds. That is the bliss about spiritual encounters. Ask Nicodemus. Jesus' response, do not marvel that "I" said you must be born again. Oh, no Kristen you're "quoting" scripture again. Fast forward if you need to, to the first couple of paragraphs in the chapter called the "Watchmaker." "I permit you." yikes! The perils of quoting! The dangers of interpretation! The persecution of this camp and that tribe!

Did anyone ask Jesus about His conversation with Nicodemus, what we were supposed to marvel? Do you remember the quote I highlighted at the beginning of this chapter, by Grace Hopper?

"It is often easier to ask for forgiveness than to ask for permission."

I found myself forgiven but without permission to step into the things of God, walk out my destiny scroll, engage with the Kingdom of Heaven, The Unseen.

Let's break the word down, PERMISSION:
Per should reflect a prefix to my "Mission."
Per+Mission = Through & thoroughly + a vital goal or purpose that is accompanied by strong conviction; calling or vocation. PERMISSION!

Sad to say, many of our doctrines within the "four walls" are an antonym, not a prefix;
(Per) antonym = restraint, refusal. In your mission.

Just a side note to share where my voice purposes to flow.

Redemptive gifts: Like Peter, my destiny is forerunning a reformation within the church. This redemptive gift is designed to break down "walls," and bring change. I admire the teaching of Freedom ARC and how they share in regards to this particular:

Redemptive Gift: The prophet (redemptive gift, not office);

To understand the future through the use of Biblical principles. Moody, Articulate, Passionate, Generous, Intense, Keen sense of justice, Loves the underdog, Creative, Judgmental, Extreme.

There are both strengths and weaknesses present. Ask my husband or parents. Living alongside and during the maturing of these gifts can be trying and challenging. Prophet, self-proclaimed or otherwise; I didn't want anything to do with it. For years I wrestled against the "Prophet Redemptive Gift" fuddling through my negative mindsets and Church labeling. I appreciate Freedom ARC and the discussion on their blog about two principles within the Prophet Redemptive Gift.

Principle: Design - the art of weaving principles together to produce change. Will display a picture of God so dynamic and real that it moves people out of their comfort zones (which can become prisons) and into a journey that will bring them to the fulfillment of all God created them to be.

Wow, what a reformation.

Like you, I love the church, in both heaven and earth. I love gathering, worship, miracles, healings, growing, praying, communion, prophetic words, fellowship, conferences, revivals, bawling and being undone together: Also to include how heaven is jointly responding with angels, beings, realms, the cloud of witnesses, supernatural manifestations, men in white linen. Please forgive me if I ruffle your feathers. I, too, usually read books that stir up truth: I prefer an awakening and stretching. Transition and transformation bring forth fruit that would not come forth without different elements present. Some friction is needed to create change.

"Again, it is easier to ask for forgiveness than permission." I spent years asking for permission, staying in "order." The same mindset also was woven into my relationship with God. I was working to get His permission, an orphan spirit if you want to tag it. I was searching for something that looked like me, that is only found in the "yes, yes and amen" in Him.

Funny haha, just want to share a real writing place. I'm sitting outside trying to finish the last 150-word goal for the day, focused. You've figured that out about me by now. Don came home early from a dental appointment. Over and over my mind keeps regurgitating the words: my affections, my affections, as Don interrupts my thoughts with reading out loud a blog post about, about, about; see? I give in. Don says look at this; Roman Holiday: a tour of Italy with select cigars. The day and beautiful weather, under our pergola, together. I think I will stop at 908 for the day. My affections are for him.

A new morning. Recap.

The heart of Cornelius offerings is still opening divine doors for this age of "Peters" still up on the roof today receiving revelation which is changing the framework of "church." *Sheets, of a supernatural nature, are being encountered that ask us to "Eat" what yesterday we thought unpalatable.* [The framework of the Gospel in our understanding is in constant change.] The "Good News" just keeps getting "Gooder"! I must experience His goodness so the life, testimony, and witness can increase His government. Which has no end!

Faithful Pastor, Pastor Whiting at the time of my "conversion" I would suggest very strongly, had no "grid" that the Spirit of God and unique company (Jesus, Moses, Elijah, Angels) came to meet with me that day. *He had great faith in things he did not see, just no faith for witnessing the unseen. That is a good word. Let's look at it again. He had great faith in things he did not see, just no faith for witnessing the unseen.*

I'll suggest: Jesus, Moses, and Elijah come to meet with "all of us"? At His mountain of transfiguration.

Isn't that our beginning into life, from Jesus' "finished work" on the cross? *For if while we were enemies we were reconciled to God through the death of His Son much more, having been reconciled, we shall be saved by His life.*

Romans 5:10 NASB

For God so love the world that He gave His Only Son, that whosoever believes in Him shall not perish but have eternal (eternity is not framed in death) life.

John 3:16 NASB.

I'm getting preachy, I can feel it. *This soapbox is supposed to reveal a view of a kingdom so dynamic it changes us. Let's begin where Father God's Son was "given" back to Him. Death is defeated, we should start at Victory.*

Ask the question, Shall not perish? Eternal life? Is that within our timeline or His?

Breakaway *(seven thousand three hundred and fifty words to halfway)*
5:00 am

Chapter 5

Vision Care

Some of the greater things in life are unseen, that's why you close
your eyes when you kiss, cry, or dream. - Anonymous quote

I have only been asleep for a few hours. The Lord woke me up saying. "Kristen, I want you to write about "Seeing in the Spirit" and call it, Vision Care". It is His strategy to help readers be restored to their inheritance of spiritual sight.

We have a healthy Vision Plan given to us "through" heaven. Plainly, Jesus' conversation with Nicodemus declares it as our inheritance. Let's discuss two passages:

Ephesians 1 and Matthew 5
15 For this reason I too, having heard of the faith in the Lord Jesus which exists among you and your love for all the saints, 16 do not cease giving thanks for you, while making mention of you in my prayers;17 that the God of our Lord Jesus Christ, the Father of glory, may give to you a spirit of wisdom and of revelation in the knowledge of Him. (Ephesians 1:15-17)

Highlighted prayer

SPIRIT OF WISDOM = HOW TO USE WHAT YOU PERCEIVE
OF REVELATION = WHAT YOU ARE PERCEIVING
KNOWLEDGE OF HIM = HOW IT REFLECTS HIM

The "eyes" (many) of the Lord, open up in this passage the functioning of 3 "sights" or 3 lenses, found in the prayer of Ephesians 1, each glass is to see with, each an eye of the eyes of the Lord, many.

I pray that the eyes of your heart may be enlightened so that you will know what is the hope of His calling, what are the riches of the glory of His inheritance in the saints, 19 and what is the surpassing greatness of His power toward us who believe. *(Ephesians 1:18-19 18)*

My conversation with the Lord shared that early morning was about His Vision Plan or Care, the purposes of seeing in the spirit realms. The heart condition is imperative towards our perceptions. Jesus always went up to the mountain to "experience" and see what the Father was doing. It may have been a real place that He got alone with God, similar to my pattern of sitting on my prayer pillow in the front room. But He activated His spiritual eyes and ascended or stepped in to apprehend the Father's heart. This morning Jesus was reiterating the How, What, and Reflection, and how He practiced and developed His spiritual eyes. The Lord asked me to accompany Him into a very famous passage and hear the How, What, and Reflection He experienced that day before having to minister to the crowds.

The Sermon on the Mount: The Beatitudes Matthew 5

> *When Jesus saw the crowds, He went up on the mountain; and after He sat down, His disciples came to Him.*
> *He opened His mouth and began to teach them, saying,*
> *"Blessed are the poor in spirit, for theirs is the kingdom of heaven.*
> *"Blessed are those who mourn, for they shall be comforted.*
> *"Blessed are the gentle, for they shall inherit the earth.*
> *"Blessed are those who hunger and thirst for righteousness, for they shall be satisfied.*
> *"Blessed are the merciful, for they shall receive mercy.*
> *"Blessed are the pure in heart, for they shall see God.*
> *"Blessed are the peacemakers, for they shall be called sons of God.*
> *"Blessed are those who have been persecuted for the sake of righteousness, for theirs is the kingdom of heaven.*
> *"Blessed are you when people insult you and persecute you, and falsely say all kinds of evil against you because of Me. 12 Rejoice and be glad, for your reward in heaven is great; for in, the same way, they persecuted the prophets who were before you.*

I am guilty of only seeing this passage from an earthly perspective, a real mountain. Let's look or "see" from spiritual eyes, as spiritual mountains: Lift up our perceptions to the high places of Jesus authority where He has invited us to be seated with Him.

WISDOM = HOW,
REVELATION = WHAT,
KNOWLEDGE = REFLECTION.

Jesus saw the crowds. He really "saw." He used a spiritual heart lens to see each person; many needs, many mindsets, in the spirit, being locational in the spirit. He went up to His spiritual mountain by stepping into heaven, looked to see what the Father was doing on behalf of this crowd of people. That morning Jesus shared with me that every "Blessed" is a lens to see from a heavenly place.

This vision Plan then says to the crowd from the mountain:

Those of you who are poor in spirit come, the kingdom of heaven is yours, the mountain of the lord is yours, come, learn, rest. Let me show you green pastures and still waters, drink of the river of life.

I see those who are mourning; I know that you have lost, been hurt, bruised. Come, receive comfort: Holy spirit hangout with them, comfort them until grief is past.

Those of you who are gentle, love: Love the land, help the earth, redeem creation.

You who are hungry for right-standing take this bread and this wine, every day to bring forth justice.

You, over there with the gift of mercy, share what you have received and give it away. Here is the throne of grace, learn about this compassion, lead others here.

I see the pure in heart: they have allowed me to divide the word of God inside them rightly. They have asked me to search their soul. I'd like to introduce you to Father God.

Peacemakers rise, take your place, release your voices, wear your crowns. Your names are written on many, many papers, to calm storms, legislate justice, sit down in the courts of the lord.

For those of you who have stood in a hard place for righteousness and been judged by an ungodly spirit, here is the kingdom of heaven: make it right, receive my council, undo the accusations, bring forth justice.

Insults, those of you who have been insulted, spit upon, persecuted, wrongly accused because you believe in me, take your reward, receive gladness. Rejoice, you're invited to mingle with the prophets of old.

Spoken again: Every "Blessed" Jesus talked about is a lens to see from a heavenly place.

In simple terms: readjust where your sight comes from. Seeing is a foundation of love, from the heart. I might ask myself these questions from the three lenses mentioned.

WISDOM = HOW,
REVELATION = WHAT,
KNOWLEDGE = REFLECTION.

HOW to use what you perceive: if I see a need or desire in myself, for my home, for my spouse, within my community... it's my responsibility to look and see just like Jesus' example: how to use, on whose behalf, and what does that behalf look like?

WHAT you are perceiving: many times, in the Old Testament, the Lord asked the prophets: "What do you see." When I am in a group of people, it takes courage and faith that my goofy snippet is from the Lord. By faith as a group, we share what each one perceived. Everyone's voice adds dimension to the set of glasses a team is viewing: Each picture or perception, each view paints a picture, feeling, sense.

KNOWLEDGE of how it reflects Him: why do I want to see? Light has an uncanny ability to remove darkness. The Kingdom of Heaven is alive and also a discerner of our thoughts and motives. If the reflection I see is contrary to His image, I'm responsible for undoing the works of darkness: first in me, represent others as a priest, then I gain the charge of His courts. See Zachariah 3.

The Lord prompted me a few months ago to write my testimony of introduction to Him: share it as a blog-post. That way Holy Spirit has evidence to show/reveal those He is drawing close. It reads in part like this:

When I was 8, I asked Him to come into my heart.
When I was 29, I allowed Him to heal my heart.
When I was 30, I asked Him to introduce me to Holy Spirit
When I was 40, I allowed Holy Spirit to change me.
When I was 48, I agreed with Him what He said about me.
When I was 49, He opened my spiritual eyes to His Kingdom.
I'm now 57, and I feel like I am only beginning.

Like my question in chapter one: Jesus, what (actually) happened during my "conversion" prayer. Now with open sight, it forced me to evaluate the Gospel message, or sinner's "prayer," as we say, and rethink it. If the Kingdom of Heaven is indeed at hand, then believing is vital to what I'm shown.

ACTIVATION: I summed up what I heard Jesus saying regarding principles with these spoken words.

WISDOM = HOW,
REVELATION = WHAT,
KNOWLEDGE = REFLECTION.

Jesus, I am honestly asking you to make yourself known to me. Forgive me for putting limits on You, limits on myself. I will believe what You show me. The Bible says: "You died and rent the veil so I could know Father God; see the Father. I desire a personal testimony of your death, resurrection, and where You are alive now. I will believe what you share with me. I shall do it.

I'd call that our first activation prayer. Take a moment to ponder the confession, make it your own. Keep it simple: believe the Jesus who lives in you, repent when anything contrary argues against His reflection.

BACKSTORY: There are so many great books to read out there about seeing in the spirit. For many of you, this is old hat. We need to remind ourselves of the many God is calling in this New Era that still has a need for their "Seeing" inheritance tools to be restored.

I'd like to honor and note the first Servant that altered my course of life. He encouraged me to go into the more profound things of God. Thank you, James Goll, for writing the book: The Seer. When the spirit realm was invading my life, it was so affirming to know "I'M NOT CRAZY."

While learning to rightly divide truths and understand His language, I have noticed Father reinforcing His principles in keeping with the "Law" of first mention.

KRISTEN'S DEFINITION: You are going to the mall shopping, looking for a perfect pair of jeans. You end up going back to purchase the first pair of jeans you saw on the rack, but you spent the entire day in and out of dressing rooms instead of trusting your "first" encounter. We are to be led by the Spirit, saving us time, provision, and understanding God's first purpose. I very much enjoy the entire shopping process: just saying. God is the same yesterday, today and forever. What I am sharing is not new. Experience and intimate encounters are born out of being in Him "Yesterday", learning to orchestrate with/next to Him in "Today," and walking into revealed revelation; searching out every door, window, portal, basement, floor, mansion, cosmos... Jewish thought: lesser truths always equal a greater truth.

I do not remember the spirit realm as a child in the way I have heard the testimony of the "gift of seeing" from the mouths of different people. As children, they testify encountering/remembering the spirit realm (Kingdom of the earth) and suffered great challenges in discerning the difference between "realms." As children they perceived that everyone saw what they saw: maybe we all did? I'd suggest a missing page or two in parental handbooks and say that most parents would not have a clue how to raise and steward such gifts -of seeing. Ignorance has us shutting down the good or (angelic) imaginary friends, but exasperated, weakened, ridiculing their child for seeing monsters that are "really" under the bed. Many testimonies include being tormented or isolated as children; they begged for "Sight" to be turned off. Sadly, many never find healing or maturity of operation to open that door again, while others seek repentance to receive their inheritance anew. Just this past Saturday a former employee contacted me via messenger, confused and seeing a therapist who thinks she is "crazy." She is experiencing the heavenly realm; relatives via the cloud of witnesses are communicating with her. Who has a grid for this in church? Not many. Have we traded our Kingdom inheritance to demonically influenced physics? We have many areas in which to mature.

After years of wrestling with man's opinion, I began to just believe Jesus. Holy Spirit and many other heavenly tutors have assisted my journey and spiritual education. Learning to walk in more light: well, I'm an "eternal" student. I have been allowed to "revisit" earlier days: my childhood salvation days when the gift was activated with Him breathing on my spirit. And yes, I dealt with those reoccurring dreams: we all have monsters under the bed when we are ready to take authority over them.

Interesting note that I have come to recognize lineage wise, the undeveloped seeing gift in other family members. There is a forerunning generational blessing bestowed. Instead of asking questions and developing, we make fun via family jokes about Grandma seeing the little white-haired man driving a car alongside her on her cross-country trips. We are all guilty of dissing the unseen because of ignorance, fear, or our religious box making us uncomfortable. The story of Nicodemus will shed a little light on what His breath regenerates. See John 3, a real treasure. Many people who encountered Jesus during His earthly ministry, the "bible" writings, do not reveal what happened through their transformational story of meeting Him. That's why Nicodemus accounts are such a treasure for us. Nicodemus began as a highly positioned seeker hiding in the dark of the night. He ended as a selfless giver, in the middle of a mad political crowd, to prepare His Lord for glory. Truly, truly, Jesus said, paraphrased, you must be born of water and spirit to see the Kingdom of God. Certainly, He wasn't literal? Was He?

How, did spiritual sightedness get "turned on" in me?

Love,
Love pursues,
Love believes,
Love searches out,
Love is brave,
Love breaks rules that should be broken,
Love repents,
Love admits,
Love alters fear,
Love believes because His friendship is closer than a brother, a spouse, a pastor, a board of elders, a church!
That was a power-packed statement, Yeh!
Love costs,
Love is responsible,
Love is teachable,
Love finds the weakness in self,

Love promotes destiny,
Love grows up,
Love receives the spoon full of sugar that makes the medicine go down,
Love alters mistakes,
Love receives,
Love gives away,
Love falls in love again and again and again with the same person: Jesus.
The atmosphere of love looks like something.
Jesus says it's like this: if you have seen me, you have seen the Father.

In the record of the Bible of all witnesses having encounters with Jesus after the resurrection, none of them recognized Him from the flesh. Jesus had to alter and wake up there seeing.

Examples of the different "framework/persona" that we find written:

He appeared as a

gardener,
a passer-by on the road,
dwelling as an alien (not from their land),
beheld a spirit, lightning,
white as snow.
Not a ghost or spirit

When Jesus spoke to them, responding in a manner they were accustomed to: in His nature; sharing a meal, love recalls body language, history of the relationship, their voice, secrets only He would know.

I find it amazing that our spirit knows who visits us from the cloud of witnesses, even though they look many years younger than when we knew them on earth.

I learned over time to trust the Jesus in me. Have I made mistakes? Countless times! That is what repentance is for. Have I been right? Numerous times! That is what humility is for.

A secret that took me years to find: *The most valuable doors found seem to be located within - on the floor. Face-down is the only way to discover them.*

How I began to develop seeing faith. It's the little things, the movement of things in my peripheral vision. Wait, even before that: dealing with fear. I have always been brave. Growing up with three brothers and then raising four sons, you learn to defend and conquer. I never relished playing the nurse either. I wanted a gun to shoot the bad guys.

We need to deal with fear and disagreement, wrestle the mindsets, seek His truth in doctrine. Ask Him for revelation, but on His terms, not yours.

I love what I learned from Joyce Meyer years ago.

FEAR ACRONYM:
    FALSE
    EVIDENCE
    APPEARING
    REAL
FEAR.

Spot on, Joyce also says, do it afraid. Overcome anyway.

Holy fear works on your behalf to keep you safe, aware that He is a Holy and awesome God. If there are monsters under the bed, it will benefit me to pull my head out of the sand and learn how to deal with them. Be honest with the Lord, Ask, Seek, Knock: find out how the enemy accessed your home. Find out where was the door was left open to let them (monsters) in and close off the access point.

Ask questions: Lord are there any areas I blocked what You were trying to release?
Seasons of worship music we dearly loved until we were sick of hearing them. It's similar to that children's song we sang to the point of being unending & obnoxious, "It's a small world, after all, it's a small world, after all". My example worked, didn't it? You can forgive me at lunchtime because you can't get the irritating tune out of your head. Round and round, we regurgitate worship songs, never believing the words that were so anointed from heaven to transform us. "Open the eyes of my heart Lord, open the eyes of my heart; I want to see you, I want to see you. Oh my gosh! I want to see you". On whose terms?

Fear:
Dealing with fear of the unknown,
Dealing with the Bible, we think we thought we knew,
Dealing with the teachings that told us we couldn't?
Dealing with the demonic,
Dealing with the fear of being deceived.
Doesn't He lead us into all truth? Mindsets, they seem never to end.
I had agreed with every one of these things I have listed.

Take the time to listen and repent: break the agreement with the wrong understanding. Learn to believe what Jesus informed and showed us otherwise. Haven't we responded to the Kingdom poorly? Did we allow fear to inhibit our blessings? He is such an encourager though; I am changing my response.

Redeem His words in your heart.
Redeem = Repent, buyback, change, determine, experience, express, magnify.

See the collection of Witness Scriptures in the back of the book.

Ephesians 1: 18 I pray that the eyes of your heart may be enlightened so that you will know what is the hope of His calling, what are the riches of the glory of His inheritance in the saints,

ACTIVATION: *"Father I ask for forgiveness for partnering with fear. I repent of being fearful of Your Kingdom and fearful of darkness and all that may fill it. I regret mistrusting our relationship in the areas You desire to lead me. I ask for forgiveness for imprisoning my mind with false teachings, for limiting how You can communicate with me. I repent for not taking responsibility to ask You personally about truths and rightly dividing Your word as You reveal it to me. Holy Spirit forgive me for hindering Your ability and desire to teach me all things I am in need of. I break the agreement with (fear, and anything else He highlighted) and the power they have had over me. I put the blood of Jesus between my repentance and You Father. I declare I'm forgiven and free. I ask You to rejuvenate my spiritual and natural eyes and teach me how to see, believe, and walk in the Kingdom." In Jesus' authority, Amen*
Very proud of you for getting rid of some stuff.

Be willing to make the journey. The gift of repentance has opened more Kingdom access than any other key given thus far. I can lay hands on the sick, cast out demons, prophesy hidden personal truths, step into the courts of the Lord, encounter the cloud of witnesses, translate to un-imaginable places, earthly and heavenly. Repeatedly when I look closely at my heart, I keep finding that I have not trusted my Father. That truth plucks my heart string and transforms my relationship with Him, leading me to the kindness of His repentance.

Repentance, a gift that will open Kingdoms.

Again, it's the little things I "think" I see. The movement of things in my peripheral vision is where I recall noticing a change, felt like I was seeing movement and "Beings" walking around my house. I'd be cooking a meal, and a shift would catch my attention, stepping in front of the door threshold. I lean towards these things. The more I stopped and turned aside, like Moses did when encountering the burning bush, the more I say to the Lord: I caught that! What was that? Those little snippets, as a dear friend calls them, are the activations of champions. How many times do we recall the Lord asking a Prophet, what do you see? 99.5% of the time it was the Kingdom of Heaven, the good stuff. I rarely see the yucky stuff. They know my name. You can ask me that testimony when we meet.

Really, walking around the house? Yup! You have portals all over your home: Angels assigned to your house as well as your personal ones. It really can be a crowded place. That's just the Kingdom of the earth. Heaven is a Holy Zoo! When you begin to see, angels are so excited to be recognized, they wave flags at you during your kids' football games. You know, the 4th of July Rodeos and you are sitting up in the nosebleed section? They will alter the big screen event TV to draw your attention to them: angels, hanging around the livestock chute so that you can help-pray-release to keep the cowboy safe who is ready to burst out of a buckin' chute on the back of a 2000lb bull. Angels love being seen. It's on their destiny scroll to partner with you. The more I understand the parameters of time, The more I can't imagine having to work alongside someone who is oblivious to me.

HERE IS A TESTIMONY. You will have to ask my friend, John, about the first time we met. He was leading a prophesy activation class. I was a school bus driver in those days. I had transitioned from full time stay at home Mom to all the boys now in school. Justin, my youngest, was in 8th grade, and I had signed up to be a chaperone for the annual end of the year beach trip, thankfully not driving. Whew, may God bless school bus drivers. I was a school bus driver for eight years, and it was great to have the same schedule as my kids. Paid to pray and study: when the kids went to their field-trip destination, I was free and getting paid to be alone with the Lord. It was awesome. Bus Driving: not for the faint of heart. Anyhow, Justin's field trip: we arrived at Pacific City Beach, for the day at Cape Kiwanda State Natural Area and the kids were released to run and play. Pacific City is known for its dory boats and massive dunes. Miles of beach where cars are still allowed to drive on today. I found a large tree trunk weathered by the ocean (driftwood) and nestled down into the sand, with my bible, a self-help spiritual teaching book, and a well-stocked lunch bag. I might have been perceived by the other parents as a little anti-social, but what a day! Sand dunes about five stories high on my right, the ocean crashing in front of me and miles of sandy Oregon beaches to my left. I'm ignoring the 8th graders roaming everywhere for the sake of the story. Yes, I was watching them, lifting my nose from the pages of my book once in a while performing my parental scoping duties. I noticed at the top of the dunes some movement, a circular motion. Hmm? Blinked a few times. Took a drink of water. Refocused. Then asked the Lord, "Lord, why are all those angels flying around in a circle at the top of the sand dune? Lord, am I seeing this correctly? Lord, how should I respond here? Seriously, Lord, those look like flying angels". Well, remember I have learned to believe what He showed me and was actively engaging the crazy, test, touch, ask a million questions with the childlike faith of a three-year-old. What do you think I did? Testing sounds good to me. I got up from my cozy station in the sand and said to the Lord, "Will those angels still be there if I climb that sand dune?" I climbed the sand dune, probably with difficulty as they are very steep. When I got to the top I noticed that they were "still" circling an open crevasse that the ocean was crashing up through, rough tides had washed away the shore. There was a fence around the crevasse with signposts: "keep out, danger, washouts." Well, it didn't take this "spiritual rocket scientist" too long to figure out that people were climbing over the safety barrier and angels had been assigned there to help. How practical! Well, since we are in a testing mode, "Lord," I asked: " If I turn around and look out over the town, will I still be able to "see?" So, I did. I saw angels ascending and descending over this little seaside town. That's when I figured out I could turn my eyes on and off. It wasn't a one-time vision. I figured out I had some kind of control over what I was seeing: as if I were taking on and off a set of "lenses." How patient He always has been with me, teaching me, laughing at me, encouraging me. Instead of an on-off button, it's more like leaning in. Jesus said: "the Kingdom is at hand."

I'LL GIVE AN EXAMPLE. You are standing in your bathroom taking a shower. The curtain or sliding door pulled closed. If a family member comes into the bathroom while you are bathing, you would hear them, right? Can you determine from listening-knowing who it is? Yes, we are familiar with the way someone moves. I can pull the shower curtain aside to "see" who came in, yet I am still standing in the shower. Naked mind you! If you want to take that example deeper into moving in the spirit, your spirit is very able to step out of the shower, not just peek into the room. It is a matter of practice, believing and having fun with the Lord while you practice. Reinforce it with some great scriptures about being seated in heavenly places, coming up here, what the Kingdom of heaven is like, how scripture portrays the throne of God. Well, back to my angel-beach-trip-story.

Back to learning how "seeing" works. This is cool, Lord. With practice, I figured out that I can turn on and off seeing. Open and close the shower door!

While learning, a helpful note: A person's "heart" condition is key to the purposes of seeing. Why do I desire to have eyes to see?

Our 3 lens principles again.
HOW TO USE WHAT YOU PERCEIVE: WISDOM
WHAT YOU PERCEIVE: REVELATION
HOW IT REFLECTS HIM: REVEALING CHRIST

I love how the Lord quickly confirms what He is teaching you so the enemy or wrong mindsets won't steal the lesson. Yes, the seed and sower parable has such great value.

Well, I managed to get down that dune! The field trip was a success in more ways than one, and it was time to load up the kids and chaperone back onto the bus and begin our two-hour trek returning to Corvallis Oregon. Of course, my mind was probably just going a mile a minute. The bus was noisy for at least a half an hour until the worn-out students start to fall asleep one by one, lulled and rocked as the wheels on the bus go around and around. Aah, peace. But wait there's more!

He wants to open your supernatural hearing; the Lord wants to seal His daily "Seeing" teaching.

Several seats ahead of me there was a couple of parents talking, saying that not just two weeks earlier a young man had climbed over the warning barrier at the top of the dunes, fallen, his body never found. An excellent reason for angels to be on assignment.

I'm of the opinion that we never hear about all the people that responded wisely to the voice of His angels detouring them from making stupid decisions.

ANGEL TIPS: (honor and affirmations help Angels in their ministry and eventually bring them into apprehendable view).

So, by the end of the day, we head back to the beginning of my testimony, that prophecy class with my friend John. I think I arrived first, just John and the Pastor. Since it's my first time there, I introduce myself. John graciously attempts to break the newcomer ice and asks how my day was, anything exciting happen? I take a crazy transparent leap and share my entire day about angels ascending and descending; it is a prophecy class isn't it? John and I have been great friends ever since. I do not recommend such liberties without the unction of Holy Spirit. I think my zeal made up for their mouths hanging open and mindsets blown.

When I was learning to see, there wasn't a grid in my area of influence to discuss this. In my church environment, the understanding of the unseen was pretty much: It's unseen! Playing it safe to just leave the word "mystery" dormant on the pages of the bible.

Always a good time to repent.

I haven't read many books about seeing. I tend to choose to read subject matters related to what the Lord is currently teaching me. It helps reinforce, not overwhelm, or over educate with no experience.

I know a Pastor that would say to himself:
"That was a good word and repeated it for his own hearing."

SEEING IN THE SPIRIT HELPS:
Copied from the chapter #11: Angels on a first name basis.

I am discovering that spiritual sightedness has multiple lenses: Two lenses I feel confident to share.

A LENS OF UNDERSTANDING: *framed in knowledge from the environment in which I live, the library of my life. God reflects types, shadows, and frameworks to proclaim the kingdom of heaven in me and within Him. A river looks like a river; a room looks like a room with a building around it. Moses was instructed to build from a "pattern" he received on the mountain. His pattern also included "rooms."*

A LENS OF ENERGY, LIGHT, SOUND, COLOR, AND FREQUENCY. *I can see myself as a spiritual being with a body; I also can see myself as a spirit, a creature of light.*

Chapter 6

Earth Invading Heaven

*"Hear this, young men and women everywhere, and
proclaim it far and wide. The earth is yours and the fullness
thereof. Be kind but be fierce. You are needed now more
than ever before. Take up the mantle of change.
For this is your time." Sir Winston Churchill*

The unbelievable, unsought world is alive on the yarn woven in my heart. Unbelievability is an inadequate description, and we should probably find a different way to express "unbelievable." No longer is it inconceivable to me. Mystery; I love divine mystery. I relish discovering, asking questions, touching and feeling my way to understand the supernatural realm. Through the veil is an open door of intimacy that has led me into a face to face relationship with the Godhead, having made "studying the bible" secondhand conversation. Yes, I have already been burned "at the stake" for that comment. The bible always confirms Him and many times when I have experienced something that my understanding is struggling with, I'll respond and ask: "Could you give me a bit of a clue what that is all about?" He will direct me to a passage on many occasions. Sometimes, I'm still very much in the dark. But I'll note it in my journal that He tagged a certain passage as understanding for that encounter. Proverbs 3:5-6: Trust in the Lord with all your heart, and lean not unto my "own" understanding. In all "ways" acknowledge Him, and He shall direct your paths. I call that divine coordinates. Starting with Him, "Trust" ending with Him directing your paths. Nobody ever said it wasn't in "another realm"! My right to understanding is in a position of submission.

I can close the door or shut off the "seeing" if I would choose too. Many have closed the door through fear of the unknown; misunderstanding, immaturity, wrong mindsets and teaching. I have weighed the cost and have chosen not to be spiritually blind, feeling narrowness from an earthly perspective. Heaven has popularity from a perspective of death but not the living! A dear Pastor friend of mine describes sharing from the pulpit about Heaven from the living like this: "How to decrease the numbers in your church." Not a comforting statement as a leader, confirming that there are those "leaders" who are not alone in our mystical conversion. Heaven is real and rich in providing clear answers that my "Christianity" was severely lacking.

For years my worship was exercised in a performance-like manner. Scary to say it that way! My understanding of how God's Spirit moves or is moved was based on that I could perform and He would approve by descending into the atmosphere. Whether it was thanksgiving, praise, adoration, repentance, dance, my response to Him would pull Him into the room. We "praise" to open doors, portals. You can honestly feel the shift and the tangible presence of angels around you. Our songs "supposedly" pulled and altered heavens response. Sometimes we would get caught in quantity instead of quality. In the anointed season when "soaking" arrived on the scene, I was addicted. What is soaking? It's face-time/carpet-time prayer; I do not use any words, listening prayer you might say, supported brilliantly by instrumental music; then the words won't distract you. You commit the time to listen, love, and just be with Him. Marinate or soak.

I was addicted to soaking. At church, we had a dedicated prayer chapel with pillows and lovely chairs encouraging the one on one time with the Lord. His presence consumes you and feels, Oozy Goosy, my words you might say. It is lovely to feel the whoosh of the spiritual atmosphere. You can spend hours in His presence. I'm thankful for where it led me, led our church, but we also noticed it seemed like a one-way door. "Come on in Jesus; I like how you make me feel, would You do this for me?" When the clock ticked and time was up, how much transformation occurred? I am so thankful that grace helped us figured out through the vehicle of soaking, that it was just the evidence that the door was opened. We learned not just to lay in His presence but receive the invitation and go into His habitations. I now have invaded heaven. I bring concerns and petitions, continuing to learn to deal with them in heaven. Every praise is in heaven. Heaven is God's "White House" without corrupt administrations. I'm continually focusing on not to step out. Being seated in heavenly places with Him kicks the grasshopper mentality when it comes to "There are giants in the land." Above all principality and powers, an excellent position from which to be viewing your enemies: Learning to call the shots with the King of Kings. Amen.

JUST A MOMENT OF PAINFUL TRUTH: Remember I willingly participated/wrestled within the rules of the game. The responsibility is mine. The deception of the fear of man and acceptance of man exacted a toll.

When I mention costly, I'm not pulling punches. In the "Getting Permission" season, crossing all your T's and dotting your I's was emotionally difficult. The measure of the standard is insane. Man's check off list for the "Pastorate" is without mercy. And sad to say with many, mercy isn't available. "Lead Pastor" makes it more radical. I remember receiving an invitation to set up a booth at a meet and greet. Our "church" was recruiting for "paid" interns, with room and board. Students would pass by, a few would ask questions. I can't tell you how many young women burst into tears when I shared I was the "Lead Pastor" or carrier of the "vision." They would ask: "Is it 'really' happening? We are also called to be Pastors? In silent frustration, I fought both internal and external struggles to measure up. I was challenged in the steps you take to get all your "ordination" ducks in a row. You've grown in "His" power and can lay hands on the sick with testimonies, prophecy on cue, Holy Spirit inspired secrets that touch a person's heart, lead street evangelism, street evangelism, street evangelism. Grow up in the school of hard knocks learning to walk out your healing and brokenness. You can then find the voice of freedom to help mend brokenness and lack of trust with the sheep and begin teaching the church to rightly divide the word for themselves and discern God's "callings." A "female pastor/leader" is not out of God's order and we are not going to misuse money. I look at it now seeing how I padded my leadership so that "Beyond Reproach" was a hat worn instead of a relationship of community. A series of years of pressing and searching my heart. Crazy, sad, and unfortunate how difficult it was to get "in" the box!

Selah! We must think about that. Yes, I know, in the box!

AND THEN, GOD CHANGES THE MESSAGE:

"Hear this, young men and women everywhere,
and proclaim it far and wide.
The earth is yours and the fullness thereof.
Be kind, but be fierce.
You are needed now more than ever before.
Take up the mantle of change. For this is your time."

                                             -Sir Winston Churchill

HAPPENINGS, A CHANGE OF VIEW: invading the supernatural became a famous "in the know" word. I'm so thankful to be a part, to have had access to powerful teachings, schools, and conferences, ushering in the breakthroughs of the "Supernatural." We have seen great changes in our generation. My husband and I had the great privilege of receiving annual invitations to attend a leadership conference. Blessed to sit amongst Gods leaders, hear their stories from all over the world and hug familiar faces. That particular autumn came with much anticipation for refreshment, communion, confirmation and inspired words. We, our "small" gathering, were on the cusp of change.

That evening during the conference we attended worship services. I could hardly wait for the facilitator to get the announcements out of the way so I could leap out of my seat and join the "free moving" ones down front. Stage left, positioned next to a base speaker, in front of the prophetic artist. The music cued, words scored the monitors, and my spirit lifted and was escorted into His presence. A dancer would rhythmically step and gracefully move, as paints splash the artist canvas: An atmosphere pregnant with hope, birthing new, releasing old. My spirit shifted allowing me to go in through an artist draft; heavenly portal opened with paired perspectives. I saw Heaven and earth's brush. My feet stood on top of the atmosphere between heaven and earth. Metaphorically, the edge of the ocean and the shore of the land. A thought planted itself: The Sands of Time. From spirit to soul perceiving height, latitudes and longitudes, balance, gravity, breadth and length. I had the sensation of standing on a heavenly grid with four corners, the four corners of the earth. Like an ice-cube tray or egg carton, each had uniform compartments or realms. The grid was movable and tilted on what I perceived as an axis. When one corner rose higher, the opposite corner went lower. Standing in the middle of this heavenly platform, the "grid" tilted and the corner lifted. I quickly moved with the ascension to stand on the high angle. Weight and gravity removed, I lifted up, breaking through the ceiling that covered me. I rose through, creating a chain reaction in which I saw the anointing (both water and oil) flow down through the grid or "tilted" atmosphere. The fluid started to fill individual compartments, each chamber overflowing to the next until the liquid reached the bottom. I didn't understand anything, yet I relaxed in the familiar un-doing of being with Him. My equilibrium overwhelmed, my spirit shifted, and I cognitively returned, finding myself still standing next to the loudspeaker, spiritually dumbfounded, looking around, mesmerized towards the complexion of now painted canvas, artist, and heavenly encounter. I made it back to my seat and with limited breath, murmured into my husband's ear while pointing at the painting: "I went there!" The mystic masterpiece reflected a sky of muted golds. Held within the billowed clouds is the profile of a regal lion's head. Underneath His roar stamped three dappled white stallions rushing from heaven's view. Reared over white-capped waves on cobalt blue seas was a dapple grey rearing charger. Balanced over his silver haunches stands the rider, her arms stretched back, face in the wind, as if diving upwards, her feet rolled on toe, balanced.

"Standing on the atmosphere between Heaven and Earth." By Donna Taylor

The door was permanently opened; my heart had broken through; my life would never be the same. Little did I know that my life would never be the same. Earth has invaded heaven. Knowing, but not entirely understanding, God had downloaded something powerful in me and captured it on canvas. I picked up the sheet of protocols to acquire it. I wrote to the artist, telling her in detail the encounter that I had in the midst of her creating. I filled in the monetary line the entire - but humble - amount currently sitting in my bank account. We met, hugged and talked: Divinely complete. The painting is now hanging in my home. It has encouraged and inspired many who have stopped to gaze upon it.

My spirit-life with Him remains where He sits on a throne, wears a crown, and His government is without end. I am overwhelmed and ready to learn what change lies ahead.
Stepping through the veil is nothing "new."

Let's remember:
the message of Grace hasn't always been preached or heard in the Gospel.
Let's remember afresh, the person, Holy Spirit, hasn't always been welcomed in the Gospel "message."
Rekindle our memory of revivals; healing and the laying on hands discounted from the Gospel "message."
The word of prophecy restricted from being released in the Gospel "message."

Change has unearthed once again in the Gospel "message." Preaching about "entering" the Kingdom of Heaven is ruffling feathers even though Jesus spoke about it over 153 times. And death does not have to come knocking! Yup, God changes the message: on the other side of the veil!

How approved do you think my voice is now? About like Pastor Todd Burpo in book/movie "Heaven is Real," *grammatical pause.*

"WEARING A SKIRT"! HELP ME, JESUS!

Going from this defining encounter: To my church community, the Kingdom message changed. Not just in leadership eyes but manifested itself corporately. Together, our little church started experiencing doors in the spirit, spiritual doors everywhere. Our artists were consistently painting doors, windows, portals: beautiful windows of inviting light and streams of colors welcoming us into heaven. Paintings are like seeing the heart of a person opening up. Rivers were bursting through with treasures untold. Angels, clocks and compasses were compelling us to "Come up Here." It was interesting to realize that on the Hebrew calendar it was the year of the "Door." And as a Leader I put forth the question, isn't it obvious and don't you think we should go through it! The Door? We did. Church changed. Everything changed. Leadership changed. People who didn't want to go through the "door" were, sadly, "released." With honor and patience, the Lord asked us to "release" family members. Better to release with blessing than leaving disgruntled. It was a very "grieving season."

The epitome of "Train 161" traveling across the wilderness and people jumping off into another camp. I still mull over my first quote from Martin Luther,

> *"You want to change the world "Kristen?"*
> *Pick up your pen."*
>
> *Such "Indulgences."*

I'm excited, we are getting inches close to my halfway mark. You have mulled over that "Heaven is Accessible" with breath in your lungs. So, you may ask: what does the other side of the veil look like? Great question! Overwhelming at first. I remember the first couple of months that I finally agreed: No more questioning change, no allowing parroted doctrines to have space in my relationship with a perfect teacher and companion.
For me, meeting with Him has always been "outside" the camp.

I am now to meet with Him on the other side of the veil. It was all well and good when I could just mark it off as dreams, visions and crazy encounters. That put me in the "super spiritual" category. After learning all of the prophetic culture apostolic stuff, I'm back in pre-school again. Thankfully it's not all flushed down the toilet. The seeing lens is useful, but I discovered it could be a crutch. The Kingdom takes a walk by faith and not by sight to an entirely new level.

ACTIVATION: *A hint when "perceiving": keep your spiritual eyes closed when you first enter a "new to me" place. My other senses discern more accurately than sight does at first. Just an observation for you "seers."*

It's not a race, it's a journey, and you have all eternity to keep learning, growing and walking out your scroll. Nobody is more significant or more "spiritual" than anyone else, except Jesus. He is the beloved star of it all. A person might have more access or different keys. Those things are dependent on your scroll and maturity. For instance: I'm supposed to be a forerunner: Father wired me like the Starship Enterprise, to go where no man has gone before. It works nicely with my redemptive gift! Remember; the prophet gift (redemptive, not office) *will display a picture of God so dynamic and real that it moves people out of their comfort zones (which can become prisons) and into a journey that will bring them to fulfillment of all God created them to be.* (Description credit Jeremy Wescott).

I TRUST ITS WORKING FOR YOU!
Thirty Thousand, yippee we rolled the meter again. Thirty thousand eight hundred and fifty-one words.

On the other side, peek!
Angels: Everyone wants to see angels. They are very cool. Some are personal, some messengers, some guardians: The framework we grasp them in changes according to their assignment, order, rank. Your imagination can do a better job of discerning them than your brain can, any day. Angels come in all shapes, sizes, frequencies, colors; on the whole, more without wings. I've never encountered any that are chubby little cherub-like figures. It is best not to put limitations on God's creativity. I have humbly realized I will never exhaust my learning or discovering something new. Things in the spirit are just that, in the spirit. Outside of time and space, wings are really for other purposes: like raising in worship, doors, covering one's feet... you

get the idea: just being beautiful, light beings, radiating the revelation of His glory, for the pleasure of the Kingdom.

The Cloud of Witnesses is nothing short of miraculous. The opportunity to get first-hand knowledge from a great "bible" ambassador is an honor on steroids. The joy of meeting family members recently passed, or your generational line from centuries ago, unborn or aborted. It is humbling the many ways that we understand breath stolen, but they are very much alive and so glad to be a witness to your scroll. And do they love to have an open invitation to come to "Church"! Remember? One "Body" in heaven and earth. It appears like they are in your realm, so to speak but we are the ones who change location and ascend. A blessing of seeing is to describe a living-in-heaven loved one who walks into the room carrying a gift for their family member. They come to bring healing, encouragement, legislative witness for your deliverance and freedom.

God has many unique ways of encouraging each of us; you can feel His hand upon dreams that have been alive in your heart for years. I have gotten in His way far too many times. That is the hard part about believing, the "me" part, believing self: The challenge of accepting Jesus inside of you, learning to trust that He is the Author and Finisher of your faith. I think it is that way for most of us that have gravitated towards the unknown or unseen.

It's only unseen until it is "seen."
And then the journey begins. It's much easier to believe having seen. Again, I love Nicodemus' story. You must see the Kingdom of Heaven. A good reason why the enemy has thrown so many wrenches into the pot is to keep the body of Christ blind.

BEGINNING ANEW: this is really where the book starts to reveal "Heavenly Understanding:" *Thirty thousand one hundred and seventy-five words into it.* That is a huge amount of back-story: Your story, my story. The "wilderness" of our lives: An unsettled and uncultivated tract of land left in its natural state. The mountain of God has always been the destination. Yes, very encouraging so far.

Since I, we, "Earth" has invaded heaven, you will discover that God is quite a Strategist. The tabernacle is one of an infinite collection of types and shadows: patterns - not formulas - received on a "mountain," places of authority and rule, order, purposes, and patterns repeated. There are natural and spiritual laws that govern locations for law-making and law-releasing. I have encountered different types of "Higher Universities, Libraries, Council room's, Courtrooms, Strategy rooms. Those are just a small fraction of places of governing. Let's include the gardens, rivers and waterfalls, the Tree of Life, mansions, treasuries and secret places. It's easier to hear Jesus' words: "I go to prepare a place for you and in my Father's house are many rooms." Now take the favorite scripture fulfilled before time and look at the infrastructure of the community around you. Look at our society, from sewer system to the light posts overhead, fiber optics that run your Internet around the world, the structure of the infrastructure serves a purpose for living.

The heavens declare the Glory of God. We assumed up!

I'm not a science fiction fan, but I will watch a movie just to see how Hollywood is picking up a prophetic voice. Movie makers, computer-generated animators, get so close to representing different movements in the spirit: Negative too! Not where my eyes focus. The Heavens require eternity to explore. It's big, it's purposeful, and we are not sitting on clouds playing harps. It's time to learn to hit a curve-ball on the learning curve of heavenly "protocols" and how to get involved in activating Heaven to invade earth. I swear I hear you say, "Kristen, haven't we already done that?" Yes, but it was by grace, love, and chance. Let's get to that "Great Grace." We haven't known what it meant to "rule and reign." If He is Lord of Lords, who are the Lords? If He is King of Kings, who are the King's? Who are the "Sons" (not gender-selective but it's more than our understanding of "Heirs") that all creation is groaning too?

A RUNNING THEME: I have known for years that I was called to write. You have read my struggle and deliverance. One of the aspects I understand about grace is similar to this:

God is "vaguely" familiar with all the times I chickened out to pray for someone in public when self or fear got the upper hand: His plan included the chickening-out-side steps or delays that matured me, so when it was imperative that I obey and must act on the spot, I would. My disobedience in learning and growing develops a sense I now recognize the lesson. Those times I've "missed" obeying Him, now that lesson has its perfect work: Now! And here we are, the Now of writing; Kristen is invading heaven. Do you want to come?

Chapter 7

In Heavenly Places

*"Faith is only needed for the unseen until the evidence
of it in action becomes visible around the one
who exercises the faith." K. Wambach*

*I continue to encounter this book in heaven. I've seen many books from my
pen, but let's birth one, OK!*

An authentic prophetic word is merely reading and voicing a snippet from
a book/scroll that is already written or ordained in heaven. During that
season I was unaware of its path. When I immersed myself in the prophetic
culture; I heard, received, or gave "prophetic" voice. Words inspired in
divine breath, yes, but oblivious to the course of responsibility for getting
it written, recorded, given to angels to activate it, and onto its heavenly
journey. For several years, understanding the Kingdom of Heaven has been
the learning God has been asking the "Church" to be responsible for, from
relationship to responsibility. Intimacy is a carrier and doer of His heart.
Brides get ready for the "Big" day: Sampling, trying on, inviting, creating,
looking for a way to reflect their love. Consummation is icing on the cake
of covenant. *Seated in heavenly places, we take the journey into my
responsibility to record heavens agreement. Thus my "mandate."*

"In the spirit on the Lord's day:" Every day is the Lord's day, just trying to
be creative when introducing and sharing this encounter. I have ventured
into the Court of Angels many times and am always captivated by its
magnitude, creativity, practicality, resources, and joyful light. Today a lower
floor, which my eyes had not had an invitation to see before, opened up
to a staircase similar as you would go downstairs underneath a gymnasium.
The room or "locker-room" seemed to be round with lockers set into its
circular wall; benches lined the middle of the room just as if I were going
to sit down to dress for pickleball or tennis match. Resembling a lit marque
to an old movie theater, beamed locker number 247, so I ventured toward
it. The locker was tall and narrow, a common memory from my high-school
years, never enough room to bend over and put on your unmentionables
after your shower. Remembering; You're are sticky and wet, bent over, face
uncomfortably close, and it's accosting the backside of your neighbor - well
- too much remembering there! I highlighted before that I was focused

on locker number 247. Like those spiritual doors and portals, we better open it. I take hold of the goofy lever, pull up, and it pops open. Inside the locker hanging on a two-prong hook is a berry-red shaggy "you know it's homemade" wool scarf, one that had been well loved by its previous owner. It's a little frayed at the edges, a sure sign that the user treasured it before me. Questions and heaven go together: ask, seek, and knock as if you're playing hide and seek and want to win the game. Question: Papa, who did this belong to? A pregnant pause; Answer not offered but a Fatherly smile given. I think the "mystery name" will get unpacked as my faith activates the writing mantle and obedience puts fear to rest in the long haul of things. Either immaturity or from being overwhelmed is a good reason to keep it a mystical secret. And it is the privilege of kings to search it out. Right? While I wrap it around my neck, I notice a box of white chalk on the floor of the locker. The chalk box seems vintage, weathered, more black on the box than the green and gold Crayola-ones I remember and see in craft stores today. I do not "sense" I'm to pick up the chalk, but I can come back if I need to. Nothing else seems to be in the locker, and I am not sensing to go inside (portal,) of the locker (important note: everything is alive in heaven, and you can engage it). When using the word "sense," I'm referencing an inner conversation with Holy Spirit like a river flowing through all my senses: Spiritual gates, Soul gates, Body gates. "I've got a River of Life flowing out of me!"

Hence, to the best of my ability, I am receiving written direction. "Sense/sensing."

I close the locker door, look around the room, clean, bright, and circular, head back up the stairs. I still need the assignment of an angel to my book project. Angels get assigned when a mandate has been given, agreed on or sealed and recorded.

(**MANDATE:** *an assignment received "relationally" that activates your heart into "responsibility"*). They are always in line with your destiny. Keep it Simple: God asked me, or I asked Him, and we agreed.

As I climb up the stairs to the landing, a breath of thought swishes her name into my spirit before my eyes witness her, the angel. Her name is Kate. "Hello." As our greeting commenced, my eyes shifted. Kate changed from radiant energy of colorful light into a half pint size Scottish Dog with the handle of a small basket in her mouth. I lay the mandate inside the basket, and we are off, with a chuckle on my lips. The name Kate means pure or blessed, a good friend to have along for the adventure. Let the experience begin.

Thinking this was the "beginning" of a book, how would I describe it? I'd say that His goodness wraps us in many beginnings. Authors usually paint a picture with their words so your imagination can grasp the scene. A child's imagination is a tool, a gift from the master. Birds and animals' names and purposes came to Adam from inside him; his words declared the real matter that we behold today.

The scene set, pen in hand, or iPad positioned, this is the heavenly scene I step into to write: The sky is light blue with high, wispy clouds framed by the gentle breeze. My feet are bare; jeans rolled into an ankle-high cuff while my toes pinch and feel loose dirt that has escaped the grasp of grass seed underneath a large tree. I'm wearing my favorite grey sweatshirt that my oldest son gave me, with "Marine Corp." insignia on it. The hood of the sweatshirt is padding my neck and back from the grooves of the bark of this massive tree. Leaning against the tree, red scarf (mantel) round my neck, a new friend at my side (Kate), I'm a writing-painter with a new canvas discovering what is already (outside of time written on my destiny scroll) a finished masterpiece between Papa and me. The place I'm describing is new and I have much exploring to do. Being prepared for a "timeless" moment, there is a library of words that I have yet to hear and yet to write: Crazy prophetic beginning from halfway. Go figure. Let's laugh. Guess what? I have a chalkboard or slate setting on my lap: Heavenly iPad I suppose. This is interesting, let's see what Kate has in that basket she is carrying. Yes, faithful to start, I do need the box of chalk. Let's paint more of the picture. The tree is mature and massive, maybe ten people could sit backs up to it around its base. The light is caught like honey in an unstuck drop of dew at the pointy tip-end of each leaf not longer than the length of my hand. The vast leaf number which is hosted in its canopy, touched by soft honey light, creates an expanse of peace. The light radiance without a shadow around us: Breath stealing! Hung on a reaching, mature branch is a swing. Tethered by the twist of hemp rope: securing an adventure hugging a wooden seat maybe 2x8x24 with notched holes at each end. Responding to the invitation to "swing", I gaze out upon grassy meadows letting my eyes reach far, vast fields, rolling up and down gentle hills that kiss the beginning and the end of a robin egg blue sky. "And extending the invitation to whoever may walk into the pages of my book." But for now, in its infant stages, this living tree, me, and Kate are all that my heart can see.

Reality encases the word real.... Real defined as existing as a thing or occurring in fact; not imagined or supposed (of a substance or matter), not an imitation or artificial, genuine. Placed at the end of "Real," the suffix "ity" forms nouns denoting quality or condition "humility," "probity." My study of the English language is not without its struggles. Through my education years, my Mom has been editing my written works of art. Part of facing your fear and walking in your destiny is choosing to grow in areas of weakness. There is a cool tool called "Research" that is helping me. *Reality?* The world or the state of things as they exist, as opposed to an idealistic or notional idea of them. The state or quality of having existence or substance. *"Faith is only needed for the unseen until the evidence of its unseen-hope in action becomes visible around the one who exercises the faith."* It is easier to "believe," having seen. Doubt and unbelief take a considerable amount of work to enforce. That is why Jesus had that conversation with Nicodemus. That is all the convincing I'm going to do. The purpose of this book is not to convince but to share a journey, testimony, and tools with those who desire to walk or have already walked into heaven with breath very much still in their lungs. The cross annihilated the dominion of death, sin, and fear and recorded it by the blood of my Savior. His personal invitation to follow Him was rent through a veil thicker than any fabric I can imagine, even though people were going through it before it was rent. Time asks the question, when was it rent if He died before the foundation of the world? See, access is also outside of time? If you need convincing, take it up with Him. Otherwise, I'm going to talk and share on both sides of the veil and continue to pen how my perspectives have changed along the pathway, how people's different responses toward me groomed me and aided the testing of my faith: Which only brings great pleasure to my Father. I'm smiling at His pleasure and invite you to jump in too! However, those who by faith, bravery, and courage read this book, will find it embedded with His pleasure. It's ok if you read it with a flashlight under the covers. Nicodemus first came in the cover of the night not wanting to be challenged or get anybody into trouble or have to deal with the stuff one deals with when they can "see, hear and encounter heaven." Well, I've made plenty of mistakes too and plan on sharing them, so maybe you do not have to. Anything that has real value is worth all the attempts, the enemy has tried to steal the key. Guess what? Let's make it fun. I went to Robinett's (Corvallis historic hardware store) in the spirit and made (key) copies for you! Jesus permitted me. See I have a mandate, signed, sealed, delivered: Keys and tools assigned. The power of heaven's backing, with Papers to boot!

I BLESS YOUR IMAGINATION; *I bless your eyes to see and your ears to hear. "Mystery" is reborn and cleansed, words formed before you. Do we ever consider answering our life written in the heart of the One who is also "Unseen" till we respond wholeheartedly - no matter the cost - in allowing the Jesus that we love to come through the door we open. And He asks us to follow, and we "really" do it:*

Follow into the Kingdom. **USE THE KEY!**

Falling in love with Jesus consists of a daily living sacrifice. My heart is opened for Him to search. Jesus paid the ultimate cost for me to love, to love me, to love others and learn how to love Him from a realm that many deny.

Each time I used the key, it would open more of Him. The cost would be to deny the same old, deny the statistics, negate the rules of man and reacquaint myself with the person that I should imitate. Permission ultimately resides inside of me. How much would I give Him? How much did I relinquish to others along the path and how I was to get it back.

Jesus gives each one of us permission to rule and reign, with Him. The wilderness path that I walked seemed to have filled itself with the notion that ruling and reigning was something that one did on earth. Unfortunately, as shared from my history, it entails the "ruling over" to happen with each other: Man over women, leader over follower, husband, and wives, parents with children. Authority has been exercised by title, not dominion. I have to be aware of my "domain" to exercise jurisdiction. Only God gives dominion, through the veil. What is on the other side of the door? Your heart, His temple, and a door that should be opening wider and wider with a river running through it. Follow the river. Follow the succession of the kingdom, maturing through encounters and outworking the dominion given.

The Kingdom of heaven is an expanse of territory and terrain that is first outworked in me. (the Kingdom of Heaven within) Then I follow the river through the temple door into The kingdom of His domain, the realm of Heaven. My heart looks different than His. Therefore my perceptions of His kingdom in me will travel through a process of change, transformation, opening ideas, and portals to explore: Like the tribes of Israel and their inheritance. Each one had the different blessing and opportunity to engage the dominion of the current (wilderness king) government there.

I started to see the Kingdom because of love. My personal life was full of struggle from within and without. Jesus was the only answer, as HE is to us all. I needed rescuing, and He was the only one who had paid the price to be my rescuer.

The end of a writing day; One thousand one hundred and fifty-four words written; three thousand three hundred and sixty-four words to halfway.

Through the experiences of discovering my book, from Heavenly Places, every chapter of life, God has sent a spirit of confidence. He has drawn me, drawn you into areas of growth and believing in ourselves. What we struggle with now may be completely different from before. "Seeing" is a bestowment from your inheritance that helps you to connect in a picture framework form, where a "prophetic" word originates. Prophetic words are snippets from your scroll. Our Destiny scroll was never meant to be secret or only readable from the eyes of someone else's heart.

A HEAVENLY LIBRARY.

A few years back I was taken in the spirit to a vast, elegant library in heaven. The library has continued to be a place of growing intimacy in my relationship with the Godhead. Today I enter there because Father has set a table of communion. We eat together, and I share it in the spirit also with the people who I hold in my heart.

There are many libraries in heaven: Many! Creative and unusual ways for mystical papers, books, scrolls, DNA, to be recorded and stored for His kids to gain information sealed within it. It is part of our journey, the library: beautiful, high ceiling, pillars, ornate wood moldings, and bookshelves all similar in timber and stain, a mix of walnut and cherry: An authentic Victorian feel, not "Gaudy." In the spirit of getting bearings: The room 'front' has a massive alcove of windows, sitting just inside the bay is a beautiful grand piano, also built with the same wood as the rest of the chamber.

In spiritual lingo, the room is the same "sound."

The piano is also a library of vibration. Like public places, there are exits and entries to encounter on three walls. A central door leads to more "library" rooms.

Jesus first led me into this particular library on the Eve of a New Year. I was seeking the Lord for insight and direction. Seated in the center are large round tables conveniently placed around the room just like a university library. There is a retrieving place to set the books you have taken off the shelf and a chair to sit and study/encounter. This particular morning Jesus took me into the room and pulled from the shelf a "cookie tin" that was familiar to me. I put Christmas cookies in it every year. Inside the tin was a handwritten note saying: "New Era." I also was escorted into the same library room the following year. The word written was: "Container-ship." Together we're learning something about the significance of the library. It has recorded information about doors into future eras. I'll pause there! If you're interested, I have made available the messages during this period and if you would like to listen in on some of the ways the Lord unpacked those "words." You will find the link on the book website or go to the podcasts on Podomatic. See Northwest Bliss. Continuing. My pathway to this part of the library had been walked with the Lord a few times. I felt confident that I could begin to explore more of the vast "realm," room after room after room. This particular morning in my quiet time I walked out into the adjoining corridor which led to a landing. I discovered I was on a middle floor, finding stairs both up and down and other massive rooms on the same level. Angels were actively scurrying in and out from the different library rooms. Some places had open doors with ample thresholds. Other doors the entry was closed.

Interesting note about being in the "spirit:" The kingdom of heaven inside of you gives you a tracking system allowing you to know where you are, where to go, and where you are not, at this time, on any given "encounter."

Today, highlighted in my spirit, was a room one floor up. I could see the tall, slim door slightly ajar and a bright green hue was radiating from within its secrets. Heaven also appoints unusual "vehicles" of transportation. Walking is more meditative. I'm still standing on the landing having been mesmerized by the heavenly activity. Sometimes your emotions through your soul feel the overwhelming extravagance, meticulous and thoughtful preparation of your Divine Parent, and it may take you a few "quiet time days" to continue your discovery. Divine soaking: Let heaven wash over you. While resting, Jesus (it is easy to communicate with Jesus) enters from across the hall. He smiles with sheepish foreknowledge of our adventure ahead. He transforms in front of me into a glorious and regal Lion. It is not the first time I have encountered Him this way, but every time I am moved by His authority and roar. My hands naturally reach out to His kingly mane, "feeling" the texture of it, groomed in a "dread" like fashion. Mane-ropes convenient as I grabbed hold and He lifts me onto His back. Both hands are woven-hug around His neck and my face buried in the mane-pillow of the Lion of the tribe of Judah. Eyes closed and I'm feeling the rock, sway, and cadence of a Lion's gait. No need to look. I know where we are going: Up the flight of stairs, down the hall to the room with the door standing ajar. I'm soaking in the rhythm of my victorious King, "Devouring the memory of Oneness." Selah!

In nano-moments, I find myself through the door, standing, and Jesus my friend (now looking like a man) is watching me scour the room. I see two and a half of the walls filled with floor to ceiling bookcases, a women's wingback chair with floral needlepoint coverings, set next to a Victorian height corner window. The window curtains are cascading onto the non-book-shelved wall, loose growing vines with small trumpet-like white blossoms reaching as living wallpaper. I smell a familiar fragrance of "Mock Orange." Trellising vines attached to a leaded glass paned window floor to ceiling: Light, light, and cozier "Son" light. Jesus is delighted with my pleasure. An internal library, with shelves filled with an array of works: yet one oeuvre shined, hidden above the rest. My spirit is drawn blindly to it, nestled amongst the shelves inside this "designed-about-Kristen" room. Being that close to your work of destiny is very transforming. I lingered without words for a spiritual eternity. His attention to unique detail unwinds my negative internal threads. Emotions of freedom bathe me with His reassurance. Jesus says: "this is how I see you." Divine truth and vulnerability, for many reasons, I didn't inquire which book it was.

Selah, thirty-three thousand and nineteen words.

JOURNALING NOTE: Yippee this works!!! from my iPad right next to the PC. Fascinating, in the spirit, there is a golden trophy, like a winner's cup, set up on top of my bookshelf here in my office, next to Michael the angel, the same figurine that also sat on my Grandma's shelf in her office.

CHAPTER 8

Vulnerable Focus

"Vulnerability has "ability" knitted within her." Kristen Wambach

Vulnerable, so close, just a simple question away, on the shelf of a heavenly inner library, my book, this book. Why didn't I ask to see it? Where does courage run in a room full of Peace? What are the reasons I didn't inquire which book it was? Fear: what are you going to do with "Self" when you "actually" encounter you. No more excuses at hand. If I pull the book off the shelf, then I am committed to the contents. Unbelief has snuck into a hiding place, wedged in my mountain of dreams. The Kingdom world engaged in becomes a reality. I'm "real" in the story. Jesus is alive and inquiring after my heart. Somewhere on this journey of life I cut and pasted a false heart, as a shield of protection: A face with a smile; a mask called suck it up, be tough, overcome; a blackboard on which I erase grade point "average." If I look with eyes that want to see, will I change the words that don't describe me?

Vulnerable focus: In all my attempts to write a book: Lady in Waiting, Getting Permission, Earth Invading Heaven, The Watchmaker, I altered my confession but didn't change my decisions. Just around the bend from my halfway marker and self-motivational goals luring, I can honestly say I have been a flake to myself. I haven't believed His words to the degree of allowing transformation to transform. My schedule was the same, though writing was at the top of my list. Yet days, weeks and months passed, and I made other choices. I am learning to guard my day. Currently, the day is not a day without accomplishing a thousand words. The gift of writing is a priority. My "self" has chosen to take a back seat to the offering of destiny. Yes, all of it is like exercise and changing your eating habits. Oh no, this isn't a wellness book, is it? Ha! At some point, I had to invest in me, and that investment is there for the long haul. What I say I am going to do, I do. Let my yes be yes, and my no, no. I am indeed inside an "internal" library. I ask myself the question: Did I ride on the back of the Lion of the tribe of Judah? Or did He come to escort me, to feel the rhythm of His Kingship?

Adam and Eve, once naked and unashamed, were clothed by a merciful Father. I assumed from the text, for protection from the "elements" in a different environment. A transforming thought? What if the covering was to protect them from His holiness: Still a caring Father. I'm digging around in me.

Returning to the heavenly scene inside the "inner" library, I'm sitting on the quaint, woman's chair surrounded by a perfect environment that "speaks" my language. Questioning: as much pressing in, encountering, digging, touching and feeling in the Kingdom. What I have on my "time card": I am face to face, squarely believing what eternity says to me. I was frozen. Stayed in a room of perfection. God's will? Timing? Maybe I didn't want it bad enough? Or, if I look at it from today, this writing journey, invested time, dedication and work, some thirty thousand words +, mean more to me than when I first encountered the room. Boy, we are touching some emotional DNA right now. Selah!

When looking at the signpost of procrastination, it doesn't quite look like disobedience or rebellion; those words which make me cringe like putting tarot cards on the table. I'd never knowingly "have" anything to do with them. The truth of my heart was still miles away from the sincerity of transformation. I am becoming a Writer. I'm challenging weaknesses of poor grammar and spelling like they were Philistine's defying the armies of the Lord. Hardly life threatening, unless it is supposed to be a "life" source? Help me, for a moment, to remember when I was describing the unique Valentine heart collage items in the first chapter. Didn't I also tell you about the tiny gold snuff box? I think so. It was a gift from Melchizedek, and I placed the small trinket to the right of my computer, positioned to "correspond" divinely. I googled "tiny gold snuff boxes" and cut, pasted, and printed the photo closest to what was in my spirit. I covered it with saran wrap, backed it, and taped it to my desk. Also, I shared how I encountered the hand of God holding my hand, and together we dipped "pen" into it, which revealed it was an inkwell. Remember, I described them in the first chapters. Then we have the "if's," If I had never taken this vulnerable journey would I have missed a moment like Moses and his staff? It is just a tiny gold inkwell I saw in the spirit of things. What flesh (Red Sea) would have never parted, creating a pathway made only by the hand of God. A hard-won life source was separating us from our enemies and the mindsets of bondage. Every lie that slithered like a snake consumed by the right-hand of the Lord overshadowing mine. The learning of using a supply source that is purely mystical and unseen. These words penned are ink to page. The victory result, Goliath's weapons in my tent: Miniature ink-well, an extraordinary gift given from the King of Salem, in a room where moth and rust will never enter.

RABBIT TRAIL: My pen is momentarily halted (I'm sitting outdoors), by the sweet sight of a sparrow couple taking turns bathing. This pair, washing the day's dust in the gurgling stream falling from the basket of my "lady at the well" fountain in my garden. She's statued in the middle of our Koi pond: highlighting my bitty feathered friends, the life-source of experiencing it together. Hearing God's words stir in my heart and rumble around in my mind, penned, life-source. Man shall not live by bread alone but by every word that proceeds out of the mouth of God. Life-source, it occurred to me in my pondering while still sitting in the spirit in this "inner" library, rolled up jeans, bare feet on the floor, bum planted on a chintz-covered ottoman just next to a bookshelf. Jesus is standing mid-room watching and waiting for me to exchange.

The tipping point, the first half of the book for the second half.

Trade the doubt and unbelief for belief. I noticed, just moments before, hidden in the front pocket of my "spiritual" jeans, the snuff-box. Inside my pocket, muslin lining is bunched and resting in the bend of my thigh. I retrieved it like a kid pulling marbles from their pocket. Again, how you know things in the spirit? I give Jesus the tiny box. Simultaneously from way high up the shelf, a book mysteriously slips forward. Who pulled it forward? But a divine reflex, a booby-trapped secret. Give and receive. Moment of truth. Pause/breathe. Another door to pass through. I reached up and grabbed the book. The room shifted by the secret latch of taking it off the shelf, a weight tripped. The book, medium size, distressed brown leather with a buckle and small gold lock. A wrought-iron spiral staircase appeared just next to Jesus, leading upwards through the glass-paned ceiling. I tuck the book like an experienced explorer in the back waist of my pants, pulled my white shirt over the top and made my way to ascend the staircase, Jesus point-man. Round we climbed like stair rungs of DNA; rising as the room faded beneath. I effortlessly passed through the glass-light, squeezed past Jesus' bare feet dangling down from sitting on the spiritual ceiling. Standing on the last rung, I popped my head above into the "realm." Reminds me of a seal bobbing on the ocean; checking out the sea topside. Daft scene: Jesus seated, reveals the ceiling topside is a huge clock face, His feet still dangling into the inner library.

The epitome of the saying; one person's ceiling is another person's floor. Original author unknown.

I lift myself up and have a seat on the face of "time." Jesus says, "Let me see your book?" So I pull it out of its traveling state, hand Him the small journal size manual and wait, on pins and needles. Of course, He is the key and the lock snaps open in obedience of its "Holder." Jesus opens the book to what my spirit knows as page 93. He turns the book into my view, points to a particular line for me to read, hands me the book, I look. I see July 17, 2017, completed. 07/17/17 written in red. Ok, we need another "Selah" moment here.

You are not going to believe this! Well then, you are reading a book about heaven. Let's just believe.

HAPPENINGS: Not just a week before I was sitting outside on the patio. We have a well-trafficked bird feeder hanging on an old basketball hoop pole. Our visiting bird-family consists of red-headed house finches, towhee's, sparrows, yellow finches, waxwings, chickadees and a couple of boisterous scrub jays; just to name a few at our hanging table. During my kingdom time on an earlier morning, seated nestled into my "perfectly pillowed" rattan settee, I shared with the Lord that I would be delighted to have a pair of mourning doves at my feeder. They are good at cleaning up the seeds that the blankity blank jays wastefully knock to the ground. Every morning while feeding my Koi, I call out a little sing-song, whatever little melody gurgles out.

"Calling the doves to come live in my backyard."
"Come, come, you peacefully little swifts, come, come, come and bless my yard in this."

Yup, you know where I'm going here! Just at that divine "supernatural" moment when I read the highlighted line Jesus was pointing at in the journal saying "July 17th, 2017 manuscript completed", a mourning dove landed on my patio not ten feet from me. In astonishment I flinched, raising my arms and scared her up into the safety of the tree branch. All heaven declares the Glory of God, right here Oregon USA. Oh, how He puts His seal upon our hearts. It's not just a creative imagination; it's a time marker that heaven is declaring agreement.

Well, Jesus, I guess I'm continuing to be a focused writer! Today is May 10th. That's 38 days. Divided into half of 70,750 words is 930.9......words a day. Pretty close to my original goal of a thousand words a day. Who'da thunk it and done the math. Ahead of "TIME."

Get it! We are sitting on a clock face.

Can we just take a moment to focus on Him? Jesus, you are keeping me in wonder. Jesus, I love you. You amaze me. Jesus, I'm undone at the nuances I am discovering in this writing project. Tears are such a small offering of what You are stirring. I'm wrecked in His presence. I give you praise.

> *Praise for the dove who answered my call.*
> *Praise for the journey with my All in All.*
> *Praise tho' the world be hurrying by,*
> *Praise from my backyard, cool breeze, wet eyes.*
> *Praise from the heavens &*
> *Praise in the earth*
> *Praise, now I worship and adore new-found worth.*
> *Praise in the moment and*
> *Praise out of time*
> *Praise as I sit with this King of mine.*
> *Praise in the day and*
> *Praise in the night*
> *Praise for the words to finish with might.*
> *Praise now I'm laughing, crazy to boot.*
> *Praise on the mountaintop only with You.*
> *Praise can you hear me.*
> *Praise obey quick*
> *Praise I said praise it's ready to tip.*
> *Praise overflowing and*
> *Praise from the well*
> *Praise let's get louder oh rocks won't you yell.*
> *Praise in the season of*
> *Praise You've well known*
> *Praise my impossible now un-throned*

Praise to the coming
Praise to the day
Praise the uniqueness I found in this way.
Praise we are asking.
Praise we declare
Praise I am giving your gift to the air.
Praise surrounds glory
Praise lifts His throne.
Praise to my Jesus He unlocked the unknown.

That was fun, just drinking in His goodness, before we turn the corner.

Three hundred and seventy-eight words to divide tide, mark the marker, flag the forest, split the intersection, I'd like to share in this "Vulnerable Chapter," a statement found in the chapter "Vision Care." *Blessed are they; the journey that you see on the pages of this book, enveloped with times of humble repentance. Remaining in any condition that Jesus addresses, without gaining the promise, just seats me back into the "inner library" fearfully without receiving the book.*

A vulnerability has "ability" knitted within her.

Let's frame up the word **BLESSED**: Happy, to be envied, and spiritually prosperous - with life-joy and satisfaction in God's favor and salvation, regardless of their outward conditions. Mathew 5:3 AMP. Let's measure the Pro and Con, find the tension between mindsets, allow the plumb line to weigh and challenge truths, heavens view manifest or sought. Do you hear my question and conclusion from a heavenly perspective?

Being poor in spirit is NOT blessed, not happy to be envied: Blessed is, the obvious solution to poverty, wealthy in the spirit, for theirs is the Kingdom of heaven.

*Mourning is **NOT** blessed, not happy to be envied: Blessed is, the comfort received, which heals, consoles, strengthens us towards another day.*

*Meekness is **NOT** blessed, not happy to be envied: Without inheritance demonstration.*

*Hunger and thirst are **NOT** blessed, not happy to be envied: Unless right-standing is now tasted.*

Merciful is **NOT** *blessed, not happy to be envied: Unless justice has its day in a heavenly court.*

Clean of heart, is **NOT** *blessed, not happy to be envied: Unless we desire, and in that desire "See" God.*

Peacemakers are **NOT** *blessed, not happy to be envied: If "Sons" don't answer creation's groans.*

Persecution for righteousness is **NOT** *blessed, not happy to be envied: If we remain blinded to the Kingdom of Heaven.*

Have I chosen to look through my lens, through opinions and mindsets or have I learned to accept Him looking through a holy lens with Truth adjudicating a transformed life? Just me, myself and I. In the "inner" library. What response does my "I love You Lord and I lift my voice" sound like to His ears? The gift of repentance is a gift. The word cannot be un-knit from repent. I can tell when it has arrived and shifted my heart, turned the room, altered my pen. It's the reality of the bells sewn on the high priest garment. My preparation and journey through the veil in the tabernacle will ring a tune one way or another. The heart is freely moved with the spirit to say lead me not into temptation; the head might argue, forgive those who have transgressed against me. Father, I repent for falling short of the glory you continually have planned for me.

So we have turned. Half Way...
Exactly five hundred and seventy-one. Divine freakiness.

Chapter 9

Halfway

"By writing...in the language of his society, a poet takes a large step toward it. It is society's job to meet him halfway, this is, to open his and read it. "Joseph Brodsky"

Thirty-five thousand, three hundred eighty-eight words and counting.

FOR SUCH A TIME AS THIS.

Earlier, I shared a brief story in the book about how God presented my book map. He introduced it I encountered God's Train named "161" which traveled through the wilderness. An interesting vehicle choice to represent the track of life. It was His part of the map, the blueprint of this book. The story traveled, and my life experience moving along a "wilderness" track. When we reach in chapter 14 Tools of Responsibility, I will be able to share with you more of the story of this "map" from wilderness choices, towards what I have learned beyond the veil: My responsibility to believe and how God released a prophetic word for writers that we will unpack together. Let's remember and take a moment to recall where we have traveled so far.

Martin Luther's testimony put me over the top. I finally agreed with what heaven said about me and picked up my pen. Together we have wrestled with those indulgences, shared the origins of encouragement through my heart shaped "window box."

Yesterday, after our encounter with Jesus and the "face of the clock," sitting on time, do you remember I traded Him the little gold snuff box? I'm also very practical in my prophetic mapping. Later on, that evening I sat down at my desk and removed the representation of the snuffbox cutout I had made and positioned just right of my computer, the way I saw God and my hand "dipping" into the ink. I had traded it to Jesus in return for my book on the shelf within the inner library. The snuffbox no longer was mine so, I lifted the cutout, peeling up the tape from my old teak desk. Yikes; even tho I used painter's blue masking tape to not make any other marks on this scuffed up old desk, removing it stilled ripped off a portion of the stain, leaving a mark. It's not sticky. You can't feel a residue at all, just the faded outline "watermark" of His goodness. It's still there to remind me where we have traveled thus far. I took the still sticky cutout and attached it to the corner of the paper map taped with my other collage items in the window box on the wall ahead of me. I am aware that two of the items I received in heaven's Treasury Room are "spent" so to speak, prophetically have come to pass.

Nestled in the chapter "In the Beginning God," I shared about the little corner church. My introduction to Jesus at least on this side of the veil. I wrestled with what was historically familiar to "man" and God.

From bus stories we ventured through the chapter "A Lady in Waiting," and I introduced you to the painting "Jane." These days I'm happy to wait, but it's in the audience of God; and being patient is entirely different than trying to Get Permission. Whew, I think that was the most difficult time to understand.

HALFWAY-RABBIT TRAIL: Can I talk to pastors and leaders for a minute, please? I've worn the hat, been there, done that, believed God every step of the way just like you. I feel very honored when people "address" my relationship within the church through addressing me by the title "Pastor." It is a privilege to marry and bury people. I'm uniquely different; I'd rather do the burying honors than the marrying. The brilliant benefits of "seeing," makes it so refreshing to witness the individual coming to their own "wake." Ha, ha, ha! Seeing them (in the spirit) lay hands on their loved ones. What a privilege to perceive the Kingdom of Heaven. Yes, I am a leader in a small Ekklesia and mentor other groups. In our continuing interlude, I sense there is little freedom for us to apprehend by me telling a painful story, from the top side of things regarding inner healing circles.

RABBIT TRAIL PAUSE, Wearing the Pastor's "hat" has also graciously made available to me perfect moments to ask many a wounded individual for forgiveness. We all have had our "leadership errors," and feathers have been ruffled during pursuits of the heart. Not that I was in this instance of inner healing the inflicter of pain, but asking for forgiveness brings healing to a wounded sheep. I've also been that injured sheep who has been healed and is taking responsibility through forgiveness for a "Glory shortage" in leadership or the pastorate. Time with Jesus and a heartfelt exchange has dislodged many an arrow from words and actions misunderstood. Back to my brief story with a bit of hindsight included.

Tucked in between the chapters, "Getting Permission" and "Earth Invading Heaven," Holy Spirit was opening up my spirit to see more than just angels. Hand in hand the arrival of ministry gifts, gifts to minister to the body. It's the responsibility of the "gift" holder to humble oneself to Holy Spirit, receive instruction, mature the gifts and learn how to use them. I was frustrated because no "leader" in my current circle was teaching the stuff. That didn't detour Holy Spirit from pouring and pouring. The overflow just isn't contained in any box. The river flow will leak and find the most accessible route to travel. Don and I had done the "church shopping" thing which naturally seemed to go with moving into a new town for employment purposes. I was "attempting" to be a "good" little wife, allowing my husband to lead. Note: *versus the wisdom of communion where both spouses are empowered.*

Most of my struggle was what my head was trying to grasp that was contrary to my heart. Don graciously has never usurped authority because of the doctrines either of us heard. While we were church shopping, my favorite church visited, of course, was the Foursquare since they had already worked out the flesh thing "with women in the pulpit," to a degree. Don felt like we should attend a "Charismatic," association. The lead Pastor was a hoot and could he teach! I learned so much about Romans from a gifted teacher. At a point in our pastoral relationship, he said to me: "Kristen, I love you, but I don't know what to do with you." Not the first time I had encountered that statement. A few months later he moved into a University teaching position and left the local church "canvassing" through another season of change. I have great empathy for any pastoral family that has had to endure the canvassing checklist. After a few months, a new pastor and wife accepted employment, and uplifted excitement returned within our congregation. I continued to lead women's ministries and youth groups. I fell immediately in love with the new Pastor's wife. She was a wise peach. In years before this insane season of being spiritually "misdiagnosed," I had a particular anointing flowing through me. Pastors' wives trusted me. Befriending them is not an easy assignment. They have been through the ringer, seen it all, undergone verbal assault by many wounded sheep and had to keep their mouth shut about the entire thing. So "earning" the privilege of being a confidant is huge. Mrs. Peach and I were immersing ourselves in intersession. A semi-safe place for those who are "spiritually weird"; you open enough doors in faith and spiritual stuff starts to manifest. Problems began. Her husband grew up within a respected pastoral lineage, family history. I so enjoyed hearing church stories when he let his hair down. The pastor would share crazy family stories from good ole Revival Tent meeting days. He was just a young lad then. He witnessed crazy miracles and healing revivals within the pastoral service family tree: His dad, his grandfather, pastors of great faith. The parts of the stories that many didn't hear were when man started falsifying, copying and pasting of what began as bona fide miracles, now altered by man's selfish desire. Backstage, wounded, this young man's heart changed towards Holy Spirit. He saw the made-up miracle, acted-out miracle, time and time again. Man's attempts to help God out. Take a moment to ponder the trauma toward a developing hero of the faith and Holy Spirit here. Years later in his faithful ministry, I come along, Holy Spirit fire-breathing, with signs, gifts, and healings were manifesting. What memories do you think I stirred up inside? Every "dis-" word out there. Gosh, it was hard. Can I say that again? Gosh, it was hard. I'd submitted to church leadership, whoever was supposedly in "authority" over me. The protocol was to share words of knowledge, dreams, understandings, never opening one's mouth without "permission." The chapter on "Getting Permission" was such a war. Until one day when the straw broke the camel's back. I was forced to choose, authorities consent or healing. The camel broke over someone with a collapsed lung? Both choices couldn't live in the same house together. In all that nonsense, I received one of the best directive words ever in my life, from Pastor, through a very angry rebuke. A sad day delivered, during a privately called meeting: me, board member, and Pastor. My error in hindsight is Don should have been with me. In that meeting, he unleashed a handwritten, two-page front and back yellow legal paper, lay "dis-" words and accusations accounted to my responsibility. What does one do? I sat there as every accusation spoke, line upon line until the yellow pad could only be flipped and repeated. I asked for forgiveness. Seemed like hours on the hot seat. My response, through tears, was, again and again, will you forgive me. When asking for forgiveness just wasn't paying the bill, fierce anger mounted, God's voice crept through: "There is a place for people like you, somewhere in Redding." I never looked back. The best rebuke to this day. Never underestimate the humbling power of going through the "fire" or where you might be experiencing it. I never had the opportunity to share with my good friend - Mrs. Peach - she never asked. My husband said that was enough and we left. Years later Holy Spirit allowed me to send a Christmas card to her, honoring her and husband for their encouragement into my life during that misdiagnosed season of deep birthing. I think that's enough of the back-story.

I have had the remarkable insight to sit in the pew, serve as a layperson, walk out the calling/hats of lead pastor. What would I say today? The courts of heaven were designed to receive the gift of repentance. Every high priest who comes has to deal with his accusations first before representing people. Otherwise, your "bells" don't ring! (referring to the bells on the garment of the High Priest). We do not fight against flesh and blood. Though, my blood has needed tremendous cleansing. I forgive you!

Only thirty-three thousand, nine hundred and sixty-one words to hear and write. Until tomorrow.

My pen rests

"What is the point of Halfway if we don't step over the continental divide and learn the flow on the other side." Kristen Wambach

RABBIT TRAIL: Some thoughts I sense Father wanted to be shared: for years I have been extending the hand of forgiveness from "pastor" to the "misdiagnosed"; it is a tender place. Can we walk there for a moment?

ACTIVATIONS: I, Kristen Wambach lay down all "offices, ordinations, labels, ministry names, titles, diplomas, coverings, associations and religious pedigrees: All man-made. Together, I invite you to step before the Cross of Christ.

I confess, on your behalf that I have made mistakes and have misunderstood your glory. I ask for "Your" forgiveness. I ask you for forgiveness. Selah.

I break the agreement with hurt, unforgivingness and the root of bitterness and the power they have had in your life and my life. I declare freedom, in Jesus' name.

During my quiet time with the Lord this morning I asked a question about His DNA, His blood. Scripture says that He walked entirely as a man in the flesh, laid down His divinity. That is why I asked. My DNA, a combination of father and mother, holds a family line of genetic inheritance: Good and not so good. Jesus' DNA had no "earthly" father-line blood or semen in it. It was divine. I asked how does this make you fully man? A profound question for sure. I'm certainly no DNA expert. Then He showed me a picture/vision of a Mobius curve. I drew one for you and added to the online community. I understand this as an eternal figure of eight, infinity sign. I have encountered a similar place in the heavens. Without being too scientific and outside of my experiential witness, I saw Him, Jesus, His earthly ministry, the cross positioned in the center of the figure of eight at the "crossing" over of this "Mobius curve/strip." Then the Lord reminded me of Saul, a man with heinous sins against the children of God, on the road to Damascus when He blinded him, called out to Saul, and the conversion took place. The Lord shared with me; this "crossing" over-place is where I changed his DNA. Saul/Paul encountered, "my" crossing over-place, it sheds some light on Jesus crucified before the foundation of the world. The crossing over place is part of eternity. It's the consummation of flesh when the flower fades and is blown away. Born into sin/born into righteousness. Every day in communion I partake of His flesh and blood. It is the crossing over-place. Interesting to be writing about this in the chapter "Half Way"?

With that said: we will close the chapter drafted in the wilderness. Selah.

COMMUNION ACTIVATION: spend a few moments having communion

Sitting with Papa in the New Era Library, he held my hand, and I didn't call Him Abba, I called Him Father. I have entered a season of being "fathered." I have matured. See journal post 4/28/17.

CHAPTER 10

Gateway of Three Infinite Changes

"You never know how strong you are until being strong is the only choice you have." Bob Marley

There are those pinnacle times in your walk with the Lord that leave your thinking forever changed. The veil is formally open in my heart, no going back to the old, my path is new. I see things differently. My whole outlook on life, ministry, reading the bible and God have turned earth-side pointing up. I'm on such a learning curve that I will forever be a student of heaven, a teacher of encountering, and a daughter loving to be loved by her Father. Eternity has become touchable, death a distraction that has no part in me.

THREE INFINITE CHANGES

Revelations 3:20: "Here I am! I stand at the door and knock. If anyone hears my voice and opens the door, I will come in and eat with that person, and they with me."

This door, I open it almost every day and invite Him to a place we call the garden of our heart: "The gateway of first love." Our story makes it clearer; I had opened the door before I ever encountered having a meal with Him. Jesus never vacates the Kingdom of heaven within us, but none the less, I open it, and He comes with a fresh communion every day. It "feels" like a living place on the inside of you. If you were to have a "look-see," you would discover a place of comfort, intimacy, and a place to plant "encounters": revelation experienced that when watered will grow and produce manifest fruit. Garden is a natural description. See Bible Seed and Sower passages. All take place in the garden of your heart. Jesus said some things needed to move around: Some soils that need to change.

I was enjoying a season of cultivating a Kingdom that I was no longer in denial of or hiding its glories. I came out of the spiritual "closet". If someone asked me honest and hungry questions, I shared my encounters freely. Church, though significantly smaller, was walking through a season of repentance and change. We had a tremendous mess to clean up: a spiritual mess. Areas we had partnered with man's design that had nothing to do with the kingdom. Leadership, finances, coverings that didn't look anything like what we were now experiencing in heaven. In my personal "spiritual" garden I sat with Father on the front steps of a grand, brick home: Two storeys, white shutters, right out of my love for all things Jane Austin. It was my gateway of first love, where the temple door from Ezekiel's vision exists. I am the gate, and my head is lifted up. Your garden and dwellings are kindred to your likes and dislikes. We'd talk, Father God and I. Jesus would show me other places in heavenly realms, I'd bring the encounter back to talk with Father and plant it in my garden. This Kingdom within me was growing and building my confidence in the spirit, and my spirit or mind of my heart was expanding and being built up in my most holy faith. I tend to "outwork" or learn to understand spiritual things with my hands here in the natural. I'm a kinetic learner. Our backyard garden changed as well. I'd arranged landscaping to be similar to the things I was experiencing and seeing. Heaven has an array of tutors: His throne, Sea of glass, Seven Spirits, Sapphire under His throne; Throne of Grace; Courts and councils. Gardening helped me to sit in His presence and ponder the things that were "mystical." I was learning to call Him Abba. Indeed, a child learning, loving, being disciplined, heavenly "hands on." I was entering and coming close to a God as an adoring parent: Dealing with inadequacies that we might recognize as "Father issues." In my yard or home, if I could prophetically create it, busy were my hands. I love designing heavenly living-in reminders, creating a living "David's tent" around your home. I was sitting with Father one day, talking as we do, and realized that I had never stepped inside this lovely brick house as we sit on the front stairs. I'd been shown many rooms and mansions elsewhere in His kingdom, but despite my "discovering" personality, I had never looked on the other side of this particular set of "white" double doors. Father knowingly watched my ah-ha moment. I stood to my spiritual feet, put my hand on the gold lever handle of the door, turned the knob and whoosh! Like in "Ezekiel's Vision" the temple door opening and the River of Life is held back no longer. I was underwater, and my garden was submerged (in the spirit you do not need diving equipment to breathe). Everything I had planted, the blueberries in the urns, the trees, treasured gazillion spiritual memories in this garden underwater and by the way, where is God? How am I supposed to sit with God on the steps now if it is all flooded and submerged? Weirdness, to say the least, happens in the spirit. Well, what does one do if under the water? Yup, come up for air. Again, my head is bobbing on the ocean of who knows where. Insane how these crazy encounters take you a few days to process. Now, where am I supposed to meet with God? The morning would come, my usual quiet time, and I'd look from the outside in at my "former" garden of first love, and it was still quite under water. Yikes! So, what does one do? Tread water! I got pretty good at treading water in the spirit. My understanding was still confused, I was grieving the flooding of an intimate place. Here I am bobbing around like a seal in the middle of the ocean: By the way, this experience didn't hinder my ability to visit other kingdom territories; God's garden, Wisdom heights, so many eternal places, but not my gateway of first love. Then one encounter day, I was treading water and who do you think comes walking on water towards me? Jesus! Sometimes you just have to laugh at the similarities of Jesus acting just like Jesus in the Bible. He is a living Type and Shadow. Haha! He offered me His hand, pulled me up out of the water and now I'm standing on the water with Him in the middle of what seems like an ocean. I can barely see the shores on the horizon. Well, what's a good question to ask Jesus now? I asked Jesus about my "Destiny Scroll." Seems a bit pertinent after flooding your spiritual near and dear (treasures,) I'd say! Asking: "Can you remind me again of where I am going," Jesus reached into the invisible sky around us and pulled a glass screen, as if it had been hidden in a secret envelope all this time, and set a window for the scene. Mind you, we are still standing "on" the ocean. But there it is, my own private, ocean-side-view, "spiritual" white-board. He had my undivided attention. Then He, Jesus, reached over, putting His hand inside my heart, and pulled out my scroll: So similar to an architect spreading the blueprint open to view the plans. He proceeded to pin "my scroll" to the white-board/screen. Joining in, we uncoiled and spread this rolled up parchment, Jesus queuing me by grabbing my hand to hold up the opposite side. Brilliantly it stuck like paste, with I-don't-know-what, and it adhered to the transparent white-board, "In the middle of the sea, and my garden flooded." Aah! It seemed like now we were getting somewhere, and I would get some answers. Not! Jesus peeled of His white linen robe, kicked of His sandals, and dove into the sea. I'm left with my scroll attached to a mysterious glass wall and His shoes and clothes piled in a heap! On the ocean! He swam out of sight. So, I adapted to this absurd situation since no one was watching, and stirred up a magnificent idea. Behaving like an inquisitive little kid with nothing else to do, I played dress up and tried on His clothes. Meditative type and shadows were going on here. Ha! Wrapping myself into the glory of His coverings, the fabric full of weight and light. I basked in Royal Robes of righteousness. The arms of the garment are too big for me, His rustic sandals over-sized for my small feet: Now what? I tied His belt around my waist. My spirit was still crying out

S.O.S; help! And where does the scripture come in now: "My help comes from the Lord". He just swam to God-knows-where. So, I sat down, in His clothes. Again, I'm waiting, thinking Jesus will come back, at least for His clothes, right! His clothes are lovely: Robe, white and creamy, gold thread belt, the fabric thick but sheer, full of the light of a million candles, though homey, comfy like flannel, it was weighted liquid. Oh my gosh I know where "earthly" designer's got the design for "Birkenstock sandal." Argh! (I have just said to my dear friend Julie if you ever catch me in Birkenstock's please put me out of my misery!). A severe fashion faux pas! So, I'm setting on a spiritual ocean, in Jesus clothes. That took me a couple of mental days to process. Whew, this is a suitable place to say: Selah.

Thirty-eight thousand five hundred and seventy-three words.

Since yesterday's writing, I have been pondering what I remember in my journal entry about seeing my scroll. I know that there was something particular He wrote on it. Encounters in the spirit remain alive. We can re-encounter them again and again, as the Spirit leads, for our training. I have had my iPad for four years. Before that, my journals entries were penned the old-fashioned way: pen and paper. I searched for the original post to jog my memory. I'm struggling to remember the time frame of the initial encounter. Also, my handwritten journals are packed in boxes with other "church" office supplies in storage.

RABBIT TRAIL: I suppose I should have another side note here. I mentioned it much earlier but didn't unpack any back-story at all. The timing of writing this "Unfinished Book" is with fear and trembling, misunderstanding, celebrations, and the faithfulness of my community of believers. Sadly, relationships have dwindled while embracing the mystery we found on the other side of the veil. Our lean number of church family also decreased, changing our financial budget, which included salaries. We are now walking on a "cellular level," shaking the core of what we believe, having accepted "Heaven" and submitted to "Truth," challenging every mindset. After months of "standing firmly" in what we heard, saw, encountered. With mixed emotions we moved out of our downtown "church" location, putting everything in storage. It was an excruciating season that I do not understand. Back-story in hand it adds a little more to the trials of having more "time" to write. In every shape of the matter, He has my undivided attention! I brushed up my resume and began "sending" it out into the mass e-communication of "No-face pedigree." For over ten years my hat was that of a Pastor, a Visionary, with and without income. Interesting how employers view that experience. Our church family continues to meet in a home-church environment. I wish I understood more answers about all that. As much as the ache-of-giving your all, part of me wanted to say; I'm finished, been there, done that, was obedient. I still see that mandate of (Re-educating the Educated): even the name of the "vision"/blueprint came with a price. The words are still alive. It's uncomfortable to pen what feels like a non-success. A very vulnerable place to share without a measure of a relationship established with you. What responsibility does the reader have to such personal information?

I'll let you ponder that question.

PERSPECTIVE REVELATIONS: I opened my computer the other morning, and something caught the corner of my eye, an insignificant gem, hidden in the beautiful architecture of historical library pictures I chose for screen-savers. Not an encounter, yet? My Screensaver. I did a Google search to see if I could find the name and location and was unable to retrieve information about this historical photo, regal library room, dusty old books housed on cherry wood bookshelves, floor to tall ceiling. Each aisle of shelves had a portable ladder attached and able to slide on ladder-tracks connecting to the roof of the gallery. There is a white bust of an outstanding individual set as a marker between isles. As daily sitting at one's computer, maybe I had not noticed in the screen-saver picture the rungs on the ladders. Imagine climbing to the top in search of a particular book. But there aren't any more rungs at the top! The last two steps in the rhythm of the design were missing. I'd never noticed that before. Makes sense in the practical way of things: what use is a stair or rung on a ladder if you run out of head-space? What sparks a gem of a moment, even though in this "library" it appears that you are at the top of the ladder: Logic might dictate you can't climb any further because of the impending ceiling. In the Kingdom, questions lead to principals, and it doesn't mean you won't find another access or measure for ascension. Truth often is revealed much like this flooding encounter in which I find myself sitting in the middle of the ocean, waiting for the next invisible "rung": Gems of encouragement when sharing openly about controversial dimensions. I'll hide it in my heart.

Returning from our relative rabbit trail, three infinite changes continue: currently, I am on a spiritual ocean, waiting for the next "rung" on the ladder. Jesus has vacated the scene (for some reason), and my most intimate place of communication has flooded. Did you pick up that I finally sat down? Like the missing rungs on the library ladders, I didn't see it at first either: A spiritual "Duh" moment. I'm sitting down! On what? What could one possibly sit on in the middle of a sea? So I looked and it appeared to be a rock. More questions, why is there a rock under my backside, to sit on in the ocean? Maybe this is why Jesus went for a swim: sometimes you are more inquisitive and brave when you are not relying on the one with ALL the answers. It reminds me of the heading quote attributed to Bob Marley: *"You never know how strong you are until being strong is the only choice you have."* Sometimes your teacher wants you to mature and walk in the lessons He has been teaching (I finally figured out that this wasn't an irrelevant rock I was sitting on). In the current light of things, I just wasn't aware; I only knew that this doesn't feel like a "happy" (flooding), which it turned out, was a promotion. I have officially had a Noah encounter, a marker of a perfect type and shadow. After a forty-day like Ahha, I've come to rest on a mountaintop: Re-start, Re-plant. The waters began to recede, my spiritual eyes shifted into more light, and my mountain was now next to the Mountain of the Lord. A great mountain range to belong to. After that, my affection for my old garden was satisfied. People often ask me: "Where does your Mountain reside?" What is the up and down of it all? Well, I see it in two places. I perceive my mountains as seven areas of influence in the spiritual earth realm. That is where I decree, and learn to rule and reign. I also see my mountain in the heavens with Him, that is, the recognized authority in the Kingdom of Heaven that He has given to me: Father-daughter, relationship to responsibility, King and Priest, Rabbi to the student, and students do have exams.

Thirty-nine thousand five hundred and eighty-five. Time to make dinner.

Quick note for us to ponder in the "allusion of hierarchical" thought: when Paul said that he saw a man who went up to the third heaven, he is sharing a perspective, writing from a perspective. Fiction, non-fiction, whatever platform you work within, spiritual writing is through a lens of the author's experience, or we write to illuminate the reader's frame of reference. Jesus is the plumb line, period - lesser truth equals greater truth - it's still true, but there are more "rungs" on the ladder. You must admit the little "missing ladder rungs" nugget has become helpful for us to grasp a concept. A Greek-mind assumed third heaven was a mathematical equation. If there are three, then there must be one and two. Without "experience" we never discover the possibilities of four, five or more: Not, hierarchical, just more. Three is a pattern of redemption: Body, Soul, Spirit; Father, Son, Holy Spirit; Outer Court, Inner Court, Holy of Holies; Kingdom of the Earth (physical), Kingdom of Heaven (spiritual), Heaven (Light); Faith, Hope, Love. All-encompassing the Father's great care and love before creation spoke. Higher "up" is just a measurement word to explain that there is also depth, length, breadth, width, and height.

I remember His redemption path: Jesus led captivity captive. Love's desire never keeps people out, 2 Peter 3:9: The Lord does not delay [as though He were unable to act] and is not slow about His promise, as some count slowness, but is [extraordinarily] patient toward you. Not wishing for any to perish but for all to come to repentance. His Fatherly patience and plan, has reached farther than our perceptions of "perishing."

THREE INFINITE CHANGES CONTINUE.

Daily I open the door and invite Jesus to come in. Truth: Jesus continues to move me into greater truths. He dwells inside of me, and that dwelling is under-construction. What did I glean in my "Noah" experience? A "heavenly baptism." We breakthrough into new realms/understanding/mindsets and find ourselves sitting on different floors that we used to look at as a ceiling. Where our baptism /flooding focus should be directed? The debris that washed down the tub drain or who made me so clean?

SHARED ACTIVATION: Jesus, I open the door and invite you in:

WELCOME TO MY 50S KITCHEN. I'm serious, welcome. Have a seat. Even Noah had a mountaintop to discover. The waters receded to reveal a cleansed land, a washed mindset: communion always remains but where you meet with Him transforms (You dine within you, the Kingdom within, and you also feast at His table in the Kingdom of Heaven).

Just let Him lead and prepare the place you eat at. His body and blood are always the perfect provisions no matter how He serves it. Don't over think it! My journal notes say, regarding my "50s" kitchen: My Yoking up destination. Learning His face as the Ox, being yoked with Christ: Learning to carry, work together, trading, walk together, unity and oneness, how He plow's and works the kingdom. It is a different place of being taught of the Lord. I spent time in the garden before we entered the house. His yoke is easy and His burden light. *Come to Me, all who are weary and heavy-laden, and I will give you rest. Take My yoke upon you and learn from Me, for I am gentle and humble in heart, and you will find rest for your souls - For My yoke is easy, and My burden is light.* (Matthew 11:28-30).

When I look through His word, it is a season to learn to enter rest. Who would have thought the face of the ox would teach you rest. The living memory (50's kitchen) I'm describing is familiar just like the farmhouse in which I grew up: Quaint, painted white cabinets; a window over the sink with gingham curtains; chrome-trimmed, grey and white table with four chairs. It had a vintage refrigerator: with rounded corners, and a mud room leading to the back door, with slamming screen door. The small kitchen garden out back was attached to a large farm field, with a line of oak trees on the north boundary. It was a small, intimate cottage to meet with the God-head. Where does one start? I spent a little over two years sharing communion here with all of "Them." The gate of first love, my fellowship place as a transformational altar.

The end meets with the beginning at the "Crossing over place." Yes, my place of learning how to be yoked with Christ was uniquely transformed. This season helped me to understand what He was doing in me, what to plow and when to leave fallow. The text for this is found in Hebrews 9 about the earthly tabernacle. *Verse 7: but only the high priest entered the inner room, and then only once a year, and never without blood, which he offered for himself and for the sins the people had committed in ignorance. 8: By this arrangement, Holy Spirit was showing that the way into the Most Holy Place had not yet been - disclosed as long as the first tabernacle was still standing. 9: It is an illustration from the present time because the gifts and sacrifices being offered were unable to cleanse the conscience of the worshiper...portions of my mindsets were unable to be conscientiously cleansed.* (Hebrews 9:7-9).

"Now faith is the substance of this hoped for and the evidence of things not yet seen." (Heb. 11:1) Relationship in Him is learning the depths of the gifts and sacrifices He gave. Faith produces proof of transformation.

I had mindset areas, rooms, understandings, blockages that were still standing like the first tabernacle. Holy Spirit is always showing the way into more of God. During this tremendous change, God taught me about resources: "Seeing" the vintage refrigerator always full: The cupboards in the kitchen always filled. Good thing as resources in the natural transformed too. Entering rest is as close as the kitchen table: Learning to eat, and to receive from His goodness. Everything flows from love. All that I was learning was flowing from love as if you were eating a hearty bowl of chicken soup and a slice of buttered homemade bread. The drift of the River of Life flowed through our little kitchen transforming me and changing the world around me. I have, yes, I said "have" fond memories in this kitchen. You sure can get to know someone when you "eat" with them every day.

I chuckle at this, thinking of Don and my coffee this morning. Time, marriage, causes you to know someone well to the point you trigger when their repetitious morning "slurp" finds a touchy note!

"Oh, 'Change' when will you have your fill?" I required this season of closeness.

A SIDE NOTE ABOUT TRANSFORMATION: The blood of Jesus is the most powerful force we have interceding for us. However, without the employment of the blood, the redemption it provides is like a court ruling not being enforced (See reference page for resources on the courts of heaven).

Interesting how my place of first love has changed, the realm that holds feeling, purpose, and spiritual memory. Shouldn't Jesus on the inside of you promote transformation? Sometimes the furniture just needs to be rearranged, upgraded, donated, or binned. The concept of a "Kingdom" being in you is bizarre, unfathomable. It has a framework with many similarities found in the tabernacle design: Outer court, inner court, most holy place: Body, soul, spirit; Fantastic Kingdom patterns.

My original framework was beaten down and confused. Life and circumstance may speak loudly. I have experienced many different tools of inner healing ministry over the years. It's interesting how genetics, traumas, wrong understanding, the enemy, can create blockages that stop the flow of the river of God in your life. I have added several links in the reference page of ministries that personally benefited me. I can teach you how to step through the veil, engage the courts of heaven, protocols of heavenly government, gateways of your spirit. I would instead support you asking for yourself. One of my favorite scriptures: *Search me O God and know my heart; Try me and know my anxious thoughts and see if there be any lousy way/vexing path in me, and lead me in an everlasting way: All righteousness.*   *(Psalms 139:23, 24).*

I continually invite Him to search, transparently trust our relationship. I listened to His counsel, admitted to wrongs partnered with, and the road changed. The veil thinned on the perceptions of my heart: Jesus took on everlasting flesh. You might ask how can a "veil" become thinner when it was rent? Great question! Experiencing great encounters is not the focus. Heaven is a place to live. If I invited you over for a barbecue, you might admire our garden, learn more about my family dynamics and gain understanding through our choice of décor: Our family stories hidden in the treasures tucked into our nooks and crannies. You would enjoy a wonderfully prepared and cooked meal. Each room has a purpose: the kitchen is for preparing; the dining room for eating; the bathroom for care, maintenance, and refuge; the living room for sitting, visiting and laughing; the bedroom for sleeping, intimacy, and restoration; the family room for unwinding, learning, and sharing. The house always needs cleaning and upkeep. The thinness of a veil is the Father revealing the relationship with the bride.

THREE INFINITE CHANGES CONTINUE:

I said I have fond memories of my 50's kitchen, past tense. When I got earnest about writing - I mean *70,750 words* genuine - I committed to moving towards and take responsibility for what I had witnessed on my destiny scroll. Distractions in self or otherwise that had hindered my yes-yes-and amen changed because I changed them. Transformation is revealing once more. Might as well figure it's a divine pattern that my communion place, gate of first love, will continue to transform, until my love looks like His love. I do love interior design.

That day a mood must have been stirring in me. Quiet time with Him is not necessarily hushed. Thanksgiving was singing, and desires that had been spoken for many years shaking at the thought how will life divinely change.

Stirrings were looking forward into the moment when I can say Lord, the book is finished, removing the "Un" finished, forever. Your turn! It's all You God here's the pitch, hit away!

That day I asked another profound, Kristen-are-you-listening-question?

Father, why does my gateway of first love look like a 50s kitchen? Oh, His infinite gesture of body language reacting with a smirk - that means look out, revelation is hitting the ground. Selah.

My spirit leaped forward like a bulldozer and pushed down the 50's kitchen, cottage, and archaic structure. Whoosh! And it was gone. I knew the answers to my questions simultaneously to my spirit's demolition. It didn't look like me! Nothing in this "place of first love" that I had spent so much time with Him seemed like what I would choose personally. It didn't have my DNA as my home does: No Kristen's flare, no "Bow and Poof ministry present." My flooding emotions (not ocean-water this time) melted at the truth. The inside of my "love" had been formed by the opinions of the era I was born in, 1959. When tears subsided, and His overwhelming goodness allowed me to stand again, all I saw in the spirit was my rectangle glass dining table and four chairs: Just like the one I chose as my office desk at church. The dust settled: Not a board, nail or remnant of the 50s cottage remained. My glass table was smack-dab-center to a foundation no longer there. My yoking up place, field, and garden remained. I am sitting here today and the offerings He has brought to the table during this project, His spiritual remnants resting inside of my Valentine collage heart, are on the wall before me. He said "tell them about the pink tulips." I am Father.

RABBIT TRAIL: *Well we're back at the beginning when the Valentine made its appearance from Don, and I chose not to put my two cents into the matter saying that chocolates were counterproductive. Father knew exactly what my heart wanted, Pink Tulips. I went to many different garden centers to find just the delicate hew of pink I could see in my spirit. Finally, stashed in their back stock, a nursery-woman showed me the tag of these not yet budded tulips. We looked up the name and picture on the computer. I brought two 10 inches planters home with joy towards their bloom. And they didn't bloom last spring, so disappointing. So Father gave me some in heaven. A secret, during proofreading, they are making their spring arrival this year nicely. Maybe their timing of blooming glory will be on the day of publishing. So soon!*

Every jot and tittle I treasure:

- On my spiritual desk sits a bouquet of pink tulips
- Map of this book,
- Precisely drawn on a sheet of spiral notebook paper; a "Craftsman door" penciled by contractor friend Steve,
- The picture of the gold inkwell, I gave to Jesus,
- David's sword, which has also been given away,
- Cover design for when the book was going to be named The Watchmaker,
- My Valentine's heart collage.

What shall we say? 58 years and my places of love are beginning to form between me and the Author and Finisher of my faith.

The heart is the same, but the "collage inside," what was put into my spirit, made it metamorphose. I'm beginning to look like the Kingdom He placed inside of me!

> *"You never know how strong you are until being strong is the only choice you have." Bob Marley*

Forty-one thousand eight hundred and seventy-six words.

CHAPTER 11

Angels on a First Name Basis

Angels.
I am steadily amazed at the creativity God knit into all creation,
the beings of light which serve together with us, without recognition
so that we can fulfill our collective destiny, and have a conversa-
tion with a loving Father. Beings of light traveling through dimen-
sions carrying the residue of His glory. K. Wambach

CONFESSION: *Forgive me, Father. I was also hiding in ignorance and blindness from within the beloved, denying Your creativity and helps, when (for inconsequential reasons in the light of eternity) my relationship was broken, and heaven hindered.*

VALUABLE LESSONS AND A FEW ENCOUNTERS ON A FIRST NAME BASIS.

THREE "WAKEY WAKEY STORIES" I initially heard the first testimony while attending a women's conference at Bethel Church, Redding Ca. (See reference for the link to Beni Johnson's blog).

MY VERSION. Early in the days of discovering Bethel Church and their lovely prophetic culture, I was invited to join a group of women attending a women's conference. Much anticipation was felt by all as we got organized. Wives and mom's checked multiple "family" lists: filling refrigerators with food, cookie jars with sweets, all to get out of town for a glorious weekend; new friends waiting and old friends enjoyed. A fond memory, this was my first time at Bethel. I remember being a bit overwhelmed by the multitude of like-minded women there. The campus was abuzz with excitement. My favorite place to this day is the Alabaster Prayer Chapel: Many memories of angelic encounters while basking in His presence. From the platform, Beni Johnson was sharing that particular session, unpacking a story about one of their BSSM students from Wales. The young girl had been awakened by the spirit of God and asked to go to Moriah Chapel and say 'wakey wakey.' I'm sure in the girl's testimony she had many thoughts running through her head and felt the sense of importance that "requests" like this do not come about every day. She arrived at the Chapel surprised at the unusual amount of people present for that time of the day. She whispered 'wakey wakey,' concerned about being heard by others. "Is that how much you want revival in Wales?" God said to her. Taking a deep breath and mustering up her courage, she yelled "wakey wakey"! Nothing occurred for several minutes. Maybe she started to step away: nothing in the testimony reported the reaction of people who would have surely heard her. After leaving the scene, wondering about God's directive, she turned back and looked again. There was a huge angel, yawning as he stepped out of his slumber. All she witnessed were his feet: he was enormous. She asked his name. He answered that he was the angel from the 1904 revival and that she just woke him up. I'm sure Beni went on to share a few more details about the story but that's what I can remember. Considering my recent (Angels at the Beach) discoveries in "seeing", the testimony was like dangling brown sugar dipped carrots in front of me. I do not remember when on the roster of the conference, the story was shared. We had a brilliant time and drove home, refreshed and breathing fire-faith. It must have been after 10 pm when I was dropped off at home, thoughts of the testimony rolling around in my head the entire drive home. Ideas were arising: what about "now" thoughts - "How" thoughts? We lived in an 1873 Victorian house that had a beautiful widows-walk on the roof; I pondered, could climb up there! Except for my unkindly neighbor, who I was sure would call the cops on me. Hmmm, Lord, where could I discharge my faith? A light popped into my head, the football field! We lived just a few blocks from the high school my boys attended: Visions of the fifty-yard line swirled in my head. I threw down my suitcase and purse, said a quick hello to the family, "I'm home," and excused myself saying I needed to unwind from the road trip and take a walk. My son Jacob who is very intuitive said, "Mom, where are you going?" "The football field to pray" I said. How else would you gently describe you are going to do something way out of "normal." "Wait a moment; Mom, you're not going alone at this time of the evening," and he retrieved his long-board (skateboard). We were out the door, and I briefly filled him in on the testimony and what I was planning on doing. Yes, my kids have thought I had had a few marbles missing at times until they started encountering angels.

LESSON LEARNED. Angels respond in an atmosphere of honor and welcome.

My quizzical invitation, already in the works via heaven, was divinely arranged; we found the gate unlocked. Jacob remained on the sidewalk riding and practicing moves on his long-board (determination), and I walked across the cinder running track, onto the grass and stopped, centered, at the fifty-yard line. An eerie internal feeling surfaced: No one there, black of the night, with a sleeping community surrounding. I inhaled a healthy farm girl breath and hollered "wakey wakey" three times. I waited, sensing, trying not to over think it! The night sky from behind me shifted, the hairs on the back of my neck raised. I was standing frozen and entirely creeped out with two things on the testimony list left to do? Turn around and ask his name. Mind you I hoped I wouldn't wet my pants! OMGosh! He stood regal, serious, and heavily armored, with no expression on his face. His expressionlessness sent a bit of discomfort down my spine. Now, what have I done! The field goal H (stand) stood about shoulder height. His sword was drawn firmly in his right hand, with a battle-marked shield in his other, sword off guard and pointing down, but "drawn" nonetheless. The helmet reminded me of the samurai soldiers in the movie "The Last Samurai." He was not there for conversation. My spirit (probably because my breath evaporated) asked him his name: Caisson. How fitting. According to dictionary.com here are three of the definitions given. Caisson:

1. A two-wheeled wagon, used for carrying artillery ammunition
2. An ammunition chest
3. A wooden crate containing bombs or explosives.

LESSONS LEARNED: Names reveal purpose, sometimes rank and assignment.

Well, the story gets a bit more extravagant with a curious twist. We both stood looking at each other, probably less than a minute and then Caisson was gone. I took a moment to regain my sanity, startled by movement out of the dark. I checked my surroundings with more of a wary look. Jacob was still hovering just outside the chain link fence, over near the front of the stadium. Then I noticed, shadowed in the blackness of the night, the outline of a young man leaning over to tie his running shoes. We were on a track. Spooked and unnerved a little, how did I not see him? He certainly would have seen me and "heard" my "wakey wakey" activity. Thoughts jumped around in my spirit; had the angel changed? Caisson changed? The timing of it all, had the angel transformed? Without entertaining any more questions in my spontaneous brain, I boldly walked over to the young man who was still fidgeting and now stretching, as if preparing for a workout on the track: In the dark? I don't remember verbatim what I said, we chatted,

I mention my unusual activity, and he acted unaware of my outburst in the lateness of the day. He stated that he was an agriculture student at the local university. A measure of disbelief filled my heart, and I asked a few more prodding questions, which he answered without offense. To this day, I kick myself for not asking the obvious: Are you Caisson, the angel?

Society is a bit more familiar with the "order" of manlike angels.

LESSONS LEARNED: Beings of light can transfigure.

Three things I remember from the conference today: the prayer chapel, the friends that also attended, and the angel story. Having told the story, I'm sure that I wasn't the only individual that night "waking" up angels. I do have a question though? Who was waking up whom? Oh Lord, give me eyes to see and ears to hear.

ARMORED ORDER OF ANGELS: wakey wakey continues. My husband Don is a master technician. One side to the benefits of having a mechanic in the house, acquiring cars is never an issue. The other side is timely repair versus "infinite" storage. At the time, I was driving an adorable old white Saab convertible. The top was a little worse for wear, and it had a great sound system with an iPod adapter. Pinch me I'm in heaven. Year round the top of my car was open if it wasn't raining; during the winter, seat heaters turned on high. Tunes cranked. I was born a convertible girl. It was a beautiful late spring day in Oregon, with my faithful little Yorkshire terrier companion, Nikki. Early in the morning, a friend of mine had invited us for a walk along the Willamette River. I gathered my checklist: water, snacks, beach chair, and Nikki and I were on our way across town. I was cruising southbound through downtown Corvallis, music loud, top down on the car, just about to pass the historic Benton County Courthouse.

Let me set the scene: It's about lunchtime, pedestrians are filling the sidewalks, car windows are rolled down, drivers arms extended, while traffic halted at the light. Typical Oregonians finding every excuse to soak up some vitamin D: Driving slow city-speed, my peripheral view captured the site of a senior man seated with a life-size cross resting on the sidewalk bench just before the Court House steps. My spirit screamed "ping, ping, ping" (Submarine sending out radar sound=ping). Not a moment to question, I was making a right-hand turn heading around the block before I realized distraction had taken over.

Zipping around the corner, parking spot available directly in front of this audacious display. I'd heard about "cross-walkers" reports before via the evening news. Cross-walkers, surprising in Corvallis yes, and a ministry declaration that you do not come upon every day. Parked and engaged, I asked the healthy looking senior man if I could sit with him for a while and began to ask him about his path. His name slips my memory, retired state trooper on a passionate quest to walk and pray at every County Court House in Oregon. Glad to share, he was lit up with two sides of devotion. One, he had dealt with all of society's mishaps & misfortunate as a law-enforcement Sheriff. Two, his heart was reaching out in partnership with God to make a difference: A loud silent statement. He was delightful company. Not many days had passed since my "wakey wakey" story had made a display in my heart. You could feel the intercession anointing he carried, so I shared with him my recent "angel testimony." He was intrigued: We both felt a consecrated moment at hand. So I asked him if I could join him on the Court House steps to pray and decree. Corvallis was still a bustle of afternoon scurry. He stood to his feet, parked the "wheeled" cross on the lawn, and we climbed the flight of stairs stationing ourselves at the one hundred and twenty-nine-year-old threshold which dictates county legislation. It felt monumental. We prayed and released the heart of God for our country, then a pregnant pause. I took a deep breath. Tuning out and ignoring the passers-by, I belted out "wakey wakey." I think I startled my new friend a bit. We waited. Bizarre, not an urban soul seemed to hear or see our antics as if we were invisible. I had yelled a healthy farm girl holler! From the unseen to seen, I heard, crash, clank. This time I heard his armor jangle as he stepped through into this realm in response. My hearing and seeing honed in on this imposing angelic soldier. He was similar to Caisson, of the same order or "troop." Austere were his eyes glaring at me from under his helmet. I'm sure the word was out. His sword was still in its sheath, thank God! With an upward head nod, he signaled he was "on it"! I explained what I was encountering to my honorable friend. Also, I thanked him for his faithful intercession.

LESSON LEARNED: faith increases by "seeing" God's strategic force, angel armies on duty. They are accommodating to our learning curve.

SPIRIT OF MOSES: *the last time, I called "wakey wakey."*

Summer is an active time: Gardening both beauty and vegetable, water sports, picnics and patio events, and do-it-yourself projects, weddings, parades, rodeos, leisure walk along the shores of flowing water. And there is the annual "family camp": Providential or sending chills down your spine, five days, no showers only outhouses, campfires, sleeping in a tent; well those of us without an RV. More dogs than family members, an overdose of cured pork, and grandma always wants us to move the gazillion-pound park tables closer together. Families are an ever-changing foundation we call love, with a few other emotional tics in there. My folks through their RV-ing "Recreational Vehicle" years, have graciously reserved a group campsite at Timothy Lake (Mt. Hood range,) closing in on twenty-seven plus years. It has been a re-occurring event ever since "Bob" was in a box! That's an inside joke for when my niece, Geordie, was a wee babe on her first camping trip. Her folks put her in a cardboard box because there was no elbow room next to the fire. It was raining cats, dogs, and elephants and all the young moms were holding toddler size jeans and boots over the fire which was covered with a fraying blue tarp. Oh, the memories. As a family, we have tried, off and on, a few other camping locations but returned to the peaceful, non-motorized lake with so many activities accessible in the shadow of magnificent Mount Hood. My boys, all pretty self-contained at this juncture of life, trekking the great outdoors, only showing up for displays of blood or hunger. Don balances a hammock or fishing pole. With so many people around, taking walks was my way of finding some quiet time with the Lord. Still very Jesus zealous and feeling fair to middling, and in-good-physical-shape, I set my sights to achieve a solo run, hiking the thirteen-mile trail around the lake. All that lovely nature, peace, and extra time with Him! Churning of course is the thought, wakey wakey! The trail was situated on what I would classify as a spiritually logistic route, the Pacific Crest Trail: Two thousand six hundred and fifty miles, stretching from Mexico to Canada. This portion of the trail was a relatively flat hike, keeping you close to the lake, then up the rock wall with cascading headwaters, easy to find many places to rest off the beaten path and miles and miles of old growth forest. I'm starting my venture a little late in the morning, before the heat of the day, backpack stocked with water, snacks, walkie-talkie, mountain money, and a change of socks. My preparation was not complete without counsel from my husband and gossiping, "Under their breath," between the family if I will make it or need rescuing? Not my first time over the years to hike this trail, but this is my first solo performance. I head towards the rock wall portion first, then the rest is just putting one-foot in-front of the other. Sun is shining, lake a sparkle of blue. As I trekked through the other campsites a smell of late breakfaster's bacon and pancakes floated upon displaced dust. Trekking the trail, rounding the rock wall with departing encampment voices, it's Jesus, me, the breeze, ascended osprey flying the updrafts from the lake, infrequent voices of fishermen in their hidden holes, and bouncing echoes. Up the ridge, occasional mountain bikers and hikers greet you on the trail: Perfection. So, this "wakey wakey" call has been a gas up to now; I'm up for another adventure: Seeking the perfect place to let 'er rip.' I stopped and listened for other hikers: Seems secluded and "free to be me." This time I asked Jesus His opinions, and ideas, with anticipation my heart started to flutter. I waited, inhaled, then at the top of my lungs: "wakey wakey." "wakey wakey," "wakey wakey." Catching my breath, I listen and wait. Simultaneously, speeding down the trail that "I thought was clear," came a college-age mountain biker. Hitting his brakes and halting before me, with a weird look on his face, saying: "Where is everybody else?" I said: "Excuse me?" He reiterated: "Where are all the people I just heard?" I responded with an unsure look on my face;

"It's just me!" He stepped back onto his pedals, tires gripped the ground, and departed turning his shaking and confused head with a last look at me. Never expecting that distraction, Holy Spirit smacked me in my thinker with what the biker may have heard! Heaven! I was laughing now, probably started walking, conversation under my breath, "how cool is that?" The ground began to shake. At least the sound I heard felt like it was shaking. My spiritual eyes were opened to see the valley below Mt. Hood. This huge, gigantic, enormous – reminding-me-of-Father-Time angel, sat up from under the earth. The broken sod was falling off his white garment. His seated legs stretched across the valley below. It was like he had been laying there for many ages. He looked me straight in the eyes; I'm an ant on the trail. Boldness rose up in me, and I said: "Hello, what is your name?" Instantly I heard in my spirit, "The Spirit of Moses" and he was gone. My spiritual lens closed. There came a barrage of doubt, questions, and the thought, you are absolutely off your rocker this time. Spirit of Moses? Oh, that is "too biblical," I need to send my imagination to the loony bin. I do not think I said anything audibly to the Lord the rest of the hike. Thoughts were bantering back and forth. I made it back to family camp in under four hours and never saw any of the money from the family bet. My spiritual mouth was closed, probably acted a bit buttoned up around the campfire that night too, nobody the wiser. Didn't even tell my husband. As the evening was ending, nestled in my sleeping bag, I thanked the Lord for His love, glad to rest my well "exercised" mind & body. Ah, sleep.

Unconscious of the time having been asleep. I was fearfully awakened! A horrific stench and a twisted face were coming in the doorway of our tent. Set on edge by this spiritual intruder, he boisterously announced himself, "I'm Leviathan!" I said firmly, "In Jesus name get out of here!" He was gone!

Forty-four thousand nine hundred and twenty-three.

My Mind was racing around the track of disgust, yay for the finish flag of Jesus that "kicked Leviathan's butt." Sleep, with all the endorphins speeding, seemed impossible. I have experienced dark visitors before, and like any monster under the bed, Jesus is my source. Who opened that door anyway? Morning arrived, early to rise sister-in-law releasing coffee smell inviting, I emerge in a sweatshirt, down vest, sweatpants, morning camp hair, rolling out of the sleeping bag, a "faux" fashion display. Coffee! Questions mulled around the daily words for my journal post. Breakfast consumed, I helped to clean up. Aah, I pull up my favorite camp rocking chair, slide it over by my tent, sending out a silent message "momentarily unavailable."

RABBIT TRAIL: Setting my "writing scene." I'm on my second cup of coffee, a thousand words set as a writing goal for the day. My body, a bit stiff, the morning after planting half of my vegetable garden: Ouch! The house windows are open, and a gentle fresh, new-day breeze blows in, bird feeders hung just out my window (I planned it that way). I hadn't noticed before from my office window angle, being a perfect perch, the cable connecting power-line sneaking through mature red gum tree, two small American Goldfinches, "twitterpating." Well, at least he was toward her. Fluttering his wings in a seated romance dance. Cooing chirp, face to face. Highlighted from on high, the birds on a wire. Jesus just pours His love, His opinion, of how He feels about you with words that nature is ever so happy to write. Just had to take a moment to soak in His glory. What's twitterpated?

My fondness springs from a quote from the Disney movie, Bambi.

"Friend Owl": Yes. Nearly everybody gets twitterpated in the springtime. For example, you're walking along, minding your own business. You're looking neither to the left nor the right when all of a sudden you run smack into a pretty face.

"Twitterpated." Excited or overcome by romantic feelings. Dictionary.com.

BACK TO OUR SPIRIT OF MOSES STORY.

I'm back at the campground with a bible in hand, seeking some answers about a souvenir day. Jesus, I have some questions. Still not addressing the angelic encounter on the trail nor the audacity of an enemy spirit so brazenly announcing himself. Leviathan? Word search. Every Greek and Hebrew trail I could manually search sent me back to the enemy in the wilderness: plagues and pestilence in Egypt all had roots linked with Leviathan. My spirit gathered that what was meant to disturb me, only confirmed whom I encountered the day before was indeed the Spirit of Moses.

LESSONS LEARNED: The enemy reveals his hand by what he is trying to defend. Hindsight. In this season of learning, zealousness opened a door guarded by the "wrong" camp. Grace protected me from getting spiritually "slimed" meaning: attacked because I was outside my realm of authority at that time. I have engaged the Spirit of Moses a few times after our wakey wakey experience. I later sensed that the Spirit-of-Moses angel's scroll assignment was with the first pioneering missionaries that traveled to the Northwest Territory: Jason Lee, April 28, 1834, Methodist minister. He was as exciting, and awakening as wakey wakey was in my history.

LESSONS LEARNED: Remember, this is the last time I ever called wakey wakey, I have since learned that my responsibility when receiving a scroll/mandate from heaven, after receiving counsel and agreement includes, sealing, and recording: then protocol takes the document to the Court of Angels for assignment. I am a witness to who is getting assigned and sent. Or, if an existing scroll also has my name on it (all scrolls have the names affiliated with them over time & ages), introduction to the angelic will occur. Hence, the Spirit of Moses.

It's far more important that I "WAKEY WAKEY UP" myself to the Kingdom around me instead of the faithful angels already assigned.

CHAIRMAN: CEO. There is a back story to tell here. To this day, God can easily remind me to be ready in and out of season quite uniquely. We lived in the Victorian house 1441 NW Grant Ave. Corvallis, one of the original dairy farm homes that stretched 300 or so acres to the Willamette River. Acclaimed in its day, many visitors traveled by horse and carriage to see the "dog" churning butter and buy from the Dairyman's wife, her famous apple butter. From the stories I have heard, the little dog ran on a belt which propelled the churn up and down: Clever dairyman. So many memories in this lovely house. The kitchen of this Victorian charmer was refurbished about ten years before us living there. Oak cabinets with windows and stain-glass insets, a dual-purpose counter workstation on one-side, stool seating the other: Brick tiles remain of an old chimney stove flue, and many access points were provided by the back door, patio porch door, bathroom door, and dining room door. In all the homes I have lived, this 1884 Victorian style has suited my "style best." This season represented being between unfinished and aborted books, "Getting Permission" and "Earth Invading Heaven": keeping my encounters to myself, learning, and discovering, without any peers to discuss the journey. It was early in the morning, and I'm heading to the kitchen to make a pot of coffee and have my quiet time with the Lord before the house woke up. To my disgust, there was a huge timber slug/banana slug, crawling on my kitchen counter. Aah, how'd he get in here: Gross? They can reach up to 10 inches in the Pacific Northwest, leaving a trail of slime behind. I mentally went through all the practical possibilities on how he had access. I hadn't brought any flowers or landscaping materials in from outside. Can't figure this one out! It made me feel disgusting and unkempt, and that feeling followed me throughout my day. Later on, I went to the local thrift store and spent some time putting together a new-to-me outfit, dyed my hair, and shook off the sluggish "frumpies." The next day a dear friend of mine called me at 10:00 am and ask if I was going to the first "Global Legacy" meeting in McMinnville? She had just hung up the phone with her daughter, who was attending the ministry school and had heard about the upcoming gathering. The meeting started at 12:00 pm with lunch, an excellent opportunity to meet other ministry leaders. I was all in, excited. I called the host church to make sure there were still tickets available, and they assured me there were. McMinnville is an hour drive away. I still had my morning clothes on and needed a shower. I hung up the phone and got myself into gear, "supernatural timing" here I come. Thankfully I arrived right on-time: Whew. A couple of new friends were also there, so we sat together catching up on the newly revealed to me Jesus info, miracles and healing's news. Worship proceeded with a small team, keyboard, and acoustic guitar, a lovely sound. I was quickly lost in Jesus. It had been a while since I had worshiped corporately. Then, there (he) was, grinning at me from ear to ear, right where the drum set was positioned on the platform. I bravely shared with my new friend what I saw, and in her excitement, she started firing off questions to me: What does he look like, what's his name, why is he here. Every-time she asked a question I heard the answer? I shared freely with her in hushed tones, as the speaking part of the meeting was about to commence. His name is Chairman: One of the most royal native American looking angels I have seen. You just knew he was important. His skin was brown, and the satin fabric used on his head-dress, vest, and pants was yellow, trimmed in several bright colors. The pants were bloused and came just above his ankles, no shoes. He had a leather pouch attached to his significant waist belt with seven vials in it and carried a treasure box with files inside. Did I mention his smile? Big bright white teeth, grinning from sea to shining sea. You could almost hear the rumble of joy rolling in his belly. Chairman seemed to remain in my seeing the entire meeting: we kept exchanging smiles. He never put down the treasure box. We broke for lunch, and when we met back at our seats, my friend said that she had shared what I saw with the host church head intercessor and said: "Be ready." It's possible you might be asked to share. Not moments in our seats, the MC gathering people to attention said, "Where is the lady that saw the angel?" Up I went before a crowd of respected peers, microphone in hand, sharing my encounter. Since that time when visiting that church for special speakers, many who were in that meeting remembered my testimony and gave me the nickname "The Angel Lady." As brilliant as the encounter was I felt like the purpose for which Chairman had come, had not been fulfilled. The vials were not poured out, the files not seen or distributed. And he was such a regal angel. Since that time I have encountered three similarly royal-dressed angels: Chairman, Jackson, and Helga, at other strategic places; State Capitol, corporate prayer meetings, meetings that gather surrounding leaders. I believe they are part of the angelic order, the governing force over the Northwest. Chairman is appropriately named in my opinion!

LESSONS LEARNED: God can use a slug to prepare you for the next day. He knew I would feel better about myself sporting a new outfit and no grey roots when asked to speak up front. He thinks of everything because he loves his kids. Angels can be a part of an "order" (same cut of the cloth) functioning in a military way or governing overseers: They bring gifts and tools. It is sad (that day) they have to "hold on to them" for an unspecified time because we are immature about their ministry.

Forty-six thousand five hundred and twenty-nine words. Ninety-six point eighty-eight pages to go.

BRIAN-NIXON: A messenger having aroused me from my sleep, in the spirit I find myself sitting across the table from Brian-Nixon, a no-nonsense, plain-dressed, clipboard-in-hand tutor. I encountered three teacher angels. In a room that had an ornate high ceiling, and gave the feeling of being in a particular temple hall. The ceilings moldings were trimmed with elaborate fruit carvings, the floor a brushed gold with two entry doors built as high thresholds with columns framing either side. The room felt gravity-free, yet we had no problem sitting at the table. My spirit was astutely tuned in that this was a place of instruction.

The First Demonstration was about the "sensation" I perceived as gravity. Brian brought the spirit of a friend of mine into the room, released a spirit of praise and asked me to join her. When I stepped into "praise" with her, our agreement created the ability to be free of the "earth's pull." We were weightless.

Next Demonstration: With my spiritual bearings altered, they escorted me into an "outer court" with many rooms attached to it. This "gravity-free zone" also illuminated my spirit outside of our frame-of-time. In the courtyard, I saw gathered all the people with whom I actively have a relationship, within my sphere of influence, most recognized from "church" fellowship. I could see their spirits, their joy, and concerns. They were not experiencing a "gravity-free zone." A large monitor screen (scroll) appeared overhead and began to play a video, and the people in the room were unable to see the "screen." Several videos played: the one I remember today was a scene of people attending church, the church as a whole.

They were walking down carpeted hallways to classrooms, and the carpet was unkempt, unraveled and covering a sub-flooring that was not up to code.

Next Demonstration: Still in the outer courtyard, the TV screen's disappeared. There were indistinct conversations of my church family with angels moving around in the room and exterior rooms. During this demonstration, I could be in more than one place. Still, in the courtyard, I was also aware of one of my angels being reprimanded or discouraged in an outer room, so I stepped into the chamber and defended my angel, saying that she was faithful, attentive and the information reported was brought forth inaccurately. When I was supporting and saying positive things to her (my angel), she seemed to grow and got more powerful.

LESSONS LEARNED: Angels are teachers in the kingdom, sent to instruct in how to partner with them and the agreement is a legal document that seats us in heavenly places, changes atmospheres, and places you above time, situation and circumstance. Heaven's assistance helps you to be able to divide, "see" and receive truth rightly. Angels are ever working to bring transformation to the body of Christ. They know the "holes & hindrances" in our foundations. They are teachers of spiritual dimensions, translocation, and spiritual sightedness. Angels are more productive with "active" agreement, supplies and reinforcements, which imbues them with more power. Honoring angels and their ministry acknowledges God's goodness in creation and affirms His handy-beings-of-light sent to help. They are happy to confess that Jesus is Lord and came in the flesh.

RABBIT TRAIL NOTE: Spiritual sightedness I am discovering has multiple lenses. Two lenses: I feel confident to share.

1. THE LENS OF "MY" UNDERSTANDING: A glass framed in knowledge from the environment in which I live. In the library of memory, God reflects types, shadows, and frameworks to proclaim the kingdom of heaven within me, within Him. A river looks like a river; a room has characteristics like a room with a building around it. Moses was instructed to build from a "pattern" he received on the mountain. His received design also included "rooms."

2. A CONTACT LENS OF ENERGY, LIGHT, SOUND, COLOR, AND FREQUENCY. I can see myself as a spiritual being with a body; I also can see myself as a spirit, a creature of light.

EDWARD: Chief Scribe and recorder. I have been learning the value of following heavenly protocol. Those agreements with heaven require recording. Jesus took me from the court of King's into a large office complex: The Court of scribes. At the writing of this chapter, I have only discovered one floor thus far with corridors and storage cabinets used just like files in a library. It has multiple realms with a sky-bridge. The meanings of their names are also very revealing. Edward: Wealthy guardian. Edward was actively working from his "cubical." It seemed like he had an entire floor of "office workers" under his charge. To me, Edward looks like a mix between a "Bookie" and a "Newspaper-man." He seems a senior at his position, wears a small visor and has coverings to protect the forearm of his shirt sleeves. Always happy to see me, Edward remembers everything and has a calendar that marks pivotal points of progress. He belongs to an order of angels. I have introduced him to group ascensions, and people have "adopted" him into their family of heavenly beings.

LESSONS LEARNED: documents require recording for implementation: Following heavenly protocol brings "earthly" results. Heaven has times and seasons. Scribes have access to resources and prior recorded materials that may be attached to your mandate. Angels are efficient at their jobs.

SANDRA: Exquisite Doorkeeper: Beauty second unto Lady Wisdom, Sandra one of the most beautiful being I have ever beheld thus far. Her assignment is that of an entry door in the Angelic Court; her wings function similar to a massive handheld fan. Opening and closing, each unfolding of Sandra's wing-door-access is an ethereal explosion of rainbow colors dispersed in a mist, Heavenly Fourth of July. The wing's movement reminds me of a peacock spreading its tail. The droplets of mist are filled with eyes of discernment. She is a cheerful divine greeter. I can only imagine how what I perceive as her beauty might change in the light of defending her territory. She has also greeted others during heavenly ascensions and revealed the mirror on mirror depths of her beauty.

LESSONS LEARNED: I appreciate feeling welcomed by a being of light. Just a look at her beauty holds me in awe of Him. Access takes on new meaning. Entry is a well-guarded door,

RAPHAEL: Heavenly Overseer. I met Raphael for the first time after a personal commencement. He was part of the ceremony. When personal and painful court proceedings occur where I have poured myself out in repentance, Raphael has always stepped in and taken responsibility to suggest angelic assignment. He is likable, easy to approach, and a discerner of love in your heart. I encounter him more as a being of light. A 5-star general is aware of the supplies and provision needed for battle. My regard for him supports that he is a team player and has a particular assignment to help me: Very reassuring. Raphael and maturing love are intertwined.

LESSONS LEARNED: when love is unpacked in your life, Raphael has a part. Angels are a part of your maturing. Excellent to stand in partnership with such a respected being.

BENJAMIN: a group messenger. Sometimes in the first moment of introduction, you feel like you have previously met them. A familiar "family" kindred spirit to them. I have often wondered the length of time passed in which they have remained at your side, unaware? Benjamin certainly has a personal nature about him. The name Benjamin means, "son of the right hand": A being involved on an intimate level and trusted greatly. We met, or my eyes were opened, after completing an inner healing session. Since that time he has obligingly become part of a group I mentor. He is not at my side all the time but seems to come for encouragement and healing reasons. A particular Wednesday morning I sensed that Benjamin was to be released to visit each member of our group. Here are a couple of testimonies.

EVANGELIST GEORGE WATKINS, WASHINGTON STATE WRITES:
Hi Kristen, I thought I would give you an update on Benjamin. I supposed he would come in the evening however he showed up about 2:30 while I was on the roof of my shop patching a leak. He's an interesting fellow. Carries a massive amount of glory because of his interaction with the throne. He is well-traveled because of his position and commission. I introduced him to my 13 Angels, assuming that he didn't know them: Probably more for my sake than his. Then he began to tell me why he came. I felt the glory when he came to me on the roof. He came to give me some insight and revelation about the holy of holies and promote some things in my life that wasn't happening. He is also going to teach me some new ways to prosper. Benjamin carries an immense amount of favor with Heaven.

I decided to keep him around for a while then it dawned on me that he was going to visit some of you also. So I asked a question, are angels multi-dimensional.

Here's the answer I got. Angels are not omnipresent like God is. However, they're not bound in time, so they can be involved in many people's lives because they're framed in another realm, not in the same time limits we are.

If you have any thoughts on that, please let me know.

Anyway, the glory is increasing around me because he carries an enormous amount of God's brilliance.

Thought I would share this with you while it was fresh in my mind.

Blessings, George

LEADER KIM SNELL, TEXAS: It was November, and we were trying to finish building our house by the end of the year so we could qualify for the substantial tax break. I was leaving the granite store heartbroken because they had sold out of my granite and could no longer be able to meet the December deadline. I was upset about losing the money and paying another month's rent and all the extra expenses. Returning to the sanctity of my car, I'm delightfully surprised by a happy greeting, peaceful entity, named Benjamin. I could feel him all over my face telling me that everything would all work out and not to worry so much about the money. In the atmosphere shift, again reminding me of my earlier expectations towards this Angelic visitation. Benjamin and I just sat together outside the granite store until I was utterly comforted. Then I told Benjamin how grateful I was for his visit, turning my concerns towards my husband shared that he would be more upset than I. Benjamin reassured me that he would visit Don and again it would all be ok.

Sure enough by the time I called Don he already knew that we would not make the deadline and when I told him about Benjamin, Don indicated that he had also I talked to him stating the same enjoyable peace-filled experience. We later found another- more beautiful slab of granite, and it all worked out in January. The granite in my house is something special that God is doing...Kim Snell

Benjamin is such a personable "makes-you-feel-special-and-important" angel, focused on our personal growth and relationship as a group of gatherers. He may be part of an "order" of angels. I just appreciate his ability and assistance to meet you right where you are.

LESSONS LEARNED: Angels minister to people in "community." Angels are practical. Angels carry the residue of God's glory. Angels are personal. Just a thought! I'm sure more angels would like to be considered a right-hand man/helper.

DOUGLAS: Angel of the church of Heart of the Valley Community Church: Stepping into my seeing one Sunday morning looking very much like "Father Christmas." He is a full figured and jolly character with a green velvet long coat with white fur trim. With regal stature, he wore a garland crown on his head. When I first perceived his presence, it made me think that water was flowing. He is a uniter. He helped to orchestrate the activities of HVCC mandates, from spontaneous Sunday worship, heaven school, and leadership meetings. He also coordinated other angels that came alongside. He is faithful at teaching us/me how to work in partnership with the angelic in a corporate setting. He was instrumental to us during our transitions beyond the veil. A sad day when his assignment was complete, and we released him. Thank you, Douglas.

LESSONS LEARNED: Angelic administrators help you to understand God's call/blueprint for a body of believers. They also assist with sentinel angels to protect the "window" of heaven your church stewards.

HONOR, CADENCE & CLARIFICATION: disaster response team. They came to rebuild what we thought was lost and stayed to communicate the new!

During a season of searching our hearts (HVCC governing leadership 3/ Bench) regarding our marriages, and others we carry in our hearts, we felt the Lord wanted more for us than what we were currently walking in. Honor, Cadence, & Clarification were sent to assist with much clean up on the marriage/church mountain. They came with sleeves rolled up, ready to work, bearing brooms, dustpans and delivering to us a "standard," Isaiah 59:19 b: "When the enemy comes in like a flood, the Spirit of the Lord shall lift up a standard against him." Standard=vanish away, subside, escape; chase impels, deliver. Now those are powerful cleaning tools, yeh! Within a few weeks of their arrival, we entered into an assignment of deep repentance/ courtroom encounters. We began hearing testimonies of marital changes, breakthroughs, and old negative patterns addressed: Which is a miracle since much of the Joshua generation is over 40. Most of us are celebrating married "FOREVER"! Ha ha ha.

Let's just take a moment to revel in the glory given in their names.

    HONOR: honesty, fairness, or integrity in one's beliefs and actions: The highest respect (Honor is the leader).

CADENCE: a rhythmic flow of a sequence of sounds or words, especially the pattern in which something experienced.

CLARIFICATION: to make (an idea, statement) clear or intelligible; to free from ambiguity: To release the mind, intelligence from confusion, revive.

LESSONS LEARNED: God created angels to serve purposes of the heart, to help us and keep us on a pathway of transformation. They are carriers of His glory. Forgiveness removes the legal right that the enemy had to remain hindering relationships; it's like giving a fire hose to an angel. Honor, Cadence, and Clarification stepped into the big shoes of Douglas as angels of our Ekklesia. They carry OUR SOUND!

A GLOBAL ORDER: WINDS OF CHANGE, TRANSFORMATION, REFINERS FIRE, SOUNDS OF MANY WATERS: a few years ago we hosted Mike Parsons from Freedom ARC as a guest speaker for a conference. Part of his assignment from the Lord was to release an "Order of angels." They have remained a valuable asset to our Ekklesia.

Somebody in our group wrote four poetic declarations of our agreement with these angels and their ministry. I encourage you to read the declarations in a spirit of receiving. It's a treasure to be able to share with you. I encourage you to read her words in a spirit of receiving.

ANGEL: WINDS OF CHANGE
Thank you for your arrival.
We value and treasure your presence.
We give you a place of honor in this house.
We respect your authority and heavenly assignment.
We position ourselves as a weather-vane.
We hoist our spirit like a sail in your wind.
We step into your atmospheric waves and modulations.
We inhale your streams, swirls, and currents.
We rest in your breezes.
North, south, east and west
We call forth His heavenly wind.
His holy whirlwind.
His perfect storm.
To plant His seed across the earth.
Winds of Change,

We open the doors of our heart to you,
and thank our Heavenly Father
who has sent you!
Love,
Heart of the Valley Community

ANGEL: TRANSFORMATION:
Thank you for your arrival.
We value and treasure your presence.
We give you a place of honor in this house.
We respect your authority and heavenly assignment.
We embrace every transformation that has been
ordained in heaven.
In our hearts, in this house, city, state, and nation.

We release all that has passed away.
We humbly and joyfully purpose to learn, follow, and trust in
our Father's unfolding mysteries.
We eagerly anticipate transformation in all reaches, dimensions,
and depths as we seek to do our Father's will. Transformation,
We open the doors of our heart to you and thank our Heavenly
Father who has sent you!
Love,
Heart of the Valley Community

ANGEL: REFINERS FIRE
Thank you for your arrival.
We value and treasure your presence.
We give you a place of honor in this house.
We respect your authority and heavenly assignment.
We submit to your blazing, fiery presence.
We give permission to:
Consume the worldly, soulish nature of our hearts
Consume complacency, doubt, and insecurity
Devour impurity, independence, and pride
Purify contaminated thoughts and imagination
Pass your fiery sword through every DNA sequence
We call forth the original DNA upon our heavenly scroll. To be
conformed to His image.

To be a blazing, fireball cast upon the earth --
Living, liquid "gold" refined in our Father's Love.
Refiners Fire,
We open the doors of our heart to you
and thank our Heavenly Father who has sent you!
Love,
Heart of the Valley Community

ANGEL: SOUND OF MANY WATERS

Thank you for your arrival.
We value and treasure your presence.
We give you a place of honor in this house.
We respect your authority and heavenly assignment.
We draw near to listen, grasp, and understand
the sounds of heaven.
Open our "gates" to hear and receive.
What are the meditations of a quiet pool?
What song does the spring sing?
What announcements come with the rain?
What vibrates with the morning dew?
What are the declarations of waterfalls?
What is the groaning of ocean depths?
Who hears the galactic hymns of the Ancient of Days?
We tune our spirits to the voice of our God.
To know Him, recognize Him, and resonate with Him.
at every frequency and wavelength.
We answer the call "deep unto deep."
Sound of Many Waters,
We open the doors of our heart to you, and we thank our Heav-
enly Father who has sent you!
Love,
Heart of the Valley Community

LESSON LEARNED: I have become MORE aware of angelic presence
and ministry, listening/learning in the company of fellowship. Agreement
within the community is vital.

Forty-nine thousand five hundred and thirty-three, words.

PERSONAL ANGELS

SAMUEL: Defender of destiny

I woke up one morning having experienced being on a construction site in my dreams: White hard hat, work boots. It seemed like I had been working all day. I was covered in dirt and very tired. The location was urban, tall buildings, office complexes, and nearby was a busy section of a cloverleaf highway overpass; you could hear the cars zooming past. The building was in its infancy, lumber and steel supplies stack up everywhere. Cement trucks were parked for the evening at the end of a hard day. I assumed that I had a management role as I was last to get ready to leave the site and was heading to the makeshift mobile office at the edge of the vast city lot. I was acutely aware that I needed a shower and somewhere in my near future would make it a priority. Two men were sitting just outside the office door, didn't seem to alarm me particularly. Both had smiles from ear to ear and almost cut off the other for rights to first words of introduction. Hi, I'm Peter, he shot out his hand to shake and start the introductions. I hesitated for a moment. My dirty hands, I pretended to dust them off on my jeans and then met his firm handshake. This vibrant, inviting Peter, oblivious to my grunge of the day, at length, held my hand, bordering, on socially unacceptable. His timing was perfect, intending to make keen an impression. Easy to look at, he was virile, forthright, with a vivacious personality. To his chagrin and common courtesy, demanding our attention, then directed towards the introduction of the other man. Nobly standing up in one fluid motion, and instead of offering me his hand he offered his chair, both vying for my attention; equally confident. "This is your place" Samuel said. Dignified and graying around the temples, wisdom partnered with a peacefully surefooted countenance. I was drawn by a glory that sat upon him, communication was comfortable, and I felt an overwhelming love of the Father when in his presence. Clasped on his right wrist, I noticed a luxurious gold-watch. Samuel also observed my interest in the unique piece. Unspoken words exchanged as Peter took a back seat to our conversation and he stepped out of the picture. Knowing that I was tired and feeling unkempt at the end of my work day, Samuel seemed particular that we arrive at a date for getting together. Since it was evident, I still desired a shower before entertaining an evening out. End of the encounter.

Already awakened by heavenly interaction, the feeling of complete touchable love lingered as tears rolled down my cheeks. I stayed still to revel in spiritual, luxuriant warmth of the Father's presence: Thick, loving and unconditional. Moments passed, and I picked up my journal to note the rendezvous, also wondering about the invitation and its time and place.

This particular brush of the divine remains kindred with the essence of Father God's person-hood caressed as if His arms were around it. Almost two years later divine word of mouth sent me on a You-Tube journey, after attending an Ian Clayton conference in southern California where I had purchased MP 3 teaching titled Night Watch. In the latter part of the message, Ian shared a testimony about a church in England that was walking through kingdom transition similar in experience to our little church: How they were stepping through the veil corporately. My quest was to find who had such testimony. My search found Mike Parsons and his church in Barnstaple, England, shortly after arriving home from the conference. I emailed him the same day. His response was one of the most gracious, hospitable doors I have ever had the pleasure to find. I began searching through available teaching and a vast amount of You-Tube materials picking at random the first of which to listen. I set aside a not-to-be-disrupted-quiet-time and turned on the pre-recorded teaching. Mike and another lady via Google hangouts began a corporate ascension, walking through the door/veil and up the river of Life. I had never experienced a pathway in this manner before, (even though it was a replay: remember heaven is alive.) I stepped through, joining the journey, knowing that God would accompany me along the way. The language was a bit different but familiar, walking in the spirit and seeing Jesus. They mentioned (on this path) coming to your mountain and Jesus introducing you to the angel that has been holding your assignment, sitting on your throne until such a time that you ascended and begin the transformation of learning how to rule and reign on your (spiritual) mountain. I walked with Jesus and saw the peak of a mountain. We approached, and a glorious being of light transformed in front of me. Immediately the favorite memory re-kindled as tears burst down my face. No introductions were needed, and Jesus smiled with unspoken words, watching a portion of the fullness of His joy flow. My spirit embraced Samuel, the regal angel who has held, guarded and stewarded the spiritual realm of my destiny, without a name, unseen, unacknowledged, waiting to tutor me in the things of the Kingdom. He is a Defender of Destiny! Teacher of those who wear crowns, an exhorter of kingdom tools. Teaching me how to decree victory.

RABBIT TRAIL ON THE NOTE OF RELATIONSHIP: I visited England this last December not too long after the manuscript went into edit mode. The relationship with Freedom Church continues to grow. Amongst the favorites that welcomed me there was my Editor Laure Fabre, who hosted me, and Alice Wescott from Freedom Church. It's funny how our angels knew each other before we figured out we were kindred-folk. Hanging on my wall is a new book graphics cover highlighting the desire to write the England testimony.

ENGLAND: NOTES FROM HEAVEN. It's amazing.

LESSONS LEARNED: This chapter was a personal request by the Lord and I again put up a bit of a fuss about writing a chapter on angels. My lost argument was a desire to avoid being "teachery"; there is so much text already at hand.

I have yet to live a day in His kingdom without witnessing the angels incredible ministry. To this day, Samuel is the only angel who I encounter in the Kingdom of Heaven within me, where transformation, spiritual gateways, and intimate communion transpire. He is ever faithful to the name given to him "God has heard."

LESSONS LEARNED: for years I thought the voice or voices I perceived/ heard were always Holy Spirit, the personal daily help. I always said thank you and acknowledge the divinely helpful thoughts. With a bit of fine-tuning my relational ear and asking many questions: I have enjoyed learning to recognize the different voices and knowing who is doing the speaking. God made divine helpers to help. This understanding has increased the grace in perceiving the "Fear of the Lord." Discovering individual voices has matured me to know Him more within His personhood as a "Holy God." Without hesitation though, Abba would humbly help me in finding my lost car keys any day. The kingdom of heaven is without competition; it all points to Him.

ANGELS AROUND MY HOUSE

LESSONS LEARNED: Holy Spirit and the Godhead talk inside you or inside your head. Angels talk like you heard the sound coming from the home you are standing in or heard from a friend or family member, their voice travels to you.

SOPHIE: Wisdom's Voice being so soft-spoken, I had a relationship with her before I understood I did. She is the practical "key" finder, in so many ways. Unpretentiously dressed in white linen, she is a carrier of scrolls and accompanies me from my left. A compassionate friend, she carries a Throne-Room-glory on her. Sophie is in charge of my personal three angels. Sophie, Kelsey, and Airadon. She administers gifts and resources given and helps me to discern and learn tools purpose. Giving and receiving are her languages. It is a hoot to watch them participate while I am doing my workout aerobic step routine. They keep their joy on!

KELSEY: Sound of Psalms. Why she positions herself on my right, I have never asked? She is faithfully there: I hear her voice from the right side of my personhood. Maybe it's the way my brain works. For Kelsey is always at hand to lean into my creative self: Music, songwriting, painting, decorating, bow and poof ministry, cooking, changing the atmosphere, gardening, writing/journaling. When she does not come as a being of light, she's outfitted in Celtic attire. So if a river is going to dance, Kelsey has both hard and soft soled shoes to meet it. She is witty and humorous and always ready to worship loudly, freely with a variety of instruments besides her feet. I remember the day I heard her on a string instrument playing with me.

AIRADON: Guardian. The battles he wages I have never seen. I see him always standing in the wings, much like a bodyguard would keep a view of the surroundings. Airadon has a pleasant, reassuring look on his face. I am familiar with him in a couple of settings: From my perspective, he transforms in size, Sometimes he alters his appearance from manlike to light being, other times he is towering, standing over my home, three stories tall. During the night I see him as a light being with the same mannerisms as a swarm of bees or a pocket of air trapped under an iced-over lake. He is always present, moving, and standing nearby. When the lens is that of an "angel" he stands lean, about seven-foot-tall, long blond hair tied back, wearing white linen karate like clothes - his sword is always drawn. He makes me laugh while I am doing my step aerobics, taking two positions: One on the front lawn just outside my window or on the roof, doing a type of Tai Chi movement with his sword, keeping himself ready for battle. I see him as my guardian angel.

AIRADON, KELSEY, AND SOPHIE, as a team, have helped me cross many spiritual bridges. We do not argue who finds my keys? I am thankful for there ministry, council, teaching, patience, joy, comedy, guidance, protection, love. They travel with me, I suggest converse with my family and their angels. Their assignment supports me here, the Kingdom of the Earth.

KATE: I introduced her earlier in the book, sharing my journey of receiving this writing project in heaven and "outworking" it within the protocols I have learned over the past years. Writer's assistant; newest on the relational wheel, I mentioned her before. Kate acts more like a "healer/header" than a Scottie dog: Dog angels, go figure! She helps to keep me focused on writing projects. Her hands seem busy to bring information my way in regards to writing. A supporter of my writing destiny can make me laugh much like the goofy pup (Scottie dog) portrayed. I am not the first author assignment on her roster. She also traveled to England accompanying the book to support my Editor. I saw her in England as well. When I began sending my manuscript around for permissions and endorsements, I understood that she was part of an "order of angels." The order is assigned to accompany God's purposes where ever "The UnFinished Book" may travel.

LESSONS LEARNED: Journaling has helped me to remember how my angels have responded in certain situations, identifying the assignment and purposes. To say that God put some of His nature in them is an understatement. They know how much He loves us. They are part of unity and brotherhood more than we acknowledge. I continually remind myself to appreciate their ministry and learn how to partner together for the kingdom.

ANGEL: Mover of Sheep. All leaders have experienced the challenge of getting a group of people headed towards a common destination whether in worship, prayer or ascension. Waiting for the room to sense what He is doing can try your patience. One Sunday morning, during worship, the Lord showed me that He was taking us to a different pasture. We would be feasting, resting and drinking at a new-to-us stream. I saw the portal much like a gate onto a fenced paddock. Some people weren't paying attention; others wouldn't go unless someone stepped out ahead of them and it felt like the Lord would never get us through. That is when "Angel" showed up to help gather and herd: Much like a herding dog would bite the heels of the sheep to direct the crowd. I would see him flagged in front to get the group attention and then squeezed from behind to move the lollygaggers. Sometimes sheep like musicians aren't prepared or have failed to tune their "instruments" as preparation to follow the orchestra leader, and the leader has to continue to repeat a particular bar of music till they respond to their "cue."

LESSON LEARNED: a living sacrifice is a daily offering, as a black music note on a musical score. We are all part of and responsible for the song.

MIRNA: Guardian of my house. A dear friend of mine who is a gifted "seer" came for a visit. You can get so "familiar" to your home/surroundings that you are unaware of the ministering spirits that help with the daily responsibilities. She pointed Mirna out to me. I'm sure we have all asked for an angel to guard our home during a storm or while we are away. My home has very mature trees around it, and every time the wind kicks up I thank Mirna for protecting our home. I would suggest that they assist in bringing individual divine visitors to your home as well. Over the years we have had many a wayward teen finding our home as a safe house. I love how their names are exclusive to their ministry. Mirna means "peaceful." This summer my family completed re-roofing our home. Not quite ready to be reflective on that massive labor project. Mirna was indispensable at keeping the tiring atmosphere governed and releasing bright construction ideas. Whew!

I am surprised, looking at the end of this long chapter, how many "angel's" comings and goings are in my life. We have just scratched the surface of my glimpse into an army of helpers. I honor and welcome their ministry. We didn't touch on Healing Angels, Herald Angels, Centurion Angels, Seraphim or Cherubim, just a few of those that support us in the Kingdom globally. The list and purposes of His light beings is a pleasure to discover. I encourage you to stir up your "Now Faith."

LESSONS LEARNED: Be not forgetful to entertain strangers; for thereby some have entertained angels unawares.   *(Hebrew 13:2)*

Fifty-one thousand three hundred and four words

CHAPTER 12

The Watchmaker

*"There is something delicious about writing the
first words of a story. You never quite know
where they'll take you." Beatrix Potter*

We've been taken somewhere, haven't we!

This chapter - once thought a beginning - now takes a different position nearly three-quarters of the way to completion. Some of the personal fears discussed in other sections are still ringing, each a different tone of woe. Are they valid? Do we participate in allowing fear undo glory? Has the love of Jesus and knowing His Kingly station honestly shed light on the book journey, once so utterly foreign to where we began, or "thought" we started; eight years old, pew row seven, left-hand side.

I am challenged to challenge you.

My first paragraph's started with thoughts and sound viewed from a different beginning. It was written before Martin Luther's quote challenged the thesis of my heart. I'm asking questions to God, to myself and you the reader. Does it matter or make a difference?

What would happen if in the story I didn't tell anyone I was in heaven? How would it change the book, turn the message? What greater credibility (of heaven) could exist? I've testified of heaven: Yet the theology of life finished, ended, exhausted or stolen and can I return to tell about it? But Jesus, You did! How much of Your death am I willing to die into? Who would be the audience or who wouldn't read this book if scripture was or wasn't there to reinforce heaven's thought? If I were to shore my writing with verses, inspired writings intended to be full of peace and illumination, it might cause argument within itself, and words will be left on the page, orphaned in the midst of torment. Beauty, purpose, a transformation, will have been lost at the mercy of accusations that echo theological words deemed to have right standing but distant from personal intimacy. If eternity is real, why are there so few places to discuss it and experience it? Must Hollywood be the place to display it, argue it and create mystical scenes that give us snippets into redemptive answers? Can I write just for the sheer pleasure of the pleasure of You: The joy of thought, the invigoration of laughter, the discovery of myself, that You never lost sight. Can we discuss hidden things, conversations that have taken place at tables that kings and dignitaries have never put their feet underneath? Talking to You, I never have my feet on the ground, but I've never been more aware of the ground I walk on.

Should I not use Your Name in the book? I don't know? It's thought-provoking. Tragically, Your name has been slandered and exhausted in breath for which they do not even have ownership. I'm so focused on trying to write this book, struggling for my encounters to make sense that I am distracted because of making sense. How can I write out a map when I am the map? We each have an internal plan. The paths I know, I've walked them, tread them down and climbed staircases hidden in stories of old. I can step in and out of heaven with just a thought, with only a focus, a turning. Death's door, obliterated by the very eyes that look from my heart. Life and the living, no longer held in the captivity that time lords over them. Am I OK if others respond to this book by saying fiction & fantasy? Is my relationship with You OK, even if challenged, knowing where the words originate? Knowing the witnesses that look upon them, who share their mystery. Who has counseled and mentored me until my understanding grabbed hold? It's a crazy notion. The paint does not question a painter as he strokes on the canvas. He is caught, impassioned to blend dry medium with liquid color in an expression of his opus, but admirers might wonder his thought or prototype. Am I OK if our words, the personal stories I write, become defamed? Fiction does sound better than false, demonic, and new age. I'll be OK since You are holding my hand. If our words sing truth, then they will find the ear to hear them like a seed carried by the wind. It will fly until the breeze deposits at home.

I'll gaze at the backside of the pocket watch that has reminded me for months of the assignment You have asked.

Though fear creeps in,
evidence that something false is in the room.
The Mighty One who carries time,
inviting me into an in-vest-it-ure of glory,
He will remind me, my divine adoption already recorded,
where scribes organize heavenly files
and libraries mysteriously can be found,

while riding on the back of a royal lion.
Only those who seek will find,
those who ask will encounter the answer,
for those who knock or hear His knock,
the door will be opened.

Do I remember the first time I was lead there? I'm trying to recall, this secret place that never was intended to be concealed. It was before all my journals were on my iPad. The days when pen and paper took a little more effort than the typing of keys and the scribble of little red lines highlighted underneath when my words were incorrect. I felt the paper, and there is something in that exchange. Those journals are packed and sitting in storage currently. That may be my next book: You can ask me tomorrow. Written in the journal entries are the tears of my life, joy-filled with memories of days, the misunderstandings and the gentle path that straightens to understanding. Pages and pages of words written about conversations between my husband and me while biting my lips closed: hidden offerings and also moments when I didn't contain my tongue, and I blew up the entire weekend. Pages of hours I spent in forgiveness till the gift of repentance bathed me, and I knew the root was gone. Early morning memories, within every house which I have lived: every nook and cranny framing an altar, that I knelt before You. On bowed knees and submitted heart I dedicated and set aside time to pray. Etched is every chair, the color of each of the walls that surrounded me, my velvet floral couch, the fireplace, the rugs, my prayer pillow, the blue tarp that kept the rain off me in my 40 days of sleeping outdoors, my cherished coffee cups. I remember well meeting Samuel. No need to pull my journals out of storage. It's as vivid and alive as it was the day I met him.

I have roughly seventy or so pages till I can change the title in my heart to "The Finish Book." The ending written in heaven before I reached the halfway mark.

Dear reader, our adventure is still not complete. I have shared my questions that wrestle my realities. Are you coming?

A journey creates a returning path; grab this anchor if you desire. Take the film of my memory and deposit it in your imagination. Follow the Master: Jesus has taken me to this place prior times: It reminds me of a "Galleria" of shops in a downtown location, a journey that has many stories. There is a large central staircase in the middle and looking up, it opens under a spiritual glass ceiling. The wide stairs ascending made of white marble with ribbons of grays; the white corner posts are massive, square with moldings. It feels like an ancient structure that has been there for what my perception sees. I look around, and there are many rooms, or shops, all the same size. Each one has a different yet unique door, some colored, some plain, some carved, all so inviting. The one I am taken to has a French door. I noticed that there isn't anyone else around in the foyers or between floors yet my spirit senses attendants in each "shop." The first time I encountered this place/room, just walking inside took my breath away. The small room was no bigger than a storefront. A small-framed man was sitting at the back of the "shop" working on a table. I melt each time I visit this lovely suite. Stationed in the center lies a square bakers-height table/cabinet, white painted wood with carved moldings, four drawers on each side. Hung above the cabinet there is a piece of framed latticework for display, laid and arranged with cream ribbons, white ribbons and draped antique laces. Set on the countertop of the drawer case were different size bowls; marble urns; open metallic boxes containing pearls, diamonds and gems, all sparkling clear. There were white on white, cream to creamy, velvets and bows and hand beaded things. Built into the far wall to the right of the entry, from floor to ceiling, were large drawers with beautifully painted words in cursive writing identifying the items within the drawers: No handles or knobs, just slight cutaway handholds like an old flour bin. The room reminds me much of the ribbon shop (Millinery) in the movie "Pride and Prejudice" where the Bennett sisters ran into Mr. Wickam while shopping for ribbons and notions for the upcoming ball at Netherfield Park. It felt like I had been there many times, before.

Crazy fact: not months after I finished the manuscript of this book I found myself walking some very similar paths in England.

This cozy nook I found looked like me - everything in this shop was ideally suited for my liking. I touched things, and ooh'd and ahh' ed over the white/cream textures, satins, velvets, bobbles, and bling with the uncanny notion this all was about who I am. Jesus was standing there, just smiling and delighted that I was dumbfounded, caught in an eye candy dither. Every trim, ribbon and sparkle, handpicked for me.

I didn't understand the purpose of this place, but it brought me great joy. Fully immersed in the rooms delight's, I recovered a bit of my focus and turned my attention to a small framed man sitting at a desk in the back corner of the niche. He appeared dressed like a watchmaker: White button-down shirt with sleeves rolled above the elbows, looped around his neck a brown canvas waist tied apron, heels caught on the foot-rail of his stool, and an eye loop cupped in his right eye. I couldn't make out the treasure on which he was working. This "Watchmaker" is oblivious of anyone in the room, so buried in his time-piece. Heaven is such a marvelous realm of "awe."

I had several days of rest and meditation, as my physical "book map" or road from the wilderness that the Lord drew out for me, ended once crossing the bridge. I love technology; this heavenly "book map" I drew it with an iPad using a white-board app and printed it to hang it along with other craft collage items, in front of my desk. Great visual: However, heaven crossing over the bridge was off the edge of the paper. I am wrestling for a pattern to write about The Watchmaker's room because I have encountered it within different "time" periods. Trying to organize it chronologically is challenging me.

Did you ask yourself what about the Watchmaker? I finally did and was wondering what kept him so focused? I finally looked closer, taking my eyes away from all the beauties in the room. I must have noticed him at some point; my journal notes are unclear. I recall entering the Watchmaker's room, walking over to the back-corner workstation to get a close look at the trinket fashioned by this master of intricate movement. To my undoing, it wasn't a watch at all, but a crown. Selah.

The Watchmaker's name is Kendrick, a surname with several origins: "Royal power," "Bold power," "Chief hero," "Home ruler." The little details that move the heart by the authenticity of mystical "happenstance," confirming the core of your hearing. Being in heaven is a constant seeking and imbibing; a question I asked: What is a "Watchmaker" doing making my crown.

I think I am learning something about myself in the artistry of writing: What it feels like to write for a King and relate from the looking glass of your heart. Only transparency will reflect His voice. Words with relationship offer assistance, revelation. Words without a relationship with the frequencies of His heart are subject to misinterpretation: As per the wrestling and confrontation, I wrote in this chapter introduction. I relish the path that collections of letters, relationally "delicious" words lead us on. I've discovered a crown. A crown is a reward, yes! How do you pen the rewards of the Lord, express the sentiment and succession in kingdom authority He intended and submit your pen for writing from a position of humility? I'm so on a learning curve. In my limited experience with "crowns" outside of being in the spirit/in heaven, I have never worn one, tried one on (this surprises you? I had three brothers!) was never awarded a tiara through youthful celebrations, homecoming princess or in a pageant. Pom poms, yes: Crown only with Him. I do however like all that princessy Cinderella or Mr. Darcy stuff. I'm a hope-filled romantic! Jane Austen groupie. May I remind you that the Watchmaker's room is set in a galleria of other suites, other crown rooms. Shouldn't we ask ourselves what purpose the Lord intends for sharing something so intimate? Can we know who we are in Him without personally experiencing the royalty He deems us belonging to?

I have a new story to work through with you.

RABBIT TRAIL: This last Friday my younger brother Matt texted me and urged me to drive our folks to the Salem airport for a fly-in, cruise-in, World War 2 reenactment in which he participates. My family has an (odd) obsession with old International trucks; Matt added to the "niche" with International World War II memorabilia: The big four+ wheel kind, full military land, and sea deployment. Tank ownership is in the dream stage; half-track purchased waiting for pick up in Virginia. To our tale: I called my Mom and World War II Korean War Veteran Dad, encouraging their attendance and my willingness to be their escort. They declined from a view that their "senior" legs would not let them walk throughout the exhibits. Contemplating that it had been a while since I bestowed my "sisterly" attentions towards my younger brother, I mentally listed off my to-do list: The house was in order, and my book manuscript was in the reflective mode. My honey would have loved to attend. Sadly this was Don's scheduled Saturday to work but the day was arranged nicely. Texting my brother back, "Yes, I'm coming" Matt's enthusiastic response was, "Would you have a 1940s outfit laying around" wanting me to "look" the part. No! I'll acquire a retro costume to go along with my "rent a cowgirl" boots I wear once a year to attend your rodeo galas (Matt is a rodeo stock-man. Yes, I have a colorful family). This Saturday adventure was going to be my first time visiting his World War II hobby on display.

From what I understand this was a modest size grouping of reenactors supporting a local Aeronautics Museum Fundraiser: "WARBIRDS OVER THE WEST." The big public draw attending the fly-in was a P-51 Mustang and P-38 Lightning. At this point, I was only familiar with the planes from stories shared about Don's uncle, Harry Dowd, who flew P-38s and went down over Africa. He is my youngest son's "middle" namesake, Harry (See notes page for literature regarding those brave men). Up early to meet up with Matt at 7:00 am, rain in the forecast, catching us up on our "colder" Oregon Springtime: Golf umbrella in hand, boots, lined trench coat and extra layers. We arrived at the hospitality of a pancake breakfast inside the B-17 Museum hangar. It was an onslaught of introductions to Matt's "collecting" friends. Earlier, I had thanked the Lord for His goodness, asked His blessing on the day, had a few words regarding the weather and added, "I'll keep my eyes open for a particular Holy Spirit moment." Matt's WWII collection; jeep, duck, and a couple of large "International" haulers (H5) lined up in a row. Faithful herding dogs on hospitality duty, with "Binder" (Matt's dog) stealing the show in his olive green Sargent's shirt. Situated behind Matt's display are the hardcore reenactors with their military city setup: Tents, flagpole, cots, bedding, baseball mitts, "playing radio," supply tents and gear, authentic signs, medallions, and badges including their attire. History was well portrayed with girlfriends dressed as Rosie the Riveter. (For pictures of this day join me at my book blog).

COMMUNION MOMENT BOOK GOALS, PAUSE: *three-quarters of the way complete, fifty-three thousand one hundred and fifty-five words.*

I was very much enjoying "spreading my wings" in an environment outside my area of influence. To set a distinctive mark on the day, I purposed to collect pictures and thoughts for a blog post later. What would be my bent for the assignment? There wasn't; anyway being a "novice" I could represent the detail of the memorabilia around me. So, I watched people and listened to the stories of their mixed emotion memories from an era past. The veterans at the show presented an excellent representation. They would point at an accessory and tell their family a story from their active service past. Their faces would light up as if recounting their duty roster from "yesteryear," involving an individual vehicle, token, or remembrance. Somehow they hid the pain and loss etched in them. Dads and sons of all ages, husbands informing their wives that this bulbous yellow distressed "International" heap is a true find. In between rain threats, Matt displayed his 50cal gun standing proud like a headache rack on a lifted 4x4 truck.

Drool gathered on the lips of the good-ole-boy crowd: An impressive piece of memorabilia. Clouds accumulated in the sky, weather threatened to pour down, prayers said: "Don't you dare!"

I took a moment to ponder the "spiritual" atmosphere. Crack, in the sky just over the tarmac, lightning flashed, marking out an electric line drawing 3/4 of a window square. It had my attention. I looked around to see if any response came from the crowd: not that I could see. I stood alone and leaned into unpacking this mysterious outburst. Then I heard the angel say: "Amsterdam," his name was Amsterdam. Quickly I had an "aha" moment with the introduction to the angel of this plane. Of course, there are angels assigned to aircraft. Myrna is my house angel. I am ever learning what a thoughtful, protecting, practical Father He is.

SIDE NOTE: later on, I did a bit of research because I thought Amsterdam was quite a thought-provoking name for an angel. This particular P-38 plane never saw any wartime action. It was retired and sold to a collection of people after its initial delivery to RFC, Kingman AAF, AZ as 44-27083, February 21, 1946. The only highlighted thought I found was that Amsterdam was a "safe place" as, for centuries, the city received refugees escaping religious wars and persecutions. Hence the Yiddish name for Amsterdam: "Mokum" meaning safe-place. As an angel of peace and remembrance, he appeared dignified, honoring, a sense of recounting and healing from the past. His unusual post-military assignment was still reaching farther than war-time.

The P-51 Mustang and P-38 Lightning waited patiently on the tarmac for their aerial shows. I tried to watch people nonchalantly, and I took pictures of people taking pictures of their sons or Rosie the Riveter's sporting poses on the wing. Strolling around I took the liberty to stand with my head inside the P-38 landing gear wheel well. I winked back at the painted Latin beauty nose art, highlighted "Tangerine" (on the song charts in 1941, written by Johnny Mercer & Victor Schertzinger; see fun lyrics and link in the notes page or book blog). I investigated the hatch upfront which opened to load rounds of ammo. I noticed the different planes and how the gun mountings would alter the pilot's view/aim. People were breathless in the company of these old and rare man-made birds. I listened to my nephew's tale of admiration of this World War II glamour'd hero, feeling a bit like I was the wrong member of the Wambach family to be in this show. Here I was when it should have been my husband, looking at a restored bird that his uncle had valiantly fought with and died in, just a few days past June 6th, D-Day, a day that the Lord has marked twice with a special visitation to me. He must be up to something. The day ticked on as afternoon rounded on the clock, morning fly-by video on my phone, my feet and tummy desiring a break. I had asked Don to pack me a camp chair so that I wouldn't have to stand all day. When I mentioned bringing it along, Matt's body language said, "unheard of" and as I discovered later, unpacked from the truck were the appropriate period wood folding chairs. Oh, my; two sides to that kind of detail eeh! "Fair food" was a welcome treat, and I ate the foot-long corn dog happily but passed on the "free coupon" for elephant ears, smelling their cinnamon "Dumbo eared" breeze all day. When passers-by took an interest in the jeep, I could tell a simple story from my Dad's army company. Painted with a decal "angel" 11th Airborne 127th combat engineer (11th/ AB CB ENG), the only unit to air-jump into occupied Japan, ever! A fun day to be incognito. Just a sister: Resting in the Lord's goodness. Planes were queuing up for the afternoon show, and my nephew and his wife corralled a space along the runway fence. It was a spectacular display with a backdrop of painted blue skies and billowy clouds. Never saw any more manifestations of "lightning." Pure, showmanship in the air. I was surprised how hushed the prop engines were on the P-38 and later read about its stealth reconnaissance accounts. Planes landed and chocked, Thomas my nephew, Matt's son and I gathered at the P-38 nose like groupies to watch the pilot dismount his craft, answering questions and inviting few, specific guests on board. People got into the "follower" setting and stepped out, lacking patience. Those of us "hard-core" waited to see what opportunity might favor us. The pilot crawled out, remained on the wing, and a fit senior man was waved aboard as I corralled along with the men, "the only female on deck here" to spot this mature individual climbing up an offered ladder. Rumors on the ground were that his dad had been a P-38 pilot, a well deserving hush came over the intimate crowd as we watched him ascend the plane and descend into the cockpit. Pilot Bret answered questions and flagged a young father to allow his two early grammar school sons onto the wings. They wiggled and asked questions as dad took pictures. I took pictures of the dad taking pictures of a momentous mark in their family history. Our senior invitee was still buried in the cockpit, within his thoughts. I noticed our "in the cockpit groupie" didn't seem to have anyone in the crowd noting his auspicious moment, so I asked one of the guys to hand up my phone to the pilot to capture this moment. Now I was committed to the wait so I could exchange contact info with this senior man and forward him his photo. Something in me warmed: he was having a spiritual moment. He finally came out, and after being flagged to come up, my nephew went on board. Gathering myself towards this kindly senior, with tears still in his eyes, I boldly introduced myself, shared that I had his picture on my phone and then asked a very personal question: "You had a spiritual moment up there didn't you?". He nodded and began to share that he felt like his dad (the former P-38 pilot) was right there with him. Knowing this was a divine moment, surprised again (Father God, me of all the people to choose from) that I could respond in a heavenly language with grinning experience: "The cloud of witnesses is closer than we think!". My new friend John stood to agree still captured in amazement. John began to ask me questions about how I perceived the experience he had just encountered. We were kindred spirits for the day right from the get-go. The dust settled, the crowd dissipated, Thomas stepped out of the cockpit in glory, grinning ear to ear and joined me, delighted to be a part of this small group watching the pilot. Bret was combing his thoughts with the end of the display around the corner. His attention stopped; noticing I was still "entertaining" the enthusiasts, he asked if anyone else wanted to come up. My hand leaped airborne. He answered with a gentle "that's you" hand gesture and next, I was climbing the ladder to the wing to access the cockpit. Funnily enough, I felt like I was "cheating someone out of the opportunity who actually deserved such grace". Here I was, out of my element, given a once in a lifetime chance to fathom aeronautical defense. I tried to rush the moment and Bret said sit, no hurry. What does one inquire about in the face of gages, gadgets and large foot-pedals? Funny how those redemptive gifts kick in, I asked which ones are the triggers and which the bomb buttons. That made him laugh! I asked about his flying career and looked at the different size guns straight ahead, mirror stainless steel plaques on each side to see the landing gear situation and the generous smile from my host. I was beginning to "feel" like a hero of sorts. Pictures were taken, texted, face-booked, names of new friends exchanged: evening had come. It was a day I needed to talk to Papa about. Brilliant!

It "appears" that we have flown many miles from the beginning of the chapter. Words, written or spoken without a relationship, often miss the mark. How I feel about myself, how you might feel about yourself often miss the mark of His planned glory. He never stops talking; we limit our hearing. That night with many questions in my heart the Lord took me back in time to deal with some issues from my past. Opportunities stolen, mindsets that altered the favor He intended for my good. Together we dealt with negative learned responses. Even in my night season, I struggle with getting in the backseat of life instead of co-laboring with Jesus riding "shotgun." During my quiet time, I brought my night encounter and yesterday's "P-38" happenings before Him. Lord, can you expand and tell me about what you were doing yesterday? I am learning to ask, Spirit of God, where do you want my seeing or perceptions today? Where shall these questions be taken in Your heavenly realm? Where will Your heart be worked out for me today? My eyes/heart stepped into a place I call the council of the Fathers. It looks like an enormous modern glass urban office building. The council gathers in the open lobby with enclosed sky bridges surrounding. I recognized two people sitting in the council: Bob Jones and John Paul Jackson. I was standing in the center with my questions in hand. I see Jesus and He "feels" like a rabbi/teacher with a pointing-teaching-stick in His hand. I am the apparent student, and we are doing a "live" demonstration. Jesus nods at me. Pensively standing center of the council, waiting to see what my spirit will do, I perceive a single half-sphere banister witness stand: I step in. The witness stand feels like it goes up and down like a periscope with me riding in it. This particular "witness stand" or spherical "light" silo (I have noted similar light structures from past encounters) has often referred to God's DNA. *Spherical structures, silo-shaped, filled with strands of light, comparable to fiber optics. The light of my being transforming into the DNA likeness of Him, through communing in communion with Him.*

It appears that I am a witness today in the DNA of His light? My questions are now representing more than myself but a generation. The periscope "chair or lift" movement moves the council and me independently. I ascend and they descend. The proceedings mystically seem complete, and I'm Back to the governing floor. I step off the "DNA elevator" and move over towards Jesus. Then, directing my focus as if it is my turn to speak with the council, I'm looking at the mandate or night encounter in my hand. Something has transpired: I now witness a red line drawn through it, and the word "repentance" noted on the side in red. I proceeded to read it aloud for the proceedings that already has a "verdict." My memory in the experience: While on the witness stand, repenting: soul ties, all unhealthy un-holy, all entanglement "under the sun," nothing new happens under the sun (new occurs over the sun in sonship). My spirit split-sees a couple of spiritual-visual-screens drop into the room, multiple lens views (heavenly monitors): The council, Jesus, my night encounter all at the same time. I am reliving my night battle, and it is changing under the judgment from the courts of heaven. Forgiveness vehicle complete, justice served, my clothing changes, and I am seated next to Jesus. His forgiveness is extended to myself and my generation for the lack of perception of the gifts of God that He placed on people's lives. As heaven's representative, I received back everything that belonged to me and my generation, receiving back honor and favor. Jesus dealt with and returned my thinking anew, returned to me a crown that had fallen from my young head. At that moment my understanding came back into the council room, though I hadn't left. My heart actions were a witness. I saw a pile of crowns next to the mobile witness stand/DNA "periscope" of light. Where they came from, I do not know. They were not there when I started this journey. My spirit moved towards the royal mound, and I started picking up crowns and throwing them back into the light, returning them to their rightful owners in my generation. Tears are streaming down my face as I partnered with justice.

AS PER MY NOTES: that is why I experienced the "crown room" Galleria, and everyone (from Council of Fathers) was watching. They must have known the glories were coming to witness crowns restored. What started with a spontaneous invitation to World War II reenactment and a bad dream had drawn my heart and drawn a crowd. The sky-bridges around me had filled with the cloud of witnesses while I was standing as a "witness." Heavenly family members came to see favor and honor returned to family lines. So many crowns! The balcony appeared, and I could make out more and more people. My eyes seemed to gain clarity as an individual seemed a bit blurred but highlighted, darker sandy brown hair, thin, huge smile. With joy, my spirit knew his identity. It was Harry Dowd, my husband's uncle who had flown P-38s watching from the cloud of witnesses. I had seen his picture hanging in our den for years. He was wearing a flight suit and took off his flight cap. People from the council were coming up and shaking my hand, saying that court case was incredible. Good job. I was leaning elsewhere and focused on shaking Harry's hand auspiciously, just the next day from my P-38 happenings opening up to me. In the spirit, I moved towards the sky-bridge. I heard Harry saying: "Thank you for the honor of naming your son Justin in my memory." When I went to talk to him, I shook hands and hugged many past relatives from my family: Great aunts, uncles, grandpas and grandmas. Some I had not encountered in heaven before.

Living from eternity on earth. God, You are stunning! Don's mom Mary was standing next to her beloved brother and we all hugged. She looked just like the pictures from her younger years that I had seen: Intelligent, slim figured, full of wit and beauty. I noticed Harry reaching into the shirt pocket of his flight suit and then, with a grinning gesture, he handed me his wings. Through most of this encounter, my cheeks have been wet, as King Jesus unravels my heart. Heaven and earth have met with me inside the cockpit of that P-38 Lightning. I asked the Lord if "mantles" were given via marriage covenants. He just smiled at me as I said "Duh"! We do not fathom the realms of relationship and responsibility that He very much desires in our maturity. Unless He shows us, we agree and obey.

It has taken years of fighting the good fight of faith and practice in the spiritual realm He opened my eyes to. In times like these, it is difficult not to feel a bit of soulish sense of regret that wouldn't serve me very well. The humility that I am finally following through, following my scroll, using the perceptions that Jesus gave me, is worth a thousand lifetimes. Note: Item #6 *Pilot wings added to my Valentine Window Box collage.*

Fifty-five thousand seven hundred and seven words.

There are a few questions/thoughts I want to place on the table of writing: Meat, potatoes, gravy, spinach and cake. If crowns are a reward, can they be lost or stolen? Who recovers them? If we desire to cast our "crown" at His feet, how would one do that if a person had never received one or worn it? David was anointed King in a season of succession before he wore the crown.

There have been times in worship that I have cast/offered my crown to the Lord. Was I just being "religious"? Jesus humbly handed it back and said: "Kristen, you need this" and put it back on my head.

PURPOSES OF AUTHORITY/CROWN/MATURITY = dominion in the spirit, authority in unseen realms that govern the seen realm. The authentic maturing relationship, Lordship, Kingship, Sonship, ruling and reigning.

I have remembered a fun quote from my earlier years, listening to the heartfelt ministry of Joyce Meyer: "You can't have authority over the devil if you do not have authority over a sink full of dishes."

I DISCOVERED: THE WATCHMAKER IS GOD, my crown room/ our crown rooms are a journey of succession. I shared a very intimate encounter today; justice served, and many heaven dwellers witnessed the recovery of crowns, did I return yours?

I INVITE YOU TO AN ACTIVATION INVITATION: *Father I stand in the council of Your word. Thank you, Jesus, for your blood representing me and my entire family line. I ask that you speak to my heart if one of the crowns returned was mine or my family's? I receive my crown by faith. I remind myself that I'm seated in heavenly places with You. Open the eyes of my heart to perceive its glory and I will make a note of its unique characteristics. I'll write them here.*

POST ACTIVATION: COMMUNION AND THANKSGIVING,
Share them with our online community.

Chapter 13

A Crown for Casting

Ascertaining how to be consummately fitted with my "royal"
destiny: Receiving, wearing, understanding, transforming.
A crown for "casting." - K. Wambach

It has been a couple of years since my original encounter in the Watchmaker's room. I returned in a season of developing my spirit, which has many gateways (See notes page for more links to "gateways"). They are access points in which the presence of God or river of life flows through you.

A BIT ABOUT INNER HEALING /TRANSFORMATION: Every chapter, through my wilderness to crossing the river into heaven of the "Unfinished book" God has faithfully brought different tools of spiritual healing to my pathway. Holy Spirit began first by restoring the gift of music to me, healing me from being and feeling the separation in my relationship from the Godhead. He worked tirelessly to help me remove anything that would separate us. In all the languages of inner healing I have received, experienced, learned, taught, administered; stepping into heaven has surpassed them all.

THE EASE:

> In which the enemy goes under our feet in the courts of heaven.
> In believing i am seated in heavenly places with him,
> In which the ministry of his cross flows from death into life.
> When walking through the tabernacle to the arc of god.
> In which relationship becomes one on one.

REPEATED AGAIN: In all the languages of INNER HEALING I have received, experienced, learned, taught, administered; *stepping into heaven* has surpassed them all.

The mind of Christ lives in me, and I can encounter what the Father is doing just like Jesus shared. Seated with Him in heavenly places brings to life that I am a new creation. He encourages and monitors my growth towards maturity. In the light of eternity *(looking both forward and backward from the crossing over place of His sacrificed flesh)* the blood of Jesus has cleansed me from all sin. However the evidence of sin through iniquity, bad choices, and negative patterns, both from self and generational, has left hidden black marks and shadows. Shadows indicate that something is "blocking" the light on and in my DNA. That is to say, my **"DESTINY NOW ALTERED."**

Through relational communion with Jesus seated in heaven, He is returning my DNA to

"DESTINY NOT ALTERED" the original yarn that God knitted me within my mother's womb. The blood and water from Christ change, the blood and water of negative genetics, contrary agreements that the enemy has legally used to distract me from my path. Love's perfect work is work. Love is free, but love is responsible.

I'll share a visual scenario of "DNA hidden things" to help process the thought. Say that you/I have just purchased a new home: Closed escrow, move in, unpack, organize furniture and personal belongings. The house is brand new (the builder was God, He is an excellent craftsman) and this "house story" begins:

New house history is in the alpha stage. However, all my furniture and personal belongings come from bygone times. Some good, some not so good. I just moved them into the house. Holiness is a way of life, yet I didn't choose that way until I encountered The Way. Looking into His eyes and love began to rearrange the furniture.

Inner healing from heaven is like Jesus being invited to be your mentor/roommate/spouse while living together. He has access to your home and will have a conversation about all of its content: If we allow Him access! From the bathroom to bedroom, all drawers, shelves, closets, attics and basements, family photographs, checkbook, medical bills, computer, TV and Internet activity, refrigerator, kitchen, garage... When I made Him Lord of my life, I chose to become a daily living sacrifice, offering myself (a living stone) to Him as a part of His house. It becomes a transformed home, and He is getting His house and myself in order. House Story, His Story, History.

FROM MY JOURNAL NOTES, at least since I owned an iPad with "tagging" and search capabilities, I thought I would search and count how many times the Lord has spent focused time with me in regards to my crown:

A way to "measure" the importance of the identity He desires me to walk in. So I searched. 66! Sixty-six times over a three-year span, how long I've owned my iPad. That's 22 times a year Father brings up the subject matter of my "royalty."

Living those seasons through the Watchmaker's room, a transformation process was already underway.

I began to work through a series of spirit, soul and body gateways (see Psalm 24) asking the Lord if they were open, closed or hindered. If closed, I sought what was blocking the access?

In heaven with your spiritual senses activated, growing and practicing you actually perceive gates, door and access points.

I'll share pinnacle notes of my journey.

CROWN OF REPENTANCE: I began with the Gateways of Hope, Worship, and Revelation. I asked Jesus to show me my gateway of Hope. It looked like a simple door sealed with a black substance like tar. Using the language of scripture is invaluable and living. Tar equaled atonement and judgment. Yikes! God was sharing with me that Hope had been deferred, through unresolved issues and recurring problems.

Is anyone married out there? Do we as spouses make repetitive mistakes? Break promises? Leave our internal and external "junk" laying around just a few "years" too long? So my Hope belief system had been damaged along the way. I'd asked for forgiveness for my part of the mess and forgiven my honey for his; it's the "repetitive stuff" that shakes hope! We can hear the conversation between Peter and Jesus on how many times we are to forgive one another, right? Forgiveness is not conditional to whether the other person ever acknowledges the injury or wrong.

Sorry and repentance aren't in the same sentence. Saying sorry takes me "off the hook" of responsibility.

Forgiveness = repentance, which implements the responsibility to remove the hook that we all got "off-on" in the first place.

Hope in its purest form is feeling that what is wanted can be achieved/received. So how did Jesus remove the tar from my gateway of Hope? He used His crown: the crown of thorns, set on His head to heal my "head": mind, will and emotions.

Healing testified that same evening through an encounter in which the Lord transported both my honey's and my spirit to Paris (The City of Love). We were crossing a bridge over the river Seine.

TESTIMONY: 3 years after this encounter, God opened the door to ministry and relationship with France. Don and I have received a standing invitation to visit. Brilliant hope! France we are coming!

CROWN OF A DAUGHTER:

In the process of transformation, there are many victories. Hard work always pays off in the Kingdom. Thankfully the Gateway of Worship was wide open, so I went next to the door of revelation. It is closed, but I can see through it.

How many of us stopped here with just perception, not the manifestation?

My revelation gateway looks much like one of those industrial garage doors, but it wasn't budging. I asked Jesus to search my heart for the reason why it was not opening. I waited and then proceeded to muscle it in the spirit just enough that I could squeeze underneath it. While skootching under the obstinate door, I saw crumbs on the floor near the threshold. In my understanding, my spirit was moved immediately, reminding me the Gentile women who came to Jesus for the healing of her daughter. First He ignored her. Then at her persistence, He replied: "It isn't right to take food from the children and throw it to the dogs." She is notably quoted to respond: "That's true, Lord, but even dogs are allowed to eat the scraps that fall beneath their master's table." Bingo! That is where my heart got pricked. The Lord was showing me that I didn't feel "worthy" to receive revelation. I was placing myself in a "less than" position, from an orphan mindset not one of a daughter of the King. So I went to the court of accusations and dealt with issues of thinking myself stupid, unworthy to hear, blonde jokes, illiteracy and such. Oh, the things we agree with that contradict His plan. When I received divorce papers from those accusations, Jesus whisked me in the spirit to the top of my "personal" mountain, and Holy Spirit was placing my crown on my head. Gateway of Revelation is now open. Yippee!

Mountains and gateways were all pretty new to me in that season, the rewards of seeking and my repenting heart, desiring transformation to bear a Crown of a Daughter. *Faith is the substance of things unseen. Or should we say in the unseen?*

I was encountering the Watchmaker's work. I thought it was interesting that a watchmaker was constructing my crown. Today's hindsight would say: Those intricate "timing mechanisms & jewels" have been essential to functioning in, on, above, outside and around time itself. God is always highlighting His kid's identity.

DAVID'S CROWN

In my "far from Him" years, looking for love and acceptance in all the wrong places, I traded myself both inside and outside the covenant of marriage. When walking in the flesh or the flesh walking me, I never fathomed (in my "wildest dreams") the journey of repentance I'd walk to forgive myself. Jesus and I walked back through every indiscretion, to reclaim things I had given away. I found myself buried under a false identity that God never intended for me to wear. My thoughts wrestled with being free and forgiven. Illegal lies were whispered, constantly repeating "less than pure" videos, challenging my heart that lay prostrated before Him. The next testimony is the record of the encounter that set me free. *It's a bit more spiritually graphic, my focus is always Him, but sometimes we must face our accuser. Amen.*

When all else fails, the enemy will attack your dream life. I suffered from dreams so tormenting that my husband Don had to shake me awake and comfort tears from fear until I was conscious and aware of his safe arms of comfort around me. You know how (real) dreams can be! They play over and over in your mind all day. Your energy is spent casting them down, nailing them to the cross, over and over. I started to have victory over the same old repetitions when I stepped beyond the veil and personally saw the Lord's mediation at work in the courts of heaven. Another rough night occurred, threatening the peace of our marital chamber. Don shook me awake. Agitated, I began to cry, not wanting to share with him the living color of disgust I had gone through. I had been a faithful journaler, laying a pen and pad next to my bed, anticipating the Lord's presence in the night season. Even in dismay I journaled, which supported learning to hear His voice in all seasons. That same morning, even though I was tired and filled with unholy pictures running through my mind, my heart was determined to find freedom. Don was off to work, my two youngest, now adults had their own schedule. I found myself in a quiet house, initiating a "court appointment" with the King.

MY LIVING WITNESS: *Therefore I urge you, brethren, by the mercies of God, to present your bodies a living and holy sacrifice, acceptable to God, which is your spiritual service of worship.*   *(Romans 12:1)*

If we confess our sins, He is faithful and righteous to forgive us our sins and to cleanse us from all unrighteousness.   *(1 John 1:9)*

Armed with His agreement, I stepped into heaven and found myself waiting for my turn in the Court of Accusations. Odd, I do not ever remember having to wait! Somebody came and took me into another room, sat me down in the back of the room, where I knew I should be patient, so I began to look around, waiting. Off to the side is a black sign with white letters similar to conference signs showing which event is in which room and at what time. I have my journal entry (bad dream) firmly held in hand. In the interim, I inspect this different room and find I'm not alone. It is laid out like a small wood-paneled courtroom/auditorium having two sides of wooden chairs separated by an aisle in the middle. On the right side is a "box seat" area holding four seats with three maidens and a royal person sitting there. I do not recognize any of them, but it is evident that they have been asked to attend. I'm still uninformed and waiting. Mysteriously, someone grabbed my hand assisting me to the front of the room and told me to sit at the table which also has four chairs. I'm beginning to get a clue here that a trial is about to start and I feel the apprehensions of being the one on trial. I'm seated in the second chair from the aisle. My "Counselor" is none other than the Apostle Paul and his place is the first chair: Wonder and shock! I can now see the Apostle Peter taking the third seat, and the fourth is filled by the Apostle James. I don't have an extra moment to be amazed at this auspicious biblical entourage because the court is rising at the entry of Father God. Jesus is seated as the Mediator in the witness stand, and a host of elders are on my left. Still no adversary! So strange, two policemen are standing in front of the doors guarding them so no one can enter without permission. The public seats "you expect in a courtroom" to be filled are empty, the balcony, where the cloud of witnesses would gather, is also empty. I take this moment to shake Peter's and James' hand. Peter is a vigorous-looking man, more the outdoorsy kind, sandy hair about shoulder length, a bit unkempt. He has tan skin, muscles from labor, and well-used working hands. Larger straight nose, blue eyes, light facial hair, light eyebrows, and eyelashes almost like a redhead; broad shoulders, sandals on his feet with well-worn or well-traveled looking feet. He wears a white linen tunic cut just above the knee. He is fearless, funny, bold, even the thick hair on his arms is blonde. James looks like Jesus' brother would look. When I shook his hand, it felt warm and inviting. His hair is dark, a bit past his shoulders, thick and slightly wavy. He has an intoxicating smile and brown eyes framed by full serious dark eyebrows. I feel a sense of security as if we were already great friends. He is a full stature of a man, about 6ft. His hands are more delicate, less weathered than Peter's, with more refined features, cleaner and more manicured. He is also wearing white linen. I feel almost fearful to look at Paul, but he pats me on the shoulder to let me know I am OK. He had other things on his mind and was not paying so much attention to me but to the proceedings ahead of us. Paul's hair is light, curly, short over his ears. His white linen tunic hangs to mid-calf, and he has a red mantle like a sash scarf around his shoulder to his waist. In the spirit, I can see into his mantle, and it looks like medals of honor, row after row: A decorated and very noble man. His hands remind me of my Dad's, long square fingers. A collection of papers are sitting on the table in front of him. I can see that he is very aware of what is and will be going on today in this room. Feeling a bit more supported with my new acquaintances at hand, I exhale deeply, taking another moment to look around and wonder about this place. The maidens sitting with the king, beautifully dressed in white linen, a bit more "flowy" than what the men are wearing, have laurel-flowers crowns on their heads. The king, wanting to catch my eye, keeps smiling at me, sending me all kinds of body language. "Oh, it's David!" I had not yet seen him in his kingly attire: Red robe tied at the collarbone, with gold gilding stitched into the fabric and white linen underneath. How could that smile not be recognized? I remember the many times we sat together on the rustic bench in the *"Tabernacle in the woods," One of the first secrets "couldn't share with anyone" places* when I discovered the men in white linen and cloud of witnesses. A hush covers the room as our hearts said Shh! God is speaking: "I have gathered you here today on behalf of Kristen. She needs your help we need her help". I put the "dream paper" on the table. That was the reason why all this opened up anyway. Immediately a scribe comes and retrieves my spiritual journal notes and gives it to God who shares it with Jesus. The guards at the back of the room open the doors and a huge snake slithers in, an ugly boa constrictor or python, so large that he takes up most of the front courtroom area. He crawls onto the chairs of the opposite bench, sits down and begins to shapeshift into ugly disgusting creatures. I hear Satan saying that she (Kristen) has had sex with him. Jesus stands up to shut his mouth. Past thoughts whirl in my head. God pulls me aside and says that it's OK, I can do this. My thinking is going wild. With past indiscretions on trial here, the enemy hissed that the blood cannot cover me because my family has traded their seed with him. The enemy is spewing, writhing and whipping his dragon-like tail with spurs, up and down the courtroom aisle. I shift my eyes away from his repugnance and look at Jesus, sinking into His eyes of love, eyes of compassion and passion. The room evaporates from my attention, and I melt into Him. King David stands up from his seat and opens a secret access in front of his "window box" approaching the bench. Smiling at me as he walks past, he lays down his robe over the empty chairs along the aisle. David takes off his crown and hands it to me as he approaches God, and I can hear him saying: "Kristen has been meeting with my elders and me in the Tabernacle in the Woods for some time. I gave her my heart because she sought to have a heart like mine to please God. I witness that she knows the Lord and has been "known" by Him. This proceeding is unjustified and is a total lie. I bear witness to her profession, confession and repentance." If you could imagine a score of music compiled and played in the air, the witness words sang from the maidens, their voices lifting as instruments releasing a sound. Their witnessing sings about Proverbs 31, a psalm according to God's heart, the story of an excellent wife, her home, family, husband. Both heaven and earth are filled with my tears. I can see people/cloud of witnesses starting to enter the courtroom balcony and sit there. They have confetti in their hands that looked like strips of different colored paper, and they begin to throw them down into the courtroom. Paul picks up the "dream paper," crumples it and throws it on the floor. Jesus gets out of His seat and is now wearing David's robe. He is bending down on one knee receiving the worship from the cloud of witnesses. In my head is an outpouring of flash scenarios, like video thoughts on David's crown which is still in my hands. What should I do with it? Unsure but sure, I run my thoughts over again and again as it calls for its rightful owner. I excuse myself from the bench and step out into the front of the courtroom with the crown in my hand. I look at David nervously, could he sense the big question mark on my heart? He nods at me in unison, as we set his crown on the head of our Lord. In my spirit, we have just exchanged our crowns to Jesus. Jesus looks into my eyes further than deep has called, thanking us and receiving our worship. He rises to his feet and returns to His place of intercession. I sense that Father God enjoys watching this display in front of the enemy. Unseen hands present me with a paper/certificate that says "Renewed mind" with a gold seal. Paul finally sits down, looking at the document. He writes on it and passes it on, and, as it makes rounds to the witnesses, each one writes a word on it.

Paul writes: intellect and passes it.
Peter writes: boldness and passes it.
James writes: overcomer.
God says with humor: "I put my seal on it"!
Jesus writes: "My wife went ahead of time and consummated the marriage."
King David's handmaidens write:
Handmaiden Home = Beauty
Handmaiden Family = Innumerable
Handmaiden Husband = City Gates
King David = My heart

A scribe brings the document to Father God Who declares: "Now Satan, the Lord rebukes you!" and lightning bolts come out of His eyes melting the enemy into oblivion through the floor, gone! Father then declares: *"Kristen all these attributes we impart to you today. I give you the grace exchange."* Jesus is standing behind me and everyone is laying hands on me as Father speaks. Grace is tangible. *"From this day forward I am personally placing my favor on you. You have fought a very good fight. My grace will prove itself sufficient. Today, we pour Our blessing on you."* Jesus says: *"I bless you".*

With that, the cloud of witnesses also poured over us from above. *"I bless you, I bless you, and many will come from near and far to hear what I have placed in your heart."* Selah.

I have never encountered a traumatic dream since.

In heaven's living atmosphere, you plant "encounters" to eat the fruit of them. I often do it when the means are available to do this in both heaven and earth. A dear friend just "happened" to give me two sizeable Victorian cement urns for my garden. I planted dwarf blueberry plants inside them and placed the pots as a gateway from the backyard to side yard. They have bloomed and bear in my garden to this day.

Fifty-eight thousand seven hundred and seventy-seven.

A CROWN OF COMPLETIONS

One gets caught up in the fascination of how we learn via the Kingdom of Heaven. Sometimes I am participating in the "scene" other times I am watching the encounter. Different perspectives in receiving understandings. Wearing your crown, learning who you are in your Royal headwear, transforms you to look like the one He purposed for your crown.

The epitome of being taught by Rabbi:
You walk with "I Am" building relationship.
You follow "I Am" in an apprenticeship to His work.
"I Am" hands some of His work to you and watches you do it.
"I Am" sends you forth with His blessing to replicate the pattern. The pattern?

I am in various places of relationship with Him: confident in one area and just following in another. In the Watchmaker's room, I'm continuing to learn how I encounter His work, with my name on it. I return there again and again, a continuing confidence builder in how He sees me and how I see myself. My suggestion is that we are all a portion of His crown:

Deep calling to Deep.

Back to the mysteries of the Watchmaker's room.

CROWN OF COMPLETION: I am discovering more about myself in a place with eternity written within. "There is more" is a rudder, guiding me to continue to explore the insights and now the built-in cabinet of drawers on one of the walls. His presence washes over me, tangible and confirming. I am a student watching the mystery unfold. Jesus chooses to open a small drawer in the upper left-hand of the cabinet.

In the spirit, being tall enough to "see" up and inside is not an issue, though you might appear a grammar school student in a measure: There is no limitation of height, depth, etc.

Spiritual seeing is a lens of the heart. Jesus enjoys watching me as I discover.

The drawer is filled with small scrolls, similar to a page of sheet music rolled up, individually tied with ribbon, each containing a melody releasing a sound. Our focus changes and I hear Father saying: "Come over here. I want to show you something." In departing with Abba, my spiritual eyes separate and I'm able to discern more than one place at a time. A lens remained in sight of the scrolls Jesus has revealed, yet my spiritual body travels using a hidden portal, through galaxies into a cube-shaped realm. I have experienced this matrix "code" before, learning that God was speaking about a womb (see the notes page for links). The DNA in this realm appears, in the spirit, similar to the green matrix rain. Each divinely encoded droplet connects to the next. He painted this picture in my mind/spirit so my soul could stand in it, but my understanding is without "understanding." At the moment I still have two "sightedness."

RECAP:
1. Jesus has opened up for me the scrolls nestled in the drawer of the Watchmaker's room,
2. I'm also standing with God in divine code.
    Now God is going to be brilliant "again" to give His daughter a clue. Just when you think you're spiritual "toast" (nothing left to crisp,) your eyes are expanded to four perspectives. *My/Our experiential understanding is a "library". He indexes that library of memory to bring home the "Crown" lesson.*

4. The fourth view is an answer to an ongoing discussion and an outstanding question. What was my question? What is the difference between results and reward? Let's paint that "window," highlighting each of the four panes, revealing His voice and how He opens the windows of heavenly understanding using a practical hands-on application.

This is what I can perceive, in each pane of glass:

#1 Jesus opens the drawer of scrolls (Watchmaker's Room)
#2 standing in divine code realm (with Father in DNA rain)
#4 answering my question: "What is the difference between results and rewards?"

Kristen, you missed # 3! Totally for grammatical suspense!

Imagine with me the encounter; or you can "step in" if you desire, into the descending divine code. Heaven is very much alive. If you're unsure, ask Jesus to hold your hand.

#3: Popping into view as if an extra flat screen TV appears on your wall, the movie scene opens to tender feelings of a favored "overcomer" baseball movie: The Natural. The climactic scene: Injured Roy Hobbs (late in life rookie, years of undiscovered dreams and distractions) and villain characters "betting" against him that he would not be able to support his team playing in the pennant. The entire stadium is filled with anxious anticipation. Roy is up at bat, breath-holding full pitch count; he swings, bat marries perfectly to a home run ball, crack, rising and on its way out of the park, the ball smashes a stadium light. Crash, popping, voltaic lightning bursting over the crowd's head, dropping electrical raindrops as he humbly runs the bases home. Hobbs jumped on home plate and dances with teammates in victory within showers of light beads. That was God's answer to my question; the difference between result and reward?

RESULT: is a consistently high batting average derived from hitting the baseball after years of continual practice, in and out of season.

REWARD: is marking a moment in time when what you believe your destiny is about, is confirmed.

That is how the Godhead told me about those small tied up scrolls. They are records of completion. My spirit and emotions heard that, COMPLETIONS. Your DNA in Him is a record of confirming rewards. Your crown is a record of: "I know the plans I have for you says the Lord". And then some. Then I will come and do for you all the good things I have promised, and I will bring you home again. For I know the plans I have for you, says the Lord. "They are plans for good and not for disaster, to give you a future and a hope. In those days when you pray, I will listen. If you look for me wholeheartedly, you will find me. I will be found by you, says the Lord. I will end your captivity and restore your fortunes. I will gather you out of the nations where I sent you and will bring you home again to your own land".

(Jeremiah 29:11)

Heaven holds a record of our completions and we can encounter them ahead of time. **CROWN OF COMPLETIONS.**

How would you put that into a motivational collage?

A CROWN OF ACCESS

From the Watchmaker's room, I walked out into a hallway and curiosity compelled me to have a look around. The Galleria appeared vacant except for Jesus. The vast number of rooms - I can only imagine similar to mine, unique to each our own, were sadly un-experienced. In Him, we live, move, and have our being. In Him, simply in Him: The womb of God (Acts 17:28). In the middle of the Galleria was a large staircase ascending and descending, the Spirit of God leading. What I could feel in my spirit, I was to go outside into the midst of a great city. I could see the city outside the glass revolving doors. I ventured towards the doors, and a snippet flashed in my spirit. I went through. I saw my crown and somebody, who reminds me of a "Jeeves" character dressed in coat tails, a butler type persona. In the encounter, I am trying to determine if I am in the scene or watching, but I can sense dual spiritual places. We arrive, riding in a luxury black old European car, not a taxi. We pull aside and are let out in front of a large "state" building with a large set of internal portico stairs. The building has a high tower. This Jeeves person is carrying my crown on a satin pillow and enters the building. I follow, elegantly dressed in a beaded, long, formal, white sweetheart bodice gown. I have long white gloves and a white fur wrap covering my shoulders. The great hall has large columns at the entrance; we are ascending. I enter the doorway, give an attendant my purse and keys. On the right, I can see a great staircase and further on, a meeting room full of light. It feels like I give the attendant a ticket to enter this great theatre filled with seats and full of people. Again I show the attendant my ticket and he takes me down front, to the left-hand side. A spiritual spiral staircase (DNA) suddenly appears right next to the left end of the platform. We, myself and the Spirit of God, ascend the staircase to reach the box seats nearest the platform. *I notice we are inside a "bubble shield" unseen. This "spiritual vehicle" gives me a sense of familiarity. I have encountered it beforehand with the Father; just outside of the house with Kathrine Kuhlman and Amy Simple McPherson. It reminds me of a scene from the movie the Wizard of Oz when Glenda, the Good Witch, comes in. A bubble vehicle: Funny how movies give us a sense of understanding.*

NOTE: *for an understanding of bubble shield/spiritual vehicle, see Patricks Sheild, meditate on scripture Wheel in a wheel.*

End of the encounter.

TESTIMONY: with more to the story. During our Wednesday evening gathering, each member of our Ekklesia sensed, during ascension activation, that God was setting something before them, a gift. We positioned ourselves to receive, share and learn from each other in an atmosphere of communion. At times God can give you the strangest things. We haven't a clue about His purpose. I enjoyed hearing from everyone else and shared what the Lord had shown me: A British phone booth. Yup, a red phone booth. The group enjoyed the chuckle. We meditated on each gift given and spoke into it from a prophetic window, filling the room with humor and encouragement. Everyone felt that the "red phone booth" suggested that God was giving an "international" connection. Funny how they also have "crowns" on their phone booths. Everything was coming up as "crowns" in my life: A "royal" line. One of our leaders shared that superheroes made great use of phone booths. It was a good time shared by all. The following Tuesday I have a Skype call with a dear friend who is French and lives in England. I had not yet had the pleasure to travel to Europe at that time, at least not with my body. Did I make you laugh? My friend and I were catching up on family news, heavenly engagements and such. I shared my crazy gift with her, talking about the red phone booth, which made us both laugh. She proceeded to update my information about those "red phone booths" which have gone through significant transformation. Many have been retired from our technological phone age. Still iconically recognized, some are now being used as ATMs. Hoot, hoot! This gift is getting better and better. Who doesn't want God to give them an Automatic Teller Machine? I would have never known about phone booth updates without my European friend. A living revelation that kept informing my understanding, amen. I began to share with her the same Crown/Jeeves encounter I just bestowed upon you, retelling the details and sequences as she grinned at me, till I finally said: "what?" She declared: "Kristen, do you know what you just described? Apparently, I didn't"! "You just described the opening of British Parliament, almost to the T!" Now, who is getting overwhelmed? She sent me a collection of YouTube videos and sure enough, I had been there and followed the crown. A holy eeriness set in my spirit, with tears not far behind. Not the first time I have been, clueless in transrelocation. In my spirit, I still sensed a twin purpose here.

BRILLIANT RABBIT TRAIL: *Have you figured out that this book is alive?* I have been struggling with the editing and proofing process because things have come to pass or changed. I suggest it is much like the Watchmaker who orchestrates our crown. Within our relationship of being in Him, we are also with Him, in eternity. One of my last statements through this chapter was the insight that I sensed a "twin" purpose to the encounter: **"CROWN OF COMPLETIONS"**. Remember the drawers that Jesus showed containing scrolls of completion? My spiritual head was followed by the souls of my feet, not 5 months later, to England.

I thought **ENGLAND; NOTES FROM HEAVEN** could wait. Her Sequel and Prequel must voice a testimony sown in the pages of The UnFinished Book. God opened the door and provided completely for the trip to England. Yes, I knew that I was going, and would love to share an afternoon telling you all the delicious ways He taught me how to believe in Him for more. He wants us so to understand the concert between the unseen and the seen, and I've just begun my study of His glories. During my trip, I found myself, on a Thursday afternoon in London, with the same dear friend who recognized the uniqueness of my Parliament encounter. With so many vibrant things to see in London and only eight hours to see them, streamlined choices needed to be made. For me, that was Parliament at Westminster. We purchased one of those "Hop on Hop off" tour buses, including a river ride under London Bridge, dropping us off at the corner of Big Ben. The afternoon was drawing to a close, now a little after 4:00pm. We crossed the street, greeted Winston Churchill's statue, and proceeded to follow the gated pavilion. I notice a handful of London police personnel standing at the end of zig-zag security barriers and I had to ask if there was any way we could visit? Sadly, Westminster is only open for tours on Saturday's. The female officer must have noticed my desperate intent. She had no idea about my mystical history or Who was making the invitation for me. She looked me square in the face and said: "Are you interested in politics?" A wee bit distracted, I didn't address her question, ramblings dribbled out of my mouth. She got in my face and said: "You weren't listening. Are you interested in politics!" Spiritual slap in the face, I answered "Yes" firmly. She hands me the first of many check-ins and tickets, just like my encounter and we were in like Flynn, directed through security lines. We round a checkpoint and my dear friend started manifesting (Shaking from the power of His might), her eyes popping out in concern as we eyed the upcoming security guards carrying automatic weapons. Not a good time to be looking a bit weird, I'd say! I've been at that end of His electric glory many times before. Can't take credit for it, but brilliance just popped out of my mouth, saying to my friend: "Tell your body it can stand in the glory!" She looked at me concerned yet shaking like a leaf. I said: "Tell your body it can stand in the glory!" That is what she did! She commanded her body to stand in the glory. Immediately the quaking subsided, just in "time". With questions rolling in our brains, I quickly understood what was going on. It's a matter of quantum physics. DNA from the unseen was manifesting into the seen. My spirit had touched ground in this very place; myself unseen, identical stretches of double-stranded "helix" DNA (remember the silo/spherical things I had spoken about?). DNA, if separated, seeks each other out. Through transrelocation, I had stood in parliament and that DNA or my friend's shaking could be explained by words called electrostatic attractions. Do I understand all that quantum physics talk? Well, I'm learning, divinely! I think this is a great time to illuminate scripture, Jesus speaking: "Again, I tell you truly that if two of you on the earth agree about anything you ask for, it will be done for you by My Father in heaven. For where two or three gather together in My name, there am I with them." (Matthew 18: 19 & 20). I call that electrostatic attraction! Heaven manifesting on earth. We made it through security. Hey, are you chuckling at all through this? God has a sense of humor, doesn't He! We step into the massive entry (Westminster Hall) and "Ping!", catching my prophetic attention, the lobby sign said *"Unlocking Parliament"*! I shared this signpost picture on the website. The sign graphics were that of a big gold key aimed at opening Westminster, Haha! We walked through Westminster Hall, one of the oldest remaining parts of the building not ruined by the 1834 fire. Imagine stepping inside of Noah's ark: High beams curved like a sailing vessel, protruding angelic figureheads crowned each timber end. Because Parliament was in session, we didn't loiter at famous paintings or statues of statesmen. Greatness was echoing the hallways, and I found myself trying to absorb her sound. Photo op: up a flight of stairs, through back corridors, check backpack, cell phone, and coat. The Queen's Attendant ushered us to choose our seats in the upper gallery. Ornate wood carvings littered the room, with seats trimmed in green. A small number of MP's (Members of Parliament: elected members of the House of Representatives called House of Commons in England) were firmly debating their opinion during the waning hours of the business day. The issue at hand was compassionate/humane care of livestock regarding healthy and organic food. I pondered: This picture was missing something! Excusing myself, I quietly made my way back to the top of the balcony to ask the overseeing attendant a question: "Excuse me sir, where is the throne?" He responded with a smile: "Oh you mean the House of Lords, I'll take you there when you are finished viewing the House of Commons". My heart was shaking as we were escorted to the other side. There it was, just as I had encountered, the throne, with an audience of red trimmed pew seats lining the view. Here I am, Kristen Wambach in London England, inside Westminster, and seated in the balcony of the House of Lords, a place I thought only existed in the spirit, witnessing the proof with my own eyes that God had not only shown me in secret, but created a passport in which I traveled by more than one means. The thought explodes and boggles the religious mind. My friend asked me: "What do you see?" I said I do not need to "See" anything. Here I am, God's daughter, witnessing from the seats in the House of Lords, where members are appointed by the Queen on the advice of the Prime minister.

Father God was singing a song from "The yes I said in my heart." The yes to believe in the spirit, and the yes which brought my feet to stand in His will.

If not for this book it would be a private moment, a relationship signature between Father and daughter. The courageous responsibilities accepted to transform through the change that left behind the visions of man.

I accepted the mantles of heaven, believing in Him and what He said about me and who I am, who we all should be: Through the veil, aware, outworking and legislating from our Royal authority, wearing "A Crown of Completions".

A destiny scroll is incomplete without your crown received.

Eternity is futile without thanksgiving to the One who deserves my offering of a well-worn-crown cast before Him.

Where will yours take you?

Chapter 14

Tools of Responsibility

I am passionate about wearing a crown of relationship,
responsibility runs through my veins.
If there is a mess to clean up, sign me up for the clean-up crew.
Then find me first in line to cast my crown! - K Wambach

I am passionate about heaven. Why? Before God rested "They" - together in the work of His hands - made all things with redemption in mind. Love eternally expanded. Perfect love casts out all residue of fear. He loves His children so much that He created an absolute, sure way back to Himself. No weakness, ignorance, hate, or fear could run or ruin His Fatherly plan. Free will stands eternally: Not in time or outside of it. Our doctrines of understanding have strangled the Good News from a limited perspective. That is why He is God!

The author of all-consuming fire: He is love.

Heaven (seated in heavenly places) is where we appropriate this gracious gift with Him into a "working" redemptive plan. Jesus gave Himself in the flesh, agreeing to the mandate of His ministry "before the foundation of the world". As maturing "sons" we hold the keys to the Kingdom. They are given into my hands, your hands, as tool-belt full of

"TOOLS OF RESPONSIBILITY" for the things pertaining to life and godliness. *(2 Peter 1:3)*

I am passionate to wear a crown of relationship, responsibility runs through my veins. If there is a mess to clean up, sign me up for the clean-up crew. Then find me first in line to cast my crown!

I think activations are fabulous. They're not a one size fits all solution. It's a living testimony, living "How I did this!" Something you may harvest and place into the basket of tools the Lord has already given you. This collection of activations share the hands-on testimony of prophetic words, and how I "challenged" them to see if they were "seeded/seated" in the heavenly realms. If so, does the enemy have any right to hinder them? What is the will of the Father in the matter? How can I partner with them and experientially release heaven?

179

My first testimony: Blog post-www.inbetweenitall.com

Outworking heaven and the Chicago Cubs. Also, *(my statement months after the World Series win)*

#GoCubs maybe once again, we can shake hands in greatness.

(this post penned during the world series playoffs).

Here is the Blog Post. We have entered a new era as the church, leaving the Apostolic Age and stepping into the Joshua Generation and the Order of Melchizedek. There are a few different reference "titles" out there.

God has been orchestrating our understanding to position us to live on the other side of the veil, outworking heaven and releasing it on earth. I have a couple of questions to ask you, that I will partner with some suggested thoughts and some hands-on happenings.

1. What is the origin of a prophetic word?
2. Is there a responsibility for the recipient to bring it to pass?
3. An activation is found later in the text.

I recently heard a prophetic word that someone shared via social media and how God confirmed the word through a friend's dream. They offered the interpretation which involved a bent on a particular national past time. The "bent" would be a divine sign that God was bringing a breakthrough to a specific group and answering an obvious concern. I am not in disagreement with their desired response to prayer. No, I am not talking about the current political race though some of my thoughts could benefit many in that venue. This prophetic word I read gagged and stuck in my craw for about 36 hours after reading it. The interpretation and confirmation swayed the outcome of a significant event. This prominent team that many people have held in their hearts for generations. Its "bent" and influence was opposite from my desire. I found myself asking some questions.

What do I think about that?
Am I going to do anything about it?
Is it my place to do anything about it?
Are my desires necessarily self-centered or rightly divided?
Do I think they heard from God?
Why is this irritating me so much?

I gave up the struggle this morning during my quiet time with the Lord. "Lord, you obviously want me to respond here." In the language of the season, I call this a mandate.

At a later time.

It has been a few months since the whirl of the World Series. Yes, I am a Cubs fan. So I thought it was time to pick up this word again and share just what I experienced from my neck of the woods. I believe there are lessons to learn here and much to ponder.

The original prophetic word I saw was posted on Facebook in due "season" with a string of comments, interpretations, and agreements from friends. Yup, all the prophetic bells and whistles. There was the declaration that the Cubs were not going to win. That it was God's will at hand and it was a (sign) that breakthrough would occur regarding another national concern. I did struggle with this for a couple of days. It is just a sporting event. I have nothing to gain or lose by the outcome. Would I be overstepping my bounds in heaven, manipulating the outcome? All good questions. It would greatly bless my husband and his family who are Chicagoans. What to do? If I remember right, it festered inside of me through another series game, one the Cubs had lost before I brought it into my "prayer" closet. Father, I'm not OK with the Cubs not winning! So I stepped into heaven, beyond the veil and sat at my table of communion with the Godhead. Jesus looked at me and then asked a question (He is always asking questions): "Is this prophetic word "seated" in heaven?" I responded by saying I did not know. Jesus then asked another great question: "What do you suppose is written on each of the teams' scrolls?" Well, I thought, You are a good God and believe the best and desire the best for all that are called according to your purpose. I think that winning the World Series is written on both their scrolls. Jesus said "You are right: that is my heart on the matter". So I asked what should I do next? "Now that you know 'My Will' confirming it is 'seated' or has an agreement with My will, go and see if any accusations exist that would hinder the outcome." I responded "I can do that Lord!" If you know anything at all about baseball, you would be aware that the Chicago Cubs had a few hindrances, even in the natural realm that stuck out like a sore toe. They have not won a World Series in 108 years. And yes Lord, I have learned how to take care of curses and all that stuff. So I did a little research that morning on what I could find in the natural, yes the crazy goat thing too. You'd be amazed at the insane things people have done to break off that goofy thing. So I had to repent of all the witchcraft, manipulation, and the list went on. I think you get my drift here. Because I carried the welfare of the team in my heart, the blessing that it would be to my husband, the blessing it would be to the City of Chicago. I had found the heart-valve that gave me the authority to bring it to His throne: A confirmed mandate discussed with the Godhead.

PROTOCOL AND ACTIVATIONS:
I followed protocol like this upon stepping into heaven:
First, offering myself as a living sacrifice.
Then make sure my personal issues get cleaned up first.
Asked Father if I genuinely have the mandate to legislate on this.
Went to the court of accusation with my list of "grievances" in hand.
Honored the court.
Asked Father to call forth into the courtroom every enemy (bound & gagged) who holds legal documents against the Chicago Cubs baseball team.
I agreed with every accusation presented and "repented" as guilty.
Asked for a judgment against the enemies.
Asked for justice to be served and received a document.
Thanked Jesus for His blood, applied His blood and broke the agreement with everything which now is covered with the blood.
Took the document to be recorded. (Court of Scribes)
Asked for Angelic assignment. (Court of Angels)
Released the angels.
Decreed it from my mountain. (Personal Authority)

And you guessed it, they won. By the hair of their "chinny chin chins." My husband doesn't even know that the Lord and I had something to say about this. Again, I had nothing to gain by their win, but I was very encouraged! I'm also sure I was not the only one praying for the Chicago Cubs. What I learned in this instance was always to ask God. Go look into heaven's perspective on things: Is it "seated."

We should do the same for things of much higher importance like our prophetic words, concerns regarding our families and communities. It is God's goodness apparently written about each of us (Heaven only withholds secrets from misdirected hearts). Then grace kicks in. Ask the question, are there any accusations or enemies that need putting in their place. Remember, it is His good pleasure to give you the keys to the Kingdom. Those keys are for heavenly doors. He loves being a righteous

Judge on behalf of His kids. God always judges to life.

So I'll restate my questions:

1. What is the origin of a prophetic word? I learned the source not only of the Chicago Cubs but the Indians as well. Winning the Worlds Series is seated in heavenly places with Father's agreement.

2. Is there a responsibility for the recipient to bring it to pass? Yes, Zechariah 3 says: This is what the LORD Almighty says: 'If you will walk in obedience to me and keep my requirements, then you will govern my house and have charge of my courts, and I will give you a place among these standing here." What an Honor it is to have charge and take charge in His courts.

We call it priesthood. There you have it. I hope you learned something because I know I did. Ever-transforming into His likeness. So you Indians fans have hope and ask the Lord regarding your team.

And in this case today, the rest of the world may never know that in Corvallis Oregon, a baseball Mom helped to change history. *Go Cubs!*

3. ACTIVATION: "SEEDED" OR "SEATED"? OK, let me explain. In short, Jesus has given us the keys to the Kingdom, right! That is a process.

Keys are received through ongoing relationship, maturity, authority knitted in responsibility; encountering and outworking your destiny scroll. However, you may not need the key until you need to open the door. Jesus at times will hold the keys, teach you the pathway, and then, at a later date, give you access to the room/realm/path available. Practice on the path matures you until the realm/room/door remains open for you.

Let's look at the view of "hindsight." I use the word seeded much like when I was playing competitive tennis or pickleball. When you accept an invitation to play in a tournament, Tournament Officials add you to a playing field or category [bracket] that is comparable to the wins of the opponents you have successfully faced. If you are a novice, you are not "SEEDED." However (boasting) in my competitive days, I have been assigned as a wild-card and shook up many a playing field.

SEATED: is the position of authority given and recognized from heaven. You are sitting on a throne that has been accepted by heaven. That has nothing to do with church leadership, prophetic "Office" or associations. It is your maturity recognized by heaven and its enemies. See scripture: Acts 19:15. 1 Cor. 11:10.

1. *Is a prophetic word a viable scroll from heaven? If so then it has been agreed on, sealed, recorded, given to angelic assignment, and released.*
2. *Does it come under the authority, scroll and calling assigned to you, for you to receive/engage it?*

With that authority given to you, you can represent it in the courts of heaven

(See Robert Henderson "Operating in the Courts of Heaven" on YouTube, an excellent resource).

In your representation, it may just be "personal" about your mountains and spheres of influence. Or, as it has happened to me countless times through forgiveness/condition of my heart, which has positioned me to represent others' (Priesthood) mountains, dominions, seats with a higher authority open during the legislation; I will remove any hindrances or enemy's legal right which will block it.

TESTIMONY #2: THERE IS GREAT BREAKTHROUGH UPON THE WRITERS

with permission from Lana Vawser.

Posted on Facebook April 1st, 2017 and shared with me through a dear friend April 2nd, 2017.

"There is breakthrough upon the writers right now. Those of you who are writing manuscripts, the Lord is releasing winds of acceleration upon you, and these manuscripts are going to be birthed faster than you could ever have imagined. I had a vision, and I watched as the Lord released theses winds of acceleration and His angelic hosts to minister to you, and cause these manuscripts to come forth faster than you could imagine. Anything that has been attempting to block this manuscript, any warfare, is falling by the wayside as the winds of acceleration fall upon you and the Lord continues to breathe upon His message in your manuscript. There is a greater ease that you will find as the anointing upon you to write is significantly increasing. There is a breakthrough anointing over you as you write to move past the hindrances and move into the final stage of birthing.

The Lord showed me the Destiny Room of heaven again.

Yesterday, I released a word on the Destiny Room of heaven. As I pondered this word for the writers, the Lord showed me the Destiny Room in heaven again. He showed me the encounters that are going to open up for the writers as He opens up and reveals the Destiny Room and for some in new ways. In a vision, I saw the Lord taking many into the Destiny Room through visions, visitations and prophetic dreams and as He led them in, I saw big screens all around the walls of the room. As the writers went in one by one, He pressed play on a remote and "trailer" began to play. It was a trailer for their manuscript, but the trailer was not how THEY saw their book, it was how HE saw their book. It showed His excitement, His vision that was so beautifully crafted and displayed within these manuscripts. It also showed what HE was going to do THROUGH the manuscripts.

I watched as the writers wept and wept, being shown a "glimpse" of His heart contained in their manuscript and the people that were going to be saved, healed, set free, delivered, encouraged and brought to life through their writings. I watched as the writers fell at His feet weeping and out of their mouth came words "I praise you, Jesus! It's SO MUCH BIGGER than I ever dreamed."

The Lord bent down and grabbed their hands and with tear filled eyes, full of joy, full of love, His face beaming with such delight and His eyes shouting how proud He was of them, He spoke; "Thank you for pressing through, Thank you for continuing to steward the message that I have given you and lean into Me to write all I asked you to. Through the fire, through the storm, through the darkness, you did not give up. You continued to remain faithful to the assignment I gave you in writing. I am breathing My spirit upon this manuscript, and many shall come to life. Come to know Me, be set free, healed and delivered by My love and My Spirit. I am going to do MORE through this manuscript than you could ever imagine. Great joy shall fill your heart as you see what I am about to do. You will see the process has been all worth it."

I then saw manuscripts laid out on tables in this Room of Destiny. They were perfectly placed in frames, and I noticed the words written all along the frames. The words were purity, humility, surrender, integrity. As I looked at them, instantly the atmosphere was filled with the sense that these books were framed by the purity, humility surrender and integrity of the writers. These manuscripts were written by writers who have kept the "main thing, the main thing." They have stayed true to the message He gave them, and their eyes have been upon Him, and they surrendered deeply and believed on Him, worshiping him all the way through the process.

I watched as Jesus walked along these tables and He had a scepter in His hand. He placed the tip of the scepter upon each manuscript I saw. A quick glimpse of networks, doors, and connections of favor that the Lord had drawn up with His hand.

He turned to each of the writers, and He spoke "Be at rest, be at peace with this manuscript. I have already decreed the exact strategic places, networks, doors that need to be opened and hands these manuscripts need to fall into. I have taken care of it all. Rest, trust Me. I am going to get My messages out far and wide. Great unprecedented radical favor is being decreed over these manuscripts. Don't try and strive and make anything happen. What I am going to do with these manuscripts will leave you in awe of what I can do!"

"The process of these assignments I have given to you with these manuscripts has increased your anointing to write. You will see an increase in revelation, clarity, and insight upon you to hear Me and for further writing assignments. You have transitioned to a whole new level. Multiple births are upon many of you, and the supernatural ease and anointing I am releasing will see you write even more books than you imagined. It may not make sense in the natural, and for many, it will look impossible, but through the empowerment of My Spirit, you will do what you thought you could not do. Not by might, nor by power, but by My Spirit will be your testimony!

"Writers, this is your time!"

Sixty-one thousand, eight hundred and seventy-six.

Mirroring my intro into this chapter: If heaven released something on earth, someone has appropriated it in the heavens. That is the job of "sons." Refresh the thought and ask yourself the question, where does a prophetic word originate?

This is my personal path intersecting with the prophetic word; there is a "Great Breakthrough Upon Writers."

Oct. 8th, 2016 was the first time I encountered "Council Room of Windows" or "The Destiny Room" where I first saw The Unfinished Book.

I am working-out/out-working my part in bringing my book to fruition from a "seated" position. Seated= the authority God placed in my Destiny Scroll, and according to the maturity I have grown up into for this season.

April 5, 2017. To my dear friends who walk a God-kind-of-life with me. You are a gift. You have helped to steward my destiny, many times releasing more faith and belief in me than (at times) my wavering mindset believed regarding Him in me.

I dedicate this testimony to my friend John.

MY ACTIVATIONS:

I organized the promises declared in the Writers word before God, knowing there is a recorded scroll in heaven.

Winds of Acceleration
The angels assigned to this mandate, I release a sound, I declare my name written on your scroll.
I issue every promise, supply, and anointing spoken of via this prophetic word:
Greater Ease
Acceleration
Breath of His message in my writing
Anointing for a significant increase
Breakthrough anointing to move past hindrances, to make progress into the final stage of birthing.
Destiny Room:
Assigned encounters are opening up, new ways, taking me into,
God pressed play on the remote, "trailer" given, seeing my book.
See how God saw my book.
Experience how God feels excited, everything is crafted beautifully, showing pathways and plans for this manuscript.
See things contained in Father's heart, in my book, I engage with people touched via the book, saved, healed, set free, delivered, encouraged, brought to life through my writings.
I release response of Praise, more than I could imagine or dream

The Lord's hands,

Tears of joy, love and beaming delight, declaring how proud He is of me. I can hear Him saying thank you for pressing in, for stewardship, leaning into Him and writing about it. Through fire, storm, darkness, faithful breath of His Spirit, more assignments, joy filling my heart, the satisfaction I receive, you declare that it was all worth it.

The manuscripts you have placed on the table:

Put in frames, purity, humility, surrender, integrity is the framework.
The Lord put His scepter's tip upon my manuscript,
and it comes to life with favor: "Networks, doors, and connections".
I'm at rest, peace; my book will fall into divinely connected hands.
Great unprecedented, radical favor, decreed.
Increased revelation,
clarity, and insight for me to hear further writing assignments.
Transition up, multiple berthings.
Supernatural ease and anointing to write more books, more than imagined,
empowerment of my Spirit.
This is "my" time.
Blockage and warfare are removed, it looks like Justice,
Appropriating its divine authority and the courts of heaven,

I carried all these promises before His throne; my spirit shifted, transported into the mandates room, the room with all the "peacock" like eyes.

References: "See sketch drawing and a painting I painted after the first time I had encountered the Mandate room." Its living walls are papered with eyes.

Back to outworking the scroll: I call enemies against this scroll into this courtroom, bound gagged. I declare if they are not represented they relinquish their right to hinder the writers attached to this mandate or me. Period. All evidence will fall away and not stand.

I begin to hear accusations:

Fear, doubt, and unbelief, accusations, blame.

I paused for a moment, thinking and reminding myself that the enemy can't come to this higher courtroom. I became aware that I was "seeing" in dual realms, both the Mandate Room and the court of accusations. Cool! I continued listening from the court of accusations and standing in the Mandate Room.

I heard:

False keys, Pride, Arguments, Unforgivingness, Broken promises, Bitterness, Resolve, Religion, Negative trading floors, Curses, Victim spirit, Blood crying out, Shame and guilt, Inferiority, Nakedness, Illiteracy, Illegitimacy, False witness, Manipulation, Vengeance, Coercion, Control, Witchcraft, Apathy, Laziness, Out of bounds, Prioritizing, Distraction, Dyslexia, Morale, Crippling, Weak, Torment, Torture, Disagreement, Contention, Pain, Sacrilege, Misuse of what is regarded as sacred, Iniquity I have given place too, Wrong foundation or construction, Me; standing in God's way.

After hearing each accusation I repented, tears washing my face, anger welling up towards the enemy stealing and binding, God's goodness and presence washing over me as His hand rests on my shoulder. I saw myself taking this mandate and putting it inside my spirit. I asked Father: Judge me as I am standing under the council of "The Word." Jesus' spirit intercedes, and fire devours the accusations. Thanksgiving floods as freedom marinate inside me. I declare: Father, judge my enemies. The Lord sharpened my sight, revealing the list of names written on this word/mandate. *(A secret revealed to right hearts, releases the communion in which He prepared and served).*

For my benefit I saw, my name scribed at the top. I felt His confidence as I sought and outworked, on behalf of His purpose. Selah!

My spirit shifts and the Lord extends my eyes to "a familiar view as if from Google earth satellite" looking from the galaxies. I witness the "Writers mandate" in three places:

1. Its origination: authorized from the Mandates Room
2. Redeemed by the Lord's mediation and sacrifice in the Court of Accusations, both lenses of the mandate appeared to birth, "combine and marry," on a heavenly path, fused together in a dance of light, released on the earth.

Next, I step into the Angelic court with the mandate in hand, while passing out multiplying "copies" of personal angelic assignments to deliver and support writers.

3. Released on earth; heard and seen, declared through His prophetic vessel.

I have continued, multiple times, to encounter "The Unfinished Book," in heavenly places. God is not short on encouragement, nor lacking to get me or anyone of us off our duff and walking into your destiny.

These words you are reading, prepared for "such a Time as this."

We have learned so much together. We have so much more to learn.

Indeed a Destiny Room exists along with so many others; we are destined to unfold glories in its birthing. Any key accesses something? Use the tools you have been given: Ask their purpose and learn how to apply them. All tools support an operation. Legislation is our inheritance as the redeemed. Right standing before a Holy God is empowering.

Kicking butt: Well it's about time!

CHAPTER 15

The End of the Book

"Then all at once, there was a flutterment and a
scufflement and a loud "Squeak!"
The other squirrels scattered away into the bushes.
When they came back very cautiously, peeping round the tree--
there was Old Brown sitting on his doorstep,
quite still, with his eyes closed, as if nothing had
happened. But Nutkin was in his waistcoat pocket!
This looks like the end of the story, but it isn't."
— Beatrix Potter, The Tale of Squirrel Nutkin

(Small manifestation of encouragement: at the moment I moved
to do the final proofread of this last chapter, a chickadee lands
and rings my brass bell from Korea)

I know many of you have found my story familiar. I'm not alone on this journey. If past circumstances have hindered you, receive healing from an unseen place: I extend it. Be healed and move forward with Him. Love is worth it all, even if the cost results in momentary pain, pain that brings maturity not allowances. Ask Father God to rekindle your spiritual eyesight: The burn of purpose, bravery as a forerunner, and boldness to spy out the Promised Land. Convincing others is never our goal. Compel them to come because you have seen, heard and experienced. You are a witness to a heavenly tribe, with and without walls, enormously growing on the other side of the veil. Remember when I posted that I had written the end of the book encounter, only twenty-two pages before the halfway mark? Who writes the finished line of the book before the end? He does. The ending is supposed to read along with the beginning. It keeps us on course, filled with His desire. Grace extended, you've been divinely chosen. We have walked this journey together, as I complete my long-over-due offering. A sense of trust resounds in the hearing of His voice this morning. Before I finish the last lap in this particular race of destiny, around the track of heaven, I want to thank you.

From halfway I marked: With less than seven thousand words to pen, the day after my fifty-eighth birthday, thank you.

"LET'S STEP INTO HEAVEN."

I was consciously caught in that lucid place this morning, March second, *two thousand and seventeen, with the knowledge of how many pages are in my book, two hundred and eighty-three.*

While showering before the house wakes. Don't you just love how easy revelation is experienced while taking a shower. Looking for humor, standing in the shower, we've concluded we are naked and not alone. But I don't tend to focus on that. I am in my birthday suit, amen. I'm okay with looking like a spirit being at this time. Thank you Lord for warm showers. Thank you Lord for running water and water heater tanks at our disposal. Thank you Lord for the infrastructure of our community that builds the framework for homes with hot showers. I give you praise.

Do you recall way back in the beginning, we talked about David's sword with a leather tie around the handle? It was part of the provisions I received for the year. I love the freshness I feel whenever God asks me to accept a bit bigger portion than just for my own needs, desires and understanding. New grace - never for only my own purposes, which melts my heart.

I love "practicing": Stepping beyond the veil. Sitting on my floor pillow here in the quiet of my own home, familiar with spiritual in's and out's, I've discovered hands-on tools that help me to learn and perceive. Tools I can prophetically act out and use: Practical "going through" applications for the "realms". OUR hearts travel. I went into the garage yesterday. We had used some para-cord to shore up our temporary roofing for our pergola. It was still laying on the bench aside everyday tools that never seemed to be put away. My spirit was searching for an idea: Find something that looks like an old leather shoelace. I did not get any suggestions from my angels that I had this on hand at the house. The para-cord popped into mind. It will serve my purpose well (Para-cord or 550 cord). Many uses: It's what ties the parachute to the parachuter. It makes sense that it would need to be very secure for jumping out of an airplane, released, catching the wind at a fast falling speed, withstanding the up snapping weight of skydivers and being reusable for many jumps.

In a high testosterone house, we always have it on hand, and it is a typical go-to gift when stuffing many a "boy" Christmas stocking. So I cut myself about eighteen inches and tied it around the handle of my quite heavy sword (looks like a real medieval sword, decorative of course) that my friend John gave me years ago, the same friend with whom I initially shared my story about seeing angels at the beach. His reaction brought a smile to my face. We bring that story up again and again. In our last (church) house, the sword hung on the front wall of our sanctuary while located at the Lester home. The scripture engraved on it: Take up the sword of the Spirit which is the word of God. When I initially saw the spiritual sword at the beginning of the year, I was encouraged by Melchizedek's comment: "No one else has asked for it." I boldly took it off the wall of the Treasury Room at the beginning of the year. I was unaware of the historic "battles" it had or would engage in the future. Yes, I knew it was for defending but against which foe? From whom will the battle wage from where I am sitting and writing today. I very much appreciate that this sword has more experience at taking out giants than I do. David's sword is a living supernatural being that - in my understanding - looks like a sword. Also rumbling around my heart of hearing is the assignment attached to it. Lord, where or how will I be using this sword? Where am I supposed to take it, to offer it? *We use God's mighty weapons, not worldly weapons, to knock down the strongholds of human reasoning and to destroy false arguments*

(2 Corinthians 10:4).

My spirit shifts, I've entered a place of familiar, humbled, tears flooding my eyes everytime I am invited to return. Emotions flowing because of the honor to represent and to stand in this place. Nope, I am not going to tell you what court or what council. You go and ask the Lord for yourself. I'm a daughter of the King just like you are, an heir: No hierarchy trading here. If I have received a key, then my name is written on a mandate. Believe me, "Great Grace" is the responsible party for my appearance here. His high confidence is worth more than any of us could muster, measuring all the carpet/prostrate/face-time prayer one would log.

So let's do this together. I'm inviting you. That is why we are here, on this journey, right? "Great Grace".

Handy that I have practiced journaling (proficient typist) enough to encounter and take notes while encounters are happening. Hours of practice journaling saves on logging time. A bit of Kleenex ministry was also going on here. Selah!

Always take a moment to soak, feel, perceive what the senses He gave you are telling you. Don't rush the reading or experience. Selah! Hold His hand and journey.

His hands prepared heaven's places of justice for both of us: Judgment and Justice are very humbling. He is an "AWESOME" GOD in a right way. Like, pinch me I am here. Holy Spirit I implore your help in wearing my crown as it feels like I've just won the Miss America pageant and the crown is slipping off my head in front of several thousand viewers. Agh!

Father, I bring this sword to your Throne and Council. It's not the first time it has been given or laid before You. I honor King David and all who have interceded and fought with it. I call forth the voice of the righteous blood that has been spilled with it. Wearing contacts and crying just create problems. Keep in mind please that I'm feeling similar to an overwhelmed "Miss America." OK! You and I have communicated so much on this journey. Sometimes our greatest teaching moments come in the "Hands-on" ministry of the Master, Jesus. So I will share what I am "feeling" and write what I sense He is orchestrating on our behalf. These words are divinely alive. Earlier, I shared living stories and the journey of stepping in and out of time to experience them. How you choose to respond and "step in" is a key only you and Jesus can unlock. Now faith is the substance of things hoped for and the evidence of things not yet seen. You have already been given and received "more than enough" measure of faith to watch and believe. Mustard seeds move mountains and all that might be trespassing on them.

Back to the council: I honor all who are seated and present here. I acknowledge the four corners of the earth, the four winds that are present, Holy Spirit I ask for your help, I submit myself as an Ambassador. Father, how shall I proceed?

I sense this protocol issue. Father, my spirit senses I am unable to step onto (the readers) own mountains (spiritual spheres of influence). *The readers' mountains represent your kingdom authority. Mountains, houses, spiritual dwelling places that embody who you are and where the Godhead resides in the Kingdom of Heaven within you.*

My question or thought? I also sense that David's sword is ordained to proceed and represent the reader on their mountain. Brilliant!

The UnFinished Book is just a page in the book/scroll of this sword's history. When I saw it hanging on the Treasury rooms wall - receiving it with Melchezidek's permissions - agreements had already been declared, recorded and filed in the libraries of heaven, where you or I have the pleasure to discover, receive, or find ourselves in partnership. Time is not present, Eternity is...

On behalf of David's sword: I recall and send forth the sound that has been released to and fro. I invite that sound to this proceeding. I honor that sound. I declare that this sound has moved the scales of justice and will move them again. I can hear Father's voice speaking to the sword: "Hold your peace". I call forth every authorized Ekklesia to be equipped with the appropriate eardrum to receive and listen to the sound of David's sword.

This is what I can see: The sword has been lifted from where I laid it before the Council, before Jehovah. Its vigorous transformation reminds me of the movement of the wheels-in-wheels; the handle moves in a cued response to its target, never turning its back. Light is dispersed in the heavens as if the sword were a writing instrument, framing the earth along latitude and longitude lines. The sword is marking like a pen of fire or light, releasing ink that burns the "latitude and longitude" boundaries and shores up new dominion. I see the sword tip from an axis of light, opposite from the "natural" axis of the earth. The Four Winds pick up the "framework of light" which looks like a drawing of the earth and place it on its axis of light. The four winds adjust it three times.

The four corners are set, like tent stakes to secure the structure: Pounding them into heaven, just beyond the gathering of set-apart-ones seated at this council, this heavenly place.

My focus shifts. A simple staircase appears and Jesus steps out, descending to this gathering. The sword and all spirit beings including myself hit the floor, prostrated. Curiosity lifts my cheek to peek, to watch Him walk down. I smile as I sneak a peek with arms and elbows crossed overhead, and I notice the Father is also smiling: *A daughter apprehended, a daughter allowed.* Jesus descends in a plain white robe and sandals, with hair loose at shoulder length. You would recognize Him as any child's heart would. I can see living beings, living faces as if they were hologram figures to the light that He radiates: Mirrors upon a mirror, transparent screens upon screens. But my eye, my intimate eye, is drawn to the approachable, comfortable Jesus. The Four Winds swirl around four "timpani-like-drums" on wheels or bowls. They appear to have been brought for Jesus to engage with on His path towards the center of our gathering. He kicks their side upwards, two and four, one and three, upending them, spilling out the prayers contained. The area seems to be "at ease" as I sit up and adjust. I entertain a goofy thought (in all this grandeur) about feeling like my crown had fallen off my head when we all fell down prostrate on the floor. I roll to my knees nonchalantly seeking its whereabouts, like a kid having dropped a "toy piece" on Christmas morning. Crawling on all fours, I can see through the "floor." My crown and many other crowns are falling from heaven to earth faster than the prayers Jesus spilled over. The crowns look like weighty stars falling, ahead of "the rain of descending/poured out bowls of prayers". Jesus comes and sits at the head of the council table. David's sword - if swords have feelings - seems to have an endearment or a history with Jesus. He observes the council and everything we have called forth and encountered. He is well pleased with the "sword," this 3D living scroll. With so many things to draw your focus and wonder, in the greatness of this moment, Jesus and I catch a glimpse of each-other. Like a family seated at the table passing a serving plate around, Jesus gives me a linen handkerchief with something rolled up inside.

LESSONS LEARNED: Spiritual places and sight are governed by relational honor. You can choose to behold everything or show some restraint to hold a surprise for a later date, and you decide not to look. I put the handkerchief in my pocket for the future, with a particular surprise.

RABBIT TRAIL: While rereading this encounter for the first time, two months later, I am in the spirit of final descent, writing the rest of the end of the book. How close am I to the "UN" being removed from "THE FINISHED BOOK"? It's Sunday morning and I am sitting outside, underneath our patio. There's a bump in the pocket of my jean skirt where I happen to have a handkerchief. A couple of weeks ago, my son Justin - a cowboy - had let me choose a handkerchief from his just received order. He had purchased several packets. The one I prefer is a plaid pattern with tiny crowns on it, the brand "Christian Aujard Paris." Go figure! It's raining crowns wouldn't you say? Oh, how He tags and touches our hearts to deeper levels of believing. I took a picture of it next to my computer with the books "project targets" in the background to post on the link to the website.)

Back to the encounter: more tears! I perceive that whatever maybe wrapped in the handkerchief, I'll discover it at the "real" end of the writing of this book. I know what it feels like, but I'm not looking. It's a secret.

After the Sword and Jesus exchanged hellos, it was back to business again. At Jesus's lead, the witnesses at the gathering took their signet rings, signing like a mystical pen, writing in light onto the 3D mandate, still in full "screen"! King David was one of them.

Interesting note: This morning when I sat down to write, I deleted a little over 1800 words. There was a "copy and paste" that I had already re-pinned. So my "draft target" within my writing software, which helps me set goals and tells me how many words till my goal I reached for the day, started at a negative. I didn't choose to re-calculate. I find it prophetically interesting that I just finally crossed over into positive + countable words. It makes my "dingers" go off. Like uncountable secret words, my computer didn't even pen. Outside of time: Unfathomable!

Wow, Father! With all the glory, how shall we assign and release this "sound of the sword"? Waiting and finding: I have seen my "falling from heaven crown" as it was waiting for me hanging on the rear posts on the back of my throne (which is at the top of my mountain).

Another exciting note before I get to share, I know that a particular enemy is being taken out with the "sound of the sword."

A couple of hours ago my husband Don texted me. He asked: "Are you going downtown for National Day of Prayer? It's May 5th". I answered his text. I was oblivious to the date, I'm having my own National Day of Prayer here at home. I was not facetious! I screenshot it in my journal and shared it on the website. I haven't missed a National Day of Prayer for years, but this time I was sincerely oblivious; except that I got a special invitation from heaven.
That is what I call a National Day of Prayer!

Now, this is what I sensed. Remember I said that because of protocol I wasn't allowed to step onto other people's mountains? I meant without an invitation via relationship. Your mountain represents the authority that the Lord has given to you. It's where we learn to rule and reign. *Good news! This sword I presented - that David once held - the Sword of the Lord can stand, fight, win and declare on your mountain.*

May I remind you who David's sword beheaded? This day the Lord will deliver you into my hands, and I'll strike you down and cut off your head
(1 Samuel 17: 46)

That is what I sense is happening here in this portion of the "END OF THE BOOK." The enemy or "Giant" that has been stealing your heavenly inheritance is getting dealt with.

I release the "Sound of the Sword of the Lord" to cut off his head. To open his gullet in which he has eaten and stolen your legal provision. We recover your inheritance.

For some of you, the name of that Giant was Fear. Fear of the unseen, Fear of man, Fear of being deceived. Just like the armies of Israel you have been listening to Goliaths bellows for some time.

FINAL ACTIVATION: *Father God I ask for forgiveness for partnering with fear, in all its forms. Forgive me, forgive my ancestors. I choose to forgive those who may have instilled it towards me. I welcome the sword of the Lord to remove the Giant of Fear. Selah (take this moment to perceive what the Sword of the Lord recovered). Write it down, thank the Lord, write a declaration, and decree it from your mountain. I'd love to hear your testimonies. You may share them on the book's website. Amen.*

You have bravely read to the end of my book because the mystical is a fascinating "story". Maybe with a flashlight under the covers of your bed, but that's OK. Nicodemus had a remarkable transformation.

What we do in secret the Lord rewards openly. It is time for that reward.

What's the reward?

It's your witness. You are a witness. Together we began this journey on my mount of transfiguration experience, from pew, row seven left-hand side. In chapter 1, you witnessed and heard the Giant of Fear screaming in my ear for years. Holding me back from believing the Jesus in me. I am no longer afraid. Hope is no longer unseen because faith has been faithful. The UnFinished Book is Finished, It is seated on earth. Yes, it was a spiritual moment when I copyrighted it! Oh, the Library of Congress will never be the same.

You have witnessed the As it is... in the kingdom of heaven manifesting on the earth. With a handful of activation how to!

From the very first day, we were there, taking it all in—we heard it with our own ears, saw it with our own eyes, verified it with our own hands. The Word of Life appeared right before our eyes; we saw it happen! And now we're telling you in most sober prose that what we witnessed was, incredibly, this: The infinite Life of God himself took shape before us.

3-4 We saw it, we heard it, and now we're telling you so you can experience it along with us, this experience of communion with the Father and his Son, Jesus Christ. Our motive for writing is simply this: We want you to enjoy this, too. Your joy will double our joy!

5 This, in essence, is the message we heard from Christ and are passing on to you: God is light, pure light; there's not a trace of darkness in him

(1 John 1-5 The Message).

Thank you for sharing this living story from my heart and now a witness in yours. I have already been shown the hope, stirring for my future pen.

Did you figure out what Thesis the Lord was nailing in your life?

Blessings Kristen Wambach

Bible translations

Notes Page

FORETHOUGHTS
https://www.kristenwambach.com/

CHAPTER #1 *Introduction to Indulgences "The window box"*
1. Quotes Martin Luther

2. Indulgence: https://www.merriam-webster.com/dictionary/indulgence

3. WholeHearted Human http://wholeheartedhuman.com/the-power-of-the-pen/

4. Olly Oxen Free https://www.quora.com/What-is-the-origin-of-the-phrase-olly-olly-oxen-free

CHAPTER #2 *In the Beginning, God*
1. Shenandoah Movie James Stewart, bumping the backside of the usher at the church door https://en.wikipedia.org/wiki/Shenandoah_(film)
   Movie link: http://amzn.to/2Hj0Amq

2. Gondola Rail Cars https://en.wikipedia.org/wiki/Gondola_(rail)

CHAPTER #3 *Lady in Waiting*
1. Favorite field trips:

   https://www.oregonzoo.org/

   https://en.wikipedia.org/wiki/International_Rose_Test_Garden

   https://omsi.edu/

   https://portlandartmuseum.org/exhibitions/current/

   http://www.oakspark.com/

2. Courts of heaven:
   a. Freedom Apostolic Resources Engaging God series, http://freedomtrust.org.uk/AR/?page_id=4614

   b. Transformation Series http://freedomtrust.org.uk/AR/?product=transformation

   c. Robert Henderson operating in the courts of heaven http://amzn.to/2rsqfC8

   d. Heart of the Valley Community Church Website:
      http://www.iheartofthevalley.org/

   e. Podcast link: http://ladyinwaitingkew.podomatic.com/?p=1

   f. Kristen's Blog InBetweenItAll.com

CHAPTER #4 *Getting Permission*

1. Namdaemun open market: https://en.wikipedia.org/wiki/Namdaemun_Market

2. Mount Seoraksan is the highest mountain in the Taebaek mountain range, Gangwon Province eastern South Korea https://en.wikipedia.org/wiki/Seoraksan

3. Redemptive Gifts: https://freedomarc.blog/?s=Redemptive+Gifts Mike Parsons and Jeremy Westcott

CHAPTER #5 *Vision Care*

1. James Goll https://www.godencounters.com/ TheSeerExpandedEdition:Theprophethicpowerofdreams,VisionsandOpenHeavens

2. Dictionary.com

3. Seeing in the spirit: John 3 Story of Nicodemus

4. Jesus appearing in person after the resurrection
   gardener, John 20:14-16
   a passer-by on the road, Luke 24:13-16
   dwelling as an alien (not from their land), Revelation 1:18
   beheld a spirit, lightening, Acts 9:3-5
   white as snow, Matthew 17
   Not a ghost or spirit, Luke 24:39

5. Breakfast on the beach: John 21:12

6. The witness of Scripture: Opening the eyes of your spirit & heart
   Ephesians 1:18
   Acts 26:18
   Romans 2:4
   2 Corinthians 4:6
   Ephesians 3:16
   Ephesians 5:8
   Psalms 119:18
   Colossians 3:2
   2 Cor. 12:2
   Mathew 5: the Beatitudes
   Moses turning aside
   Exodus 3:4
   Courts Zecheriah :3

7. Joyce Meyers Do it afraid https://www.joycemeyer.org/everydayanswers/ea-teachings/do-it-afraid

8. Song Open the Eyes of my heart Lord, by Paul Baloche

9. Cape Kiwanda Oregon State Parks

CHAPTER #6 *Earth Invading Heaven*

1. Quote: Sir Winston Churchill "Hear this, young men and women everywhere, and proclaim it far and wide. The earth is yours and the fullness thereof. Be kind, but be fierce. You are needed now more than ever before. Take up the mantle of change. For this is your time." Sir Winston Churchill https://www.facebook.com/TheCrownNetflix/posts/1678257249138071

2. Painting: The Grid between Heaven and Earth by Donna Taylor Artist Bethel Redding, Owner Kristen Wambach

3. Heaven is Real: https://www.goodreads.com/work/quotes/11283577-heaven-is-for-real-a-little-boy-s-astounding-story-of-his-trip-to-heaven https://en.wikipedia.org/wiki/Heaven_Is_for_Real_(film)

CHAPTER #7 *In Heavenly Places*

1. NW Bliss: podcast https://www.podomatic.com/podcasts/ladyinwaitingkew

CHAPTER # 8 *Vulnerable Focus*

1. Mathew 5 The Beatitudes AMP

   https://www.biblegateway.com/passage/?search=Matthew+5&version=AMP

CHAPTER #9 *Halfway*

1. Joseph Brodsky quote: https://en.wikipedia.org/wiki/Joseph_Brodsky

2. Mobius Curve https://en.wikipedia.org/wiki/M%C3%B6bius_strip

3. High Priest Bells on his garment http://biblehub.com/exodus/28-35.htm

CHAPTER #10 *Three Infinite Changes*

1. Quote: You never know how strong you are until being strong is the only choice you have; Bob Marley https://quotefancy.com/quote/35454/Bob-Marley-You-never-know-how-strong-you-are-until-being-strong-is-your-only-choice

2. Gateway of First Love 50s Kitchen
   The Earthly Tabernacle Hebrews 9:8 Berean Study Bible
   http://biblehub.com/hebrews/9-8.htm

3. Matthew 11:28-30 (NASB) 28 "Come to Me, all who are weary and heavy-laden, and I will give you rest. 29 Take My yoke upon you and learn from Me, for I am gentle and humble in heart, and YOU WILL FIND REST FOR YOUR SOULS. 30 For My yoke is easy and My burden is light."

4. Reference to David and Goliath[50] So David triumphed over the Philistine with a sling and a stone; without a sword in his hand he struck down the Philistine and killed him.51 David ran and stood over him. He took hold of the Philistine's sword and drew it from the sheath. After he killed him, he cut off his head with the sword. When the Philistines saw that their hero was dead, they turned and ran.52 Then the men of Israel and Judah surged forward with a shout and pursued

the Philistines to the entrance of Gath[f] and to the gates of Ekron. Their dead were strewn along the Shaaraim road to Gath and Ekron. 53 When the Israelites returned from chasing the Philistines, they plundered their camp.54 David took the Philistine's head and brought it to Jerusalem; he put the Philistine's weapons in his own tent. (1 Samuel 17: 50-54)

CHAPTER #11 *Angels on a First Name Basis*

1. Wakey Wakey Story: Beni Johnson Bethel Redding
   http://www.benij.org/blog.php?id=1

2. Wikipedia: The Last Samurai, https://en.wikipedia.org/wiki/The_Last_Samurai

3. Pacific Crest Trail http://www.oregonlive.com/travel/index.ssf/2015/08/pacific_crest_trail_stretches.html

4. "Twitterpated": Dictionary.com Disney, Bambi. Quote Friend Owl: Yes. Nearly everybody gets twitterpated in the springtime. For example: You're walking along, minding your own business. You're looking neither to the left, nor to the right, when all of a sudden you run smack into a pretty face.

5. Oregon Pioneers.com Presbyterian Mission Jason Lee

6. Benjamin Angel
   Evangelist Dr. George Watkins Mt. Vernon Washington
   http://www.georgewatkinsministries.com/
   Leader Kim Snell Princeton Texas

7. Leadership of 3/ Bench see:
   http://www.iheartofthevalley.org/leadership.htmlOriginsofaBetDin

8. Definitions for Honor, Cadence and Clarification Dictionary.com

9. Winds of Change, Transformation, Refiners Fire, Sounds of many Waters: A global order Mike Parson from Freedom ARC

10. Ian Clayton: http://www.sonofthunder.org/

11. Royal Priesthood 1 Peter 2:9

12. Gateways: https://www.podomatic.com/podcasts/ladyinwaitingkew/episodes/2014-04-07T17_49_57-07_00
    Gateway of Hope http://www.schooliheartofthevalley.org/
    https://freedomarc.blog/2013/11/26/gateways-of-the-spirit/
    http://sonofthunder.org/ Ian Clayton

13. Kendrick "Behind the names" https://www.behindthename.com/name/kendrick

CHAPTER #12 *The Watchmaker*

1. B-17 Alliance Fly-in http://www.b17alliance.com/

2. 44-27083 *Tangerine* - Erickson Aircraft Collection in Madras Oregon
   https://en.wikipedia.org/wiki/List_of_surviving_Lockheed_P-38_Lightnings

3. "Tangerine" song& lyrics http://www.metrolyrics.com/tangerine-lyrics-frank-sinatra.html

4. "Tangerine" is a popular song. The music was written by Victor Schertzinger, the lyrics by Johnny Mercer. The song was published in 1941 and soon became a jazz standard.
   Tangerine, she is all they claim
   With her eyes of night and lips as bright as flame
   Tangerine, when she dances by, senoritas stare and caballeros sigh
   And I've seen toasts to Tangerine
   Raised in every bar across the Argentine
   Yes, she has them all on the run, but her heart belongs to just one
   Her heart belongs to Tangerine
   Tangerine, she is all they say
   With mascara'd eye and chapeaux by Dache.
   Tangerine, with her lips of flame
   If the color keeps, Louis Philippe's to blame.
   And I've seen clothes on Tangerine
   Where the label says "From Macy's Mezzanine".
   Yes, she's got the guys in a whirl, but she's only fooling one girl
   She's only fooling Tangerine!

5. Warbirds over the West. http://www.statesmanjournal.com/picture-gallery/news/2017/06/10/b-17-alliance-fly-in--warbirds-over-the-west/102713896/

6. Rosie the Riveter https://en.wikipedia.org/wiki/Rosie_the_Riveter

7. Angel info search:
   Amsterdam- Jewish history: http://www.amsterdam.info/jewish/
   https://en.wikipedia.org/wiki/History_of_the_Jews_in_Amsterdam
   Yiddish:

8. Faith of a Gentile woman Mathew 15

9. 2nd Lieutenant Harry Dowd: his story is found in this book
   Personal Stories of Ten WWII Pilots by GARY W. METZ
   http://www.randolphblues.com/

CHAPTER #13 *Crowns for Casting*

1. Faith of a Gentile woman http://biblehub.com/nlt/matthew/15.htm

2. Matrix: http://www.dictionary.com/browse/matrix?s=t
   "uterus, womb," from Old French matrice "womb, uterus,"
   Matrix Bible verses: http://biblehub.net/search.php?q=matrix
   https://en.wikipedia.org/wiki/Matrix_digital_rain
   Matrix digital rain, Matrix code or sometimes green rain, is the computer code
   featured in the Matrix series. The falling green code is a way of representing the
   activity of the virtual reality environment of the Matrix on screen.

3. The Natural Movie: https://en.wikipedia.org/wiki/The_Natural_(film)
   Picture from the Movie the Natural of broken spot lights and raining electricity:
   https://www.pinterest.com/pin/228628118566863061/

4. In Him The Watchmaker rooms Crown of Access;
   https://www.biblegateway.com/passage/?search=Acts+17:28
   Jerimiah 29:10b – 14 I will visit you and fulfill My good word to you, to bring you
   back to this place. For I know the plans that I have for you, declares the Lord,
   plans for welfare and not for calamity to give you a future and a hope. Then you
   will call upon Me and come and pray to Me, and I will listen to you. You will seek
   Me and find Me when you search for Me with all your heart. I will be found by
   you, declares the Lord, and I will restore your fortunes and will gather you from all
   the nations and from all the places where I have driven you, declares the Lord, and
   I will bring you back to the place from where I have driven you, declares the Lord,
   and I will bring you back to the place from where I sent you into exile."

5. A Crown of Access;
   Kathrine Kuhlman: https://en.wikipedia.org/wiki/Kathryn_Kuhlman
   Aimee Semple McPherson:
   https://en.wikipedia.org/wiki/Aimee_Semple_McPherson
   Red phone booth: https://en.wikipedia.org/wiki/Red_telephone_box

6. Crowns

   https://gracethrufaith.com/topical-studies/spiritual-life/how-to-win-your-crowns/

   https://en.m.wikipedia.org/wiki/Five_Crowns

   https://www.gotquestions.org/heavenly-crowns.html

   https://www.biblegateway.com/quicksearch/?quicksearch=crown&qs_version=NASB&limit=100

7. A gentleman's Personal Gentleman Jeeves
   https://en.wikipedia.org/wiki/Jeeves

8. Wizard of Oz Movie
   https://en.wikipedia.org/wiki/The_Wizard_of_Oz_(1939_film)

9. Patrick's Shield https://en.wikipedia.org/wiki/Saint_Patrick%27s_Breastplate

CHAPTER #14 *Tools of Responsibility*

1. Seated/Seeded Seven Sons of Sceva http://biblehub.com/acts/19-15.htm

2. With permission: Lana Vawser facebook A great breakthrough on Writers. https://www.facebook.com/lanavawserministries/posts/1359271497449333

3. Painting by Kristen Wambach The Mandate room: https://www.facebook.com/photo.php?fbid=102069246344170628&set= pb.1314114844.-2207520000.1499472720.&type=3&theater

4. Negative trading floors https://freedomarc.blog/2014/10/03/seven-trading-floors/

5. Robert Henderson Operating in the Courts of Heaven http://www.roberthenderson.org/

CHAPTER #15 *The End of the Book*

1. Para-cord: https://en.wikipedia.org/wiki/Parachute_cord

2. The weapons: http://biblehub.com/2_corinthians/10-4.htm

Acknowledgments

Don Wambach Husband, Here we are, took me 10+ years to make good on my word. I love living life with you. The second half is filled with more of His goodness.

Laure Fabre Editor/translator, John Bugni Co-Editor, Proof Reader. My "grammatically well read" friends. You have taught me considerably, thank you for patiently walking with me. I still struggle with colons and semicolons. Wouldn't want to write or publish without you.

Family: George & Erla Richards Parents, Joseph Wambach Sgt. US Marine Corp Son, Jace and Erika Wambach (photographer) Son & Daughter-in-love, Jacob Wambach Son, Justin Wambach Son, Korean testimony: Mike Richards Brother, Song Soon, Benjamin & Jennifer Richards. World War II reenactment adventure: Matt Richards, brother. Nephew, Thomas Richards.

Thank you for helping me to get the details correct. Thank you for pictures and links. You all make writing so colorful. You had no idea, did you? I did it!

Heart of the Valley Community (Church) and friends: Many of you live in the ink of the UnFinished Book pages. What a blessings it is to be loved and encouraged to walk out my destiny with your support. You have faithfully held my arms up. Thank you.

Freedom ARC UK. Mike Parsons, Jeremy & Alice Westcott, Waltraut Reimer. Thank you so much for your tremendous support. I'll be back visiting soon.

Pastor Tommy Barnett for your encouragement then and now.

Jane Clement, a Prophet's Reward, thank you for your permissions to share. I am so honored to be apart.

Lana Vawser "Writer's Prophetic word," thank you for your permission to share, Blessings

ProPrint: Skip Hamilton and Mona Alhamood (co-cover design), abundantly thank you for your professional expertise. Not only is the book beautiful but easy to read. Thank you

Many have imparted wisdom, laughter and hunger for more of Him along my journey. This is just a collection of those I bugged to help me remember the details. Thank you. I close the pages of this book only to turn a new chapter of life. What happens in heaven when we complete a manuscript that Jesus wrote about us? I hope we have the opportunity to exchange that answer in the future. I look forward to it! God bless you.

Autographed

Together we put our signature on the next generation

I am honored to have authored words with reader both near and far. The heart of any encounter with I Am, heaven or you, can draw us together in a moment of time and that instance of affirmation we have the opportunity to leave a mark of our introduction to transform individuals around us.
The pen is alive and changing the world.

In the journey of The UnFinished Book, should you and I have a moment in the asking for a signed copy lets make it memorable? Leave a legacy or a spiritual sound.

Our offering: Every Autographed book - SIGNATURE - is $1.00,
Matched from author $1.00
Through relationship = $2.00 given to arts.
Autographed: You Discover God when you Discover your purpose.
For more information www.kristenwambach.com

Together we put our signature on the next generation
Looking forward to meeting you.

Thank You K. Wambach

Made in the USA
Middletown, DE
23 April 2021